The

MUMMIES

of

ÜRÜMCHI

ALSO BY ELIZABETH WAYLAND BARBER

Archaeological Decipherment
Prehistoric Textiles
Women's Work: The First 20,000 Years

The Loulan Beauty
Illustration by Kelvin Wilson 1997

The

MUMMIES

of

ÜRÜMCHI

Elizabeth Wayland Barber

W. W. Norton & Company

New York • London

For information about permission to reproduce selections from this book,
write to Permissions, W. W. Norton & Company, Inc.,
500 Fifth Avenue, New York, NY 10110.

The text of this book is composed in Sabon
with the display set in Cochin
Composition by ComCom, Inc.
Manufacturing by The Courier Companies, Inc.
Book design by JAM Design

Library of Congress Cataloging-in-Publication Data

Barber, E. J. W., 1940–
The mummies of Ürümchi / by Elizabeth Wayland Barber.
        p.   cm.
Includes bibliographical references and index.
ISBN 0-393-04521-8
1. Mummies—China—Sinkiang Uighur Autonomous Region.   2. Bronze
age—China—Sinkiang Uighur Autonomous Region.   3. Textile fabrics,
Prehistoric—China—Sinkiang Uighur Autonomous Region.   4. Tarim Basin
(China)—Antiquities.   5. Sinkiang Uighur Autonomous Region. (China)—
Antiquities.   I. Title.
GN778.32.C5B37   1999
393'.3—dc21   98-18958
                                                                                              CIP

W. W. Norton & Company, Inc., 500 Fifth Avenue, New York, N.Y. 10110
http://www.wwnorton.com

W. W. Norton & Company Ltd., 10 Coptic Street, London WC1A 1PU

1 2 3 4 5 6 7 8 9 0

Frontispiece: This reconstructive portrait of the Loulan Beauty shows the woman shown in plate 9 wearing her hide skirt and moccasins, her shaggy woolen blanket wrap fastened at the shoulder with a long wooden pin, and her feathered felt hood. She is winnowing wheat with her winnowing tray, while the wheat basket and comb found with her lie by her knee. Grazing in the background are some woolly sheep at the Bronze Age stage of development, portrayed on the basis of Soay sheep (a breed abandoned on islands off the coast of Scotland by Bronze Age farmers and corresponding to the fleece type known from Bronze Age textiles). Ephedra bushes appear in the middle distance. Illustration by Kelvin Wilson, Rotterdam.

To Paul
who supported me in a thousand ways

AND

to Irene and Victor
who became valued friends
during an unforgettable expedition

Contents

Sixteen pages of full-color photographs appear following page 64

Preface

MY SINCERE thanks go first to Dr. Victor Mair, for making it possible for our group to travel to Ürümchi to study the mummies and their clothing; to Dr. Dolkun Kamberi and the Ürümchi Museum, for generously arranging for us to study their treasures; and to Irene Good as well as to Mair and Kamberi, for their support and good company during and after the expedition and for the use of their photographs. For reading and commenting on the manuscript at various stages, my warm thanks go to Paul Barber, Victor Mair, Harold and Virginia Wayland, Joseph Birman, Sharon Sprague Morgan, Ann Peters, and my long-suffering editor, Edwin Barber. Their comments, although not always incorporated, were most helpful, smoothing the text and saving me from many an egregious error. Errors that remain of course are to be laid at my own door; opinions and interpretations, where not referenced to others in the sources at the back of the book, are my own as well.

Several illustrations were subsidized by the Louis and Hermione Brown Humanities Support Fund, through Occidental College. Warm thanks to Gary Lyons of the Huntington Gardens, Pasadena, for locating samples of ephedra in the Desert Garden despite 110-degree heat; to Dale Gluckman, for the repeated and often prolonged use of her books; and to Susan Wadlow and Rodrick Owen, for helping me with the plaited bands. Bob Turring of Caltech graphic arts patiently built most of the maps for me on his computer system, while Kelvin Wilson created the frontispiece bit by bit via many E-mails and mail packets between Pasadena and the Netherlands.

So, before the eyes of history has come a nation,
from whence is unknown;
nor is it known how it scattered
and disappeared without a trace.

—Nicholas Roerich
painter, philosopher,
traveler to Central Asia, 1926

The
MUMMIES
of
ÜRÜMCHI

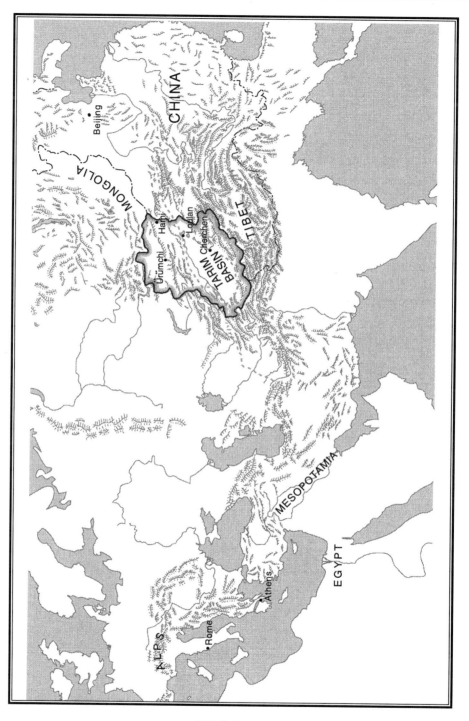

MAP I.I

1

Mystery Mummies

"Calf-length A-line dresses with contrastive piping lead the ladies' fashions, in this year of the great burial. While red and blue with dashes of turmeric yellow continue to dominate the color palette, the stunning effect of bright red trim on maroon suits along with striped leggings remains popular among the gentlemen. . . ."

SO MIGHT the fashion page of the *Tarim Times* have read, around 1000 B.C., if anyone in the Tarim Basin of Central Asia (map 1.1) had known how to read or write. The story, however, had to wait three thousand years, till Easter of A.D. 1994.

In April of that year *Discover Magazine* published a cover article laying out picture after spectacular picture of ancient mummies clothed in vivid hues of red, yellow, and blue: colorfully swaddled babies, a bearded man clad in maroon shirt and pants with white boots over polychrome leggings, women with high-peaked "witches' hats" and death grins to match. It looked more like Halloween than Easter.

This was the first dazzling notice afforded most Westerners that well-

---

Opposite page: Map of Eurasia showing the location of the Uyghur Autonomous Region, the westernmost province administered by China, north of Tibet and southwest of Mongolia. The mummies are now housed in the regional capital, Ürümchi, but were found in and around the Tarim Basin, principally near Hami, Loulan, and Cherchen.

preserved mummies existed along the ancient caravan route through the heart of Asia at a time contemporary with the much more famous Egyptian mummies. When the earliest of these Central Asian corpses nestled into the sands of the Tarim Basin, about 2000 B.C. or a little after, the pyramids of Egypt had already stood for half a millennium, but the best-known pharaohs, Ramesses II and "King Tut" (Tutankhamon), were rather more than five hundred years into the future. Next door in Mesopotamia, the Sumerians—first inventors of the art of writing—were already dying out and Hammurabi was soon to set up his famous law code; the Greeks and Romans had not yet even arrived in Greece and Italy from the northeast. On the other hand, "Ice Man," the Late Stone Age body found in 1991 by hikers in the Alps, had died well over a thousand years before. Europe and the Near East were living in the Bronze Age, a period characterized by the use of soft metals. To the east the Chinese had not yet learned to use metal but were already busy domesticating the precious silkworm that would one day lend its name to the most famous caravan route of Inner Asia, the Silk Road, along whose stretches the mummies have been found.

The colorful clothes and appealing faces of these Central Asian mummies produced an immediate response in America: people wanted to know and see more. Exactly one year after the *Discover* article featuring Jeffery Newbury's colorful photographs, *Archaeology* printed its own cover story on the "mystery mummies," and soon photographers and textile buffs were trekking out to a city their travel agents had never heard of: Ürümchi, current home of the mummies. A year later, in March 1996, *National Geographic* joined the caravan. Meanwhile, in the fall of 1995, *Scientific American Frontiers* had aired about ten minutes of Asian mummy footage on TV, the culmination of a one-hour program on Alan Alda's adventures in China.

No one who has made the arduous trip to the remote Chinese-administered Uyghur Autonomous Region, where the mummies are coming to light, would wonder that Alda himself did not go there, sending only his film crew to its capital city of Ürümchi, some sixteen hundred miles west of Beijing. The flight of sixteen hundred miles is not quite so far as jetting to Hawaii from Los Angeles, but it feels farther: flights are few and a lot more hazardous, thanks in part to killer windstorms that frequently shut down the few Central Asian airports. Flying from Beijing, one sees the countryside below soon shifting from the lush green of northern China to orange mountainous deserts as far as the eye can see, which is a long way at thirty thousand feet. An artist with only ocher and burnt umber left in his paintbox might create such a scene. In color and terrain as well as vast extent, it reminds an American of the high red deserts of Utah and Arizona and of the Great Basin in Nevada with its dry rocky crags protruding above a deep, choking porridge of sandy-looking fill. Foreigners tend to be unaware that most of the huge territory that China governs is not fit for agriculture, being either mountain or desert or both at once.

The editors of *Archaeology* had commissioned their article from someone who had traveled to the Uyghur region several times, Dr. Victor Mair, a professor of Chinese studies at the University of Pennsylvania. Mair had first seen the mummies in 1987 while guiding a group of diehard travelers through the Ürümchi Museum—the sort of people not daunted by mere dust- and gravel-storms. At that time the bodies lay in oblivion in a room so ill lit that well-equipped visitors would pull out their pocket flashlights to get a better view.

What Professor Mair recognized there stunned him. The mummies appeared to be neither Chinese nor Mongoloid in facial type; they looked, in fact, distinctively "Caucasian," with high-bridged noses, deep, round eye sockets, fair hair, and—on the men—heavy beards. According to Chinese historical documents, the Han Chinese themselves began to move into Central Asia only around 120 B.C., struggling to open up regular trade with the West. So historians would not particularly expect Chinese mummies in Central Asia in the second millennium B.C. But why not Mongoloid? Archaeologists and linguists alike had assumed that the Mongol-type peoples had "always" inhabited this entire area, ever since the spread of *Homo sapiens sapiens* around the globe at the end of the Ice Age forty thousand years ago. They also assumed central and northern Asia to be the general homeland of the Altaic linguistic group, which today includes Mongol and the various Turkic and Tungusic languages (see fig. 9.7). (Northern Central Asia was of course the heartland from which emanated the great invasions of Turks and Mongols during our own millennium; see map 9.9.) To find Caucasians was a surprise.

Returning home, Mair could not forget those strange mummies moldering in the galleries and storerooms in Ürümchi. On the immediate level, something needed to be done to help the museum protect its priceless archaeological treasure from the depredations of fungi, vermin, and microbes. Once people have removed such mummies from the ultradry desert sands that preserve them so splendidly, any dampness at all, even that exhaled by the live human beings now working around the bodies, inevitably restarts the processes of decomposition and decay. And to a family of moths, a well-preserved mummy constitutes an edible palace, as tasty to them as the witch's hut to Hansel and Gretel. The museum sorely needed stout Plexiglas cases in which to seal the mummies with a cargo of disinfectants and bug killers, set up so that scholars and other members of the public might still see and study these important finds.

But Mair also recognized that the very existence of the mummies and the history they represented would revolutionize academic thinking in a number of fields. To tease out of these now-silent witnesses the stories of their lifestyles, customs, origins, and even perhaps languages would require experts from many different disciplines. A tireless worker, Mair set about collecting such a team from around the globe, to pick up where excavation left off.

To begin with, the corpses themselves needed expert study. How old were they at death and why did they die? The famous mummies of Egypt appear dry and shriveled, blackened like discarded walnut husks, compared with these life-like remains. Had the survivors specially treated these bodies to mummify them, or did their remarkable condition result only from natural desiccation? Anatomists, pathologists, geologists, and experts on burial could presumably answer such questions.

What about their genetics? Could the new methods of DNA analysis tell us about the nearest relatives of these ancient people elsewhere on the Eurasian continent? Could one manage to extract usable DNA samples from these re-markable corpses? Films like *Jurassic Park* make the processing of DNA appear much easier than it actually is, and the results much glitzier. Nonetheless, for sci-entists to build up an accurate picture of humanity's spread across the globe, the DNA spectrum from even a single ancient mummy is invaluable, as the work on Ice Man is showing. Perhaps such data could help solve the puzzle of where these early desert dwellers came from when they wandered into Chinese Turkestan so long ago. Professor Mair began contacting specialists in the field, such as Dr. Luigi Luca Cavalli-Sforza of Stanford University and Dr. Paolo Francalacci at the University of Sassari in Italy.

Even more difficult to determine: what language or languages might these people have spoken? Nearly a century before, scholars had discovered in this same area a variety of documents dating from the first millennium A.D. and written in a now-extinct language known as Tokharian. To everyone's surprise, Tokharian turned out to be related to the Indo-European tongues spoken in most of Europe (including English, Latin, and Greek) and in parts of the Near East (including Persian and Sanskrit). These far-flung Tokharian speakers there-fore must have penetrated into Central Asia from the west, but when or how they got there no one knew. The finding of groups of Caucasoid mummies in the Tarim Basin that clearly antedated the Tokharian inscriptions thus held out hope to the linguists that their puzzle too might finally be solved.

Then there were the objects accompanying the dead: mats, baskets, a few tools and vessels, offerings of food, and masses of clothing both on and off the bodies. These form the more usual materials of archaeological investigation, from which we can derive fairly secure dates as well as cultural inferences.

Usual, that is, except for the textiles. Outside of Egypt, you find a presentable piece of cloth in a prehistoric dig about as often as you find a ruby in your oat-meal. Yet here, and for the same reason as in Egypt, ancient textiles come out of the ground by the armload. The steady dryness of the desert in both countries preserves all sorts of otherwise perishable artifacts. Just because most archaeological sites worldwide produce no textiles doesn't mean that cloth wasn't important back then. In fact, once cloth became common late in the New Stone Age, about 4000 B.C., textile production soon swallowed more labor hours than even the production and processing of food, becoming *the* most important ancient industry. But whereas the sophisticated Egyptians labored to produce masses of plain white linen, the countryfolk of the Tarim Basin wove and bedecked themselves in garments of vivid color that has survived with astounding brightness. No one expected to encounter peacocks and popinjays in the gray sands of Central Asia.

Furthermore, the textiles from at least one of these Inner Asian sites look astonishingly like the peculiar plaid twill cloths found in the only place in Europe where ancient perishables have survived well, the Bronze Age salt mines at Hallstatt and Hallein, in the Alps above Salzburg in Upper Austria. The Austrian plaid twills had been woven by ancestors of the Celts, another Indo-European group linguistically related to the Tokharians (see fig. 6.3). The parallelism of the language and textile links forms another strange tie between the Central Asian mummies and the West. What, if anything, might the prehistoric Celts have had to do with Chinese Turkestan?

To analyze this unusual but highly informative type of material, Mair called upon Irene Good, a specialist at the University of Pennsylvania in the laboratory analysis of ancient fibers and textile fabrics, and me. Together we traveled to Ürümchi in 1995 to study the finds, aided by Mair and by Dr. Dolkun Kamberi, an archaeologist formerly with the Ürümchi Museum and one of the excavators of its most spectacular mummies.

The mummies in the Ürümchi Museum are not the first prehistoric Caucasian bodies found in Chinese Turkestan. Nearly a century earlier Sir Aurel Stein (working for the British government) and Sven Hedin and Folke Bergman (working together for Sweden) had found and published details about several such mummies from the wastes of Loulan, at the east end of the Tarim Basin, whence the earliest of the Ürümchi mummies came.[1] Amid the many crates of artifacts that these savants sent by pack animal and railway across the vast continent, some black-and-white photographs of the burials and a few specimens of prehistoric clothing had made their way back to England and Sweden, but—understandably—no mummies. The ancient bodies remained where those explorers found them, left to decay or disappear into the shifting sands once more. The possibility of studying similar mummies by modern scientific methods thus caused much excitement in the scholarly world.

---

[1] For descriptions of the work of Stein, Hedin, and Bergman, see below, especially Chapter 5.

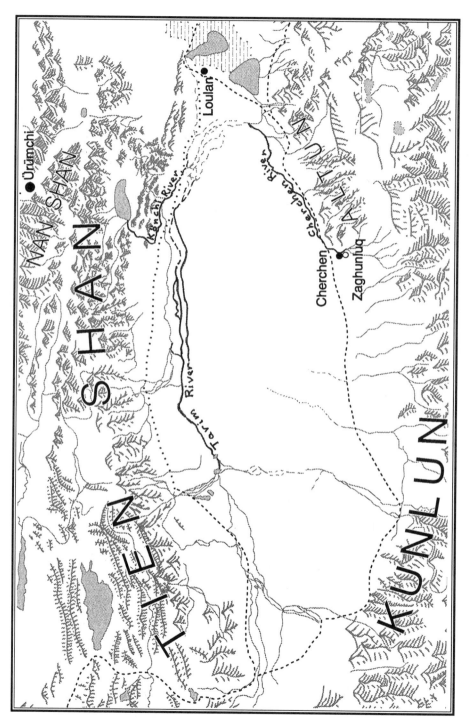

MAP 2.1

2

A Man with
Ten Hats

THE MUMMIES in the upstairs gallery of the Ürümchi Museum tax one's powers of description, so close to alive do they appear in death. They lie single file down the middle of a long, narrow chamber, arranged toe to head from oldest to most recent. Cherchen (or Chärchän), on the southern rim of the Silk Road (map 2.1), has without doubt produced the most spectacular Tarim mummies so far, and of these the most famous is the three-thousand-year-old man who occupies the gallery's dusky center (plate 1).[1]

His face is at rest, eyes closed and sunken, lips slightly parted; his hands lie in his lap, while his knees and head are tilted up—like a man who has just drifted off to sleep in his hammock. Visitors tend to tiptoe and lower their voices. A two-inch beard covers his face, and his light brown hair has been twisted—plied from two strands, not braided from three—into two queues that hang halfway down his chest. Here and there white hairs glint among the yellow-brown, betraying his age—somewhere past fifty. He would have been an

---

[1] Future visitors to Ürümchi, I am told, will find the mummies in a new gallery, differently arranged. I have chosen to leave my descriptions as I and many others saw them and as they were when the photographs and research were done.

Opposite page: Map of Tarim Basin, showing Cherchen and its ancient cemetery at Zaghunluq, with major rivers and surrounding mountains. Central area is the exceedingly dry Taklamakan Desert.

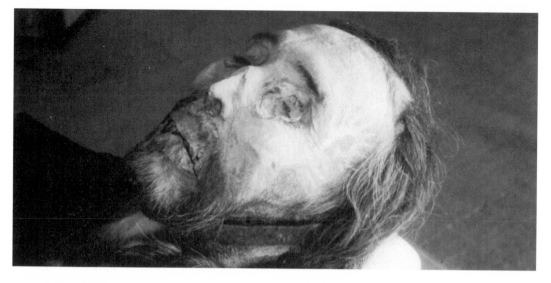

FIGURE 2.2

Face of the male mummy found at Cherchen ("Cherchen Man"), from ca. 1000 B.C., with bright yellow-ocher face paint and a red strap to hold the jaw shut. Note the heavy beard, round eye sockets, and high-bridged nose characteristic of Caucasians. (Photo I. Good.)

imposing figure in life, for he once stood six feet six inches tall (almost exactly two meters).

Bright ocher-yellow face paint curls across his temple, sprouting short rays on its outer curve and reversing its curl as it meanders down to the flatland of his cheek before climbing across the great ridge of his nose—not a low-bridged Asian nose but a veritable Sierra Nevada of a nose—to the far side (fig. 2.2). Did such markings denote rank, affiliations, piety? Did well-wishers apply it to help him during his last hours, or after his death? The finds in the tomb included "two small bone spoons with dried ocher pigment," according to Dolkun Kamberi, one of the excavators, suggesting to him that the makeup formed part of the funeral ritual. Caking of the paint around the "laugh lines" at the outer corners of his eyes, on the other hand, suggests that the man could still squinch up his face when the color was put on.

"Cherchen Man" (so the press dubbed him) also wears earrings, of a sort: a bit of bright red woolen yarn passes through each earlobe. If the thread once supported a further ornament, it is long gone.

Passing from the face, one's eye jumps between the violently colored leggings and the purply-red-brown two-piece suit that covers most of the man's body. Originally the man wore soft white deerskin boots to above his knees—the left one is still there. But the right one has torn away, revealing horizontal stripes of gaudy red, yellow, and blue that put Ronald McDonald in the shade. Knitted socks, however, had not been invented yet. This man had simply wound colored hanks of combed wool around his legs and feet, to pad them and insulate against frost, much as East European peasants still do. Insulation was welcome. Untempered by the great oceans, the weather in this basin at the center of earth's largest continent swings from unbearable summer heat to icy winter cold. Where visible, the wool has been pressed together so lightly that one can hardly call it felt, although constant rubbing inside the boots would gradually compact it into a solid material. That's all that felt consists of, sheep's wool rubbed together in a preferably warm and damp environment until the fibers are inextricably tangled. Perhaps this was how felt was first invented. (The English last name *Walker* actually means "felter" because the verb *walk* originally denoted the act of compressing wool into felt by stomping on it in a tub or stream.)

And his suit? Shirt and trousers, one would say at a glance. But the exact design of the trousers cannot be discerned because of the covering shirttails. The shirt, for its part, follows a pattern well known among folk cultures, where so much effort goes into making the cloth itself that none is wasted (fig. 2.3). Two long woven rectangles, just as they come from the loom, form the body of the shirt, one draped over each shoulder to form the two halves. Two more square swatches, sewn into tubes and attached at right angles to the first part, compose the sleeves. They will stick straight out, of course: the original "T"-shirt, with none of the gentle fitting that slants the sleeves of our modern tee-shirts into a comfortable downward angle. But simple weaving produces rectangular cloth, and any angling or sculpting wastes some of it.

FIGURE 2.3

Construction of Cherchen Man's shirt from 4 narrow lengths of cloth (left) sewn together (right). At right, the location of the seams is indicated by dashed lines and the placement of bright red piping over seams and edges indicated by dotted lines.

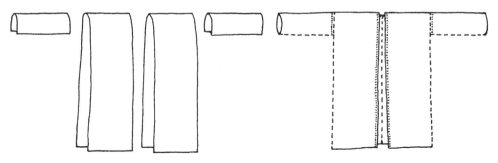

All the stranger, then, that part of the front right shirttail has been rudely but squarely torn away, so that it is considerably shorter now than its mate on the left, with a raw bottom edge. Display conditions make it impossible to discover how this problem resolves itself in the back.

Why should this otherwise elegantly dressed gentleman have his shirt so rudely torn? Pondering the possible scenarios reminded me of another ill-used woolen garment of similar date, three thousand years ago, found in a Swedish peat bog. That cloak of plaid twill had half a dozen dagger holes straight through its double folds. Brigands? Treacherous companions? Ritual killing? At any rate, mysterious violence worthy of the evening news. But with Cherchen Man the body itself shows no sign of foul play. Conceivably the rip occurred during excavation and the sundered piece never got reunited with the shirt. Among materials from the storeroom, we later saw several swatches of cloth of the same color, weight, and simple weave—the so-called plain weave, in which each thread goes alternately over and under those at right angles to it.

Most of us just grab an outfit from the closet each day, having bought the pieces ready-made from a rack or catalog. We scrutinize fashion but have never seen anyone weave, let alone make thread. We take our textiles for granted. It means nothing for me to say that your best shirt is probably plain weave and your blue jeans twill. But until the Industrial Revolution everyone knew a lot about cloth because every day in the home people worked at making thread and cloth from scratch and everyone saw the processes. Making cloth and clothing soaked up more than half the human labor hours in most preindustrial societies, more even than food production.

Although the looms used today in factories may be quite complicated, the basic process is simple. Imagine yourself prowling the grass as a wolf spider, which always trails a silken thread generated from her spinnerets (so that if she falls or gets blown off her feet, she has an anchoring safety cord). Now imagine yourself trying to make your way, thread and all, through a row of parallel grass stems felled yesterday by your landlord's giant lawn mower. Paying out silk, you climb over the first stem, then squeeze under the second, hop over the third, under the fourth, and so on in alternation. No bugs over there; you turn and come back along a parallel path. But this time you duck under the stem that you clambered over just before turning around; then you climb over the next, push under the third, and so forth till you get back to the blade you started from. Still no dinner: you turn around again, hopping over stem 1, under stem 2, etc., always alternating over and under.

As you keep laying your silk down in this manner, you are creating a plain-weave "cloth" (fig. 2.4). The long grass blades lying parallel on the lawn form the *warp,* the threads that are normally fixed in place on the loom. Your trail-

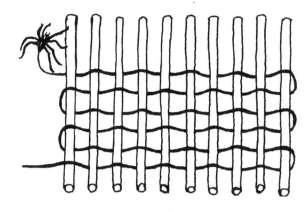

FIGURE 2.4

Diagram of the simplest kind of weave, *plain weave*, and the way that the weft normally closes the sides of the cloth (the *selvedges*) so that nothing unravels.

ing thread of silk, which interlaces with them as you hop and duck, forms the *weft,* literally "that which was woven" (from an old past tense of the verb *weave*[2]). Warp and weft: these are the two sets of threads that interlace and bind together to make a woven cloth. When the spider pulls her silken weft alternately over and under the single stems of warp, it makes the simplest of all weaves, *plain weave.* Moreover, each time the spider turns back, looping her silk around the last stem by shifting from "over" to "under" as she turns, the silken weft binds the last stem of the warp into the fabric so it can't ravel out. The neatly bound edge of the cloth formed by many repeats of this behavior is called a *selvedge* (from *self-edge*). Other weaves are possible—other combinations of how the spider pulls her silk over and under the grass blades, to form, for example, twill or satin weaves. But these are the essentials.

As with so many things associated with the mummies of Ürümchi, apparent simplicity hides much cleverness. By way of decoration on the plain-weave fabric, the tailor of Cherchen Man's suit whipped bright red yarn as a sort of piping over the seams on both the shirt body and trouser legs and around the neck and front opening of the shirt. It produces a very subtle but effective ornamentation—subtle both because the piping is so fine and because its bright red color rests against the purply-red-brown background.

If that's what one should call such a hue. Plum? Maroon? Cherrywood? This strange but attractive shade so widely used in cloth from Cherchen must have been the favorite color either of the man's social group or of his family's

---

[2] Like *leave, left.* Another word for the weft, not used much now by weavers in America, is *woof,* also derived from *weave.*

weavers. Many other cloths from this tomb bore the same distinctive color. I can compare it only to the peculiar tint obtained by a brunette who hennas her hair (as common a practice among current Uyghur women as among New Yorkers): brownish in this light, reddish in that, with a glint of beet-purple highlights. The source of such a textile dye continued to baffle me as long as I worked only in the mummy gallery.

Holding the man's shirtfront together is a waist cord plaited from yarns of five different colors: bright red, dark purply-red-brown, blue, green, and yellow (plate 2a). The threads show none of the angled structure we associate with three-strand braiding, the form of plaiting best known in our culture. Instead each emerging thread dives straight back into the perfectly round cord like a little stitch, reemerging farther over so that its color spirals slowly around and along the cord. I've done a lot of weaving and sewing but very little plaiting, so I was puzzled at how such a cord might have been made. Only later did I determine the surprising answer.

Meanwhile, Cherchen Man gave us other enigmas to ponder. Over the middle finger of his left hand he wore a white leather thong, made from a narrow loop passed through and sewn to a wider piece carefully trimmed to have an oval end. People who had nothing else to do in the gallery stood around endlessly discussing what its purpose might be. I nicknamed it Special Tool No. 893. As with the little hexagonal rod you need to unstick your garbage disposal, you'd never know its special function until you needed it or saw it used—that is, saw it in context. And we no longer have the context for this odd thing. It might have had to do with archery. My favorite hypothesis was that it once served as a tether for the man's pet hunting falcon—a pleasingly romantic notion unfortunately not yet supported by evidence, although falconry seems to have begun in Central Asia by at least the early first millennium B.C. and is still widely practiced there today.

Two items in Cherchen Man's apparel he clearly wore only in death. First, a red and blue cord tied around his wrists kept his hands from sliding off his chest, where they had been carefully posed. Similar cords bound other mummies found in the same tomb group, suggesting that the color scheme or the type of cord might have some sort of ritual significance. These ties were formed by drawing out virtually unspun combed wool into long, thin sausages, one of red and one of blue, and then twisting them around each other to form the bicolored cord. In thickness and fluffiness it resembles the bright yarns popular now for wrapping gifts.

Second, he wears a solid strap, plaited of dark red wool, that passes under his chin and around behind his head where it is tied tightly in a knot. This strap served to hold his jaw shut as the forces of decay set in, swelling the tissues. (De-

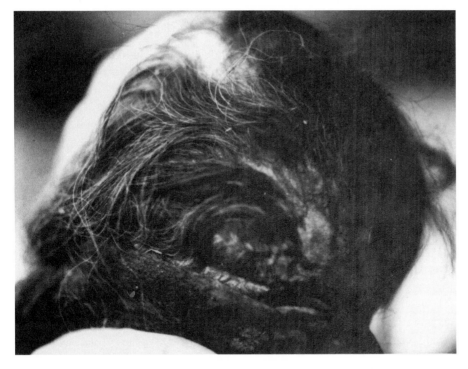

FIGURE 2.5

Top of Cherchen Man's head. The crease left by pressure from the woolen jaw strap can be seen on the scalp just above the strap.

composition can cause such bloating that even close relatives cannot identify the corpse.) It succeeded fairly well in its task, for the man's mouth came open only slightly. But the pressure was so great for a while that the strap dug into the back of the man's head where the knot is, leaving a permanent crease in the mummified scalp. Then, as the corpse dried out, the pressure subsided and the slackened strap slid down slightly in back, so that the long crease can be seen just above the strap near the knot (fig. 2.5). This two-phase process of mummification tells us more about when the man's face paint could have been applied. For if the color were put on after death, the postmortem *bloating* could squinch up the laugh lines and push the ocher paint out. Eventually the desiccation shrank back the flesh so that we can see into the empty creases again.

Most of us don't spend much time rooting about in the details of death and decomposition, so we remain unaware of the grisly events that commonly attend them. We inter, embalm, and cremate for good reasons: either to prevent these ghastly changes or to put them safely out of sight, smell, and hearing. When we chance, then, to encounter directly the effects of death, we have two reactions. Horror is one. Edvard Munch painted his famous canvas entitled *The Scream* after seeing some mummies. If bodies that mummify have *not* had their jaws tied securely shut, they display distortedly yawning mouths of just the shape captured in Munch's picture. Experts in archaeological burials call it the mummy gape (see, for instance, plate 3a).

Second, we misconstrue much of what we see. Vampire lore, for instance, grew out of misunderstandings of quite normal events associated with body decomposition. When frightened peasants dug up the dead in a search for "vampires," the body often looked plumper than before burial, and it now had blood at the lips. So the diggers would conclude that the dead person had been sucking blood from the living. A reasonable enough deduction, perhaps, if that's all you know. But in fact the gases produced during decomposition normally bloat a dead body for a while (unless it is quick-frozen like Ice Man), and the pressure this bloating exerts on the blood-rich lungs forces blood out the nearest opening, the mouth. We need no vampires. The only things alive here are the hungry microorganisms, not the bodies.

To understand certain aspects of the Asian mummies, we need to delve into details of death and decay here and there. But I will leave the curious reader with a strong stomach to learn more about the subject from the lively book *Vampires, Burial, and Death*, written by another expedition member, Paul Barber.

Paul's inclusion added expertise in interpreting several aspects of the burials themselves, including but not confined to such matters as chin straps and laugh lines. There were many questions. How came it that these bodies should be so perfectly preserved after three thousand years in the ground? Did mummification result entirely from natural conditions, or had the survivors helped the process along by artifice? One would like to add "like the Egyptians" since the Egyptians poured all sorts of fancy unguents onto the heads and torsos of their mummies to help them into the next world. Ironically, far from preserving the corpses, those liquids merely sped up the decay, so that on most Egyptian mummies only the feet remain fully intact. Some of the Tarim mummies are far better preserved than anything from Egypt in the time of the pharaohs.

At the far end of the gallery that displayed Cherchen Man and his companions was a glassed-in workroom we nicknamed The Morgue because it contained two tables laden with bodies—those under conservation. When not being worked on, these mummies lay discreetly draped with burgundy velvet coverlets. Only their bony feet stuck out at one end. A couple of large, oblong, coffin-like cases of wood contained yet more mummies in from the field, awaiting their turn on the slab. We learned to wear dust masks in that room, to keep the particles of ancient detritus and some of the faintly acrid yet sickly sweet smell out of our noses and lungs.

The Morgue also had a live occupant, a delightful and very knowledgeable young Chinese woman named Tian Lin, whose business included cleaning the mummies that came in from the excavations. Tian Lin had conserved Cherchen Man and still tended his needs, regularly changing the chemicals inside his new Plexiglas tomb and checking his body and clothes for any sign of trouble whenever the container was opened for high-paying foreign photographers.

Opening mummy cases—a process we saw twice—was no easy matter. Some of the new Plexiglas tops, which allow visitors to see the bodies clearly while affording considerable protection to both the viewer and the viewed, weigh an enormous amount. In fact it required practically all the men working in the museum to lift Cherchen Man's huge cover, shaped like an inverted box, high enough to clear the corpse (which lies on a waist-high bier), then to move the cover sideways and lay it gently onto the floor—and then back again a few minutes later. During the brief time that each case was open, Tian Lin would don a surgical mask and quickly inspect the condition of her charge, tweezers in one hand to pull back the folds of cloth gently for a better view and a small vial in the other to receive the corpses—or larvae—of any predatory insects that had somehow found their way into the case. At the last moment she would break and deposit a small vial of poison beside the body, while the men struggled to replace the unwieldy cover and seal it before anyone was overcome by the fumes intended for the bugs and fungi.

During the course of initial conservation, Tian Lin said, each of the better-preserved mummies had all its clothes carefully removed, so that the body could be cleansed of dirt from the grave and of any mold or fungus that might be setting up business anew. The clothes too were cleaned up. Then the body was dressed again to be put on display.

In the process of disrobing and cleaning the mummies, Tian Lin had made an interesting discovery. A few bodies—the ones best preserved—turned out to be covered with a strange yellow fuzz or dust that lay under the clothes, directly on the skin. Whoever had prepared the burial in ancient times had clearly painted the dead person with some substance that promoted mummification. Only after this anointment had the body been dressed and laid to rest. In its original state the "paint" had probably been a frothy goo, like whipped egg white, which upon drying and aging had turned to light dust. The earliest Tarim mummies—those from close to 2000 B.C. found around Loulan (Chapter 4)—had none of this substance. Their preservation resulted entirely from desiccation by the dry climate. But Cherchen Man and some of his companions, a thousand years later, had had some help.

Curious as to the composition of the mysterious substance, Tian Lian had scraped some off and subjected it to a series of laboratory tests. (She had re-

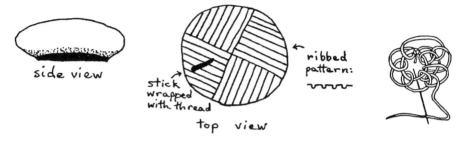

FIGURE 2.6

A beret-shaped hat constructed in *nalbinding* technique from dark red-brown woolen yarn, worked in a pattern of ribbed quadrants. *Nalbinding* uses a threaded needle (unlike knitting) to make loops interlocking with the previous row of loops (right), in an ever-increasing spiral starting from a little circle in the center.

ceived thorough training in medical chemistry in Shanghai before becoming conservator for the museum in Ürümchi.) Tests indicated it was some sort of animal protein, but she could get no further. She was intrigued to learn from Paul that mummies found in the high, dry Andes Mountains of Peru often had their skins painted with a thin fish paste, another animal protein that also apparently promotes preservation.

In all these locations, however—the Andes, Cherchen, Loulan—the extreme dryness of the climate would at least partially mummify any dead body that didn't get eaten by predators first. The same conditions also account for the splendid condition of so many textiles, color and all.

Far more cloth and clothing survive than just what the mummies wore. These grave gifts fill several cases in the museum's public gallery and countless storeroom shelves to boot. Since museum personnel had excavated the Cherchen tombs, the artifacts were kept at the museum and remained under its control. After short negotiations the staff began to bring textiles by the armload up to a small workroom where Irene and I could study them in detail (plate 5b).

The bright colors had amazed and delighted us already in the gallery, but the feel of the textiles in the study room astounded us even more. Still so supple. It was like handling fabrics from one or two hundred years ago, and yet someone had woven them three thousand years back, according to the radiocarbon dating of the tomb. What had caused such wonderful preservation?

We soon learned that the people of Cherchen had dug their graves into a geological formation of salt beds. That choice had probably been dictated partly by the fact that crops would not grow in salt, so using this space for burials would entail no loss of productive land. Furthermore, the salt, like dry heat, would suck the moisture out of the bodies and discourage microorganisms—an ideal cemetery for rapid mummification. But salt also brightens certain dye colors: it is sometimes used even today to intensify them during the manufacture of cloth and yarn.

The Cherchen people had such a fondness for clothes that they took piles of apparel with them to the next world. This single excavation, for example, produced ten hats, each different. One hat (fig. 2.6) had the shape of a beret or tam-o'-shanter, made of dark brown wool in a looped technique that at first glance looks like knitting. But knitting, so far as we know, was not invented for another two thousand years. This hat used a needle and thread method known by the Scandinavian name of *nalbinding* ("needle binding"). The skilled maker not only increased the circle to the maximum width of the hat, then decreased the diameter again to fit snugly over the brow, but even managed to work a simple but elegant ribbed pattern at the same time. A slim stick, wrapped in places with fine thread, remains thrust into one quadrant of the cap, apparently the remnant of an ornament or hatpin.

Another cap, minutely knotted of red-flecked brown wool, looks like a tiny circus tent (fig. 2.7 left). From the pointed tip, its four sides slope down and then out with a cushiony bulge toward the bottom. A third headpiece was molded from two sheets of white felt into a simple helmet shape, then decorated in front with a curving roll of felt that looks remarkably like a pair of horns (fig. 2.7 right).

The largest and most arresting hat, also plumed, looks like something that might have belonged to Robin Hood (fig. 2.8 left). The dark brown felt of its body curves up to a high, rounded peak at the top and flips over at the bottom to form a small cuff around the wearer's face. Around the edge of the cuff, thick but neat buttonhole stitching in light tan contrasts decoratively with the dark felt; similar tan stitchery continues up the center front and down the back, holding the two halves of the hat together. Partway down on one side, several big feathers were once attached.

Hats of this shape are well known in ancient Near Eastern and Mediterranean art, where they were copied from the headgear of Phrygian archers (fig.

FIGURE 2.7

Two of the hats found at Cherchen, ca. 1000 B.C. *Left:* A tent-shaped cap of red-flecked brown wool. *Right:* A helmet-shaped hat of white woolen felt, decorated with 2 horn-like rolls of white felt.

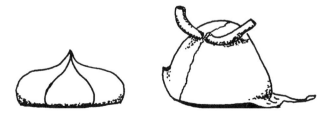

FIGURE 2.8

Left: Peaked hat of dark brown felt with tan stitching found at Cherchen, ca. 1000 B.C. *Center:* Two Classical renditions of Phrygian caps—above, from an Etruscan mirror ca. 300 B.C.; below, from a Roman grave relief ca. A.D. 170. *Right:* Phrygian cap as a symbol of French liberty depicted on Rude's sculpture of *La Marseillaise* on the Arc de Triomphe, Paris.

2.8 center), a group of people all too familiar to the Classical Greeks. The Phrygians entered history early in the Iron Age when they migrated into Turkey (map 2.9)—or Anatolia, as archaeologists call that area to avoid ethnic associations with later peoples. This region has been home to a long succession of peoples. During most of the second millennium B.C. the Hittites had ruled Anatolia, only to be ousted around 1200 B.C. by great incursions of barbaric peoples from the north. These migrations also mark the end of the Bronze Age and the start of the Iron Age, since the Hittites had kept the technique of smelting iron a secret for centuries and the demise of their rule let the precious secret out. Chaos ensued, as people scrambled to replace their bronze swords with much harder and sharper iron ones. When we get a clear picture again, around 800 to 700 B.C., the heartland of Anatolia had filled with Phrygians, an Indo-European-speaking group that had come south from the steppes, the great grasslands that stretch from Hungary to China in a broad belt across Eurasia (map 2.9). So the close similarity of the Cherchen peaked hat to the typical headgear of people emerging from the steppe zone far to the west provides an intriguing link. What, if anything, did the Tarim people know of those westerners? Did they obtain this hat through trade or gift giving? Or did all these folk share the same cultural inheritance?

The steppe, a grassland corridor some four to five thousand miles long and

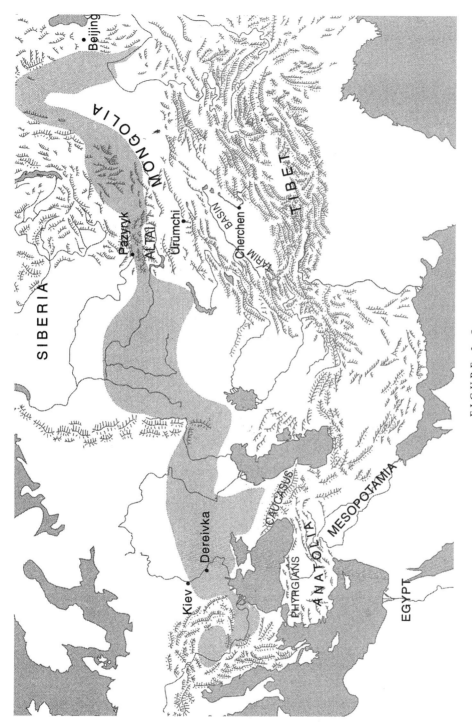

FIGURE 2.9

The Eurasian steppe zone (shaded areas), a belt of grasslands running from central Europe to northern China. Dereivka, in the Ukrainian steppe, has produced the earliest evidence for the domestication of the horse, ca. 4000 B.C. The Phrygians, originally a steppe people, moved into Anatolia (modern Turkey) around 1000 B.C., largely replacing the Hittites there. Pazyryk, where the Altai Mountains narrow the steppe zone, is the site of a series of 5th century B.C. steppe burials extraordinarily well preserved by permafrost.

of greatly varying width, has in fact formed a vital connector between Orient and Occident for millennia—ever since a few of its inhabitants got the idea of domestic animals from the Near East in the late Neolithic (around 4000 B.C.), along with a starter set of already tame sheep and cattle. As long as the grass grows well, it is far easier to herd hay-munching ruminants than to grub out the tough-rooted grass to make room for fields and then go through the endless heavy work of plowing, planting, weeding, watering, harvesting, and processing the crops. Farming is an exhausting life, herding much easier—lazier, even—especially when one can control a herd from on horseback. The steppe people themselves domesticated horses, evidently as soon as they got the concept from farther south that domestication was a possibility. A horse skull from the Ukrainian site of Dereivka, dated to about 4000 B.C., shows characteristic tooth wear that suggests the horse had chomped on a bit for several hundred hours during its life; it was not only domesticated but closely controlled. The effect of using horses to manage the other animals was tremendous, since the horse riders could move so much faster than the herds (let alone humans on foot) and thus govern such large flocks that people had no need of other forms of livelihood. The change created a completely new lifestyle that still persists in parts of Central Asia. And the life of herding is preferred. Only those who lose their flocks will farm, and they will do so only until they can build up enough capital to start a new herd. (In similar fashion, when the Native Americans of the Great Plains got horses from the Europeans, they quit farming and rode off across the prairies, the New World "steppes," to a new and more energy-efficient way of life.)

But when, as periodically happens, drought hits and the vast grassy stretches dry up, then the great herds starve and die off, and some of the humans who depend on them for food must die or change their ways temporarily. More often than not, afflicted Eurasian nomads have chosen to move, moving in particular into the greener fields of the nearest farmers—usually the Europeans or the Chinese—who, like the proverbial ants, regularly and industriously stored up grain against an uncertain future. Some such hiccup in the weather and grazing patterns may have led to the migrations that destroyed the Hittite Empire and flung the peak-hatted Phrygians into Anatolia. We will see this same pulsing rhythm of periodic migrations out of the steppes many times in seeking to understand the cultures of the Tarim Basin. Since the dawn of nomadism, perturbation anywhere on the steppe seems to have sent ripples of upheaval across the grasslands from one end to the other—from Hungary to China and back again.

A host of inventions in cloth and clothing that we take for granted have come out of this nomad culture—felt, for instance, such as that used in several of the Cherchen hats. Being merely matted sheep's wool, felt requires no loom.

Its manufacture therefore does not oblige the nomad to stay in one place. (Some nomadic groups do set up camp for several months at a time and do weave, but it takes considerable time to set up a loom and produce a piece of cloth on it.)

To make felt as a nomad does, you scatter cleaned and fluffed-up wool all over a mat in an even layer, sprinkle the wool with whey or hot water, roll up the mat with the damp wool in it, and tie the bundle to the back of your horse so as to mash and knead it as you ride all day. At night you unroll it, sprinkle it down again, reroll it the other way, and tie it to the horse for another day's punishment. Soon the wool has matted as thoroughly as you please. You can even decorate it by placing tufts of colored wool (or bits of colored felt) in a pattern on the top layer, then mash it some more. The whey and the hot water cause the tiny scales on the surface of the wool fibers to stick up rather than lie down, promoting the tangling that mats the fibers. As such they have the opposite effect from the "conditioners" that many women today put on their hair to decrease tangles. Sheep's wool is virtually the only natural fiber that will tangle so inextricably.

Nomads use felt not just for its convenience of manufacture. More important, it can be made so dense as to be nearly impervious to wind and water, yet it is far lighter than other waterproof materials like wood and metal. The herders spread great sheets of felt over light frameworks to produce their famous round tents, or *yurts* (fig. 2.10), and they use it for flooring (as rugs), bedding, luggage, saddle gear, hats, cloaks, and other clothing. They even use it to make dishes for solid foods and padded carrying cases for the china cups used for drink. Along with horse riding, felt has made the Eurasian nomadic way of life possible.

Zipping around on horses also affected nomadic clothing. Loosely flapping drapery like that of the ancient Greeks won't keep you warm on an icy winter steppe. You need garments that stay put around your body, closely fitted apparel with legs and sleeves. Many have suggested that the horse riders invented trousers, for pants seem to come into the well-documented areas of the ancient world with the steppe migrations of horse riders at the beginning of the Iron Age. Pants not only keep the legs warm, they can also minimize chafing while riding. Many cultures just beyond the steppe zone took up trousers at about this time, probably copying them from the invaders. And we know that the people of the Tarim Basin knew horses and riding by 1000 B.C., for they placed a leather saddle and the head and front hoof of a horse into the upper part of Cherchen Man's tomb (for layout, see figs. 2.14, 3.1). The peculiar thong on his finger might thus have belonged to horse-riding gear.

Cherchen Man's pants were not in a position to be studied. But another pair of trousers in the same sort of purply-red-brown woolen material turned up in the excavations at Cherchen (fig. 2.11). Between the pant legs, a square gusset

FIGURE 2.10

Kazakh shepherd family setting up their yurt, a movable felt house, in the mountain pastures of Nan Shan (Southern Mountains) south of Ürümchi, in June 1995. First they lashed together the wooden framework, consisting of curved struts for the roof, lattices for the walls (discernible inside, through the open door), and a rigid doorframe with solid, hinged wooden doors (the left one is visible). Then they tied mats to the outside of the lattice walls. Next, starting to the left of the doorway, they began raising and tying into place the great sheets of felt that cover the matting on the outside and make the tent windproof. The family is just finishing that process to the right. Then they will cover the roof with another huge sheet of felt, still lying bundled on the grass in the foreground, leaving only a smoke hole open at the top center. Finally the woman will cover the lattice inside with brightly colored felt rugs, lay more rugs on the ground for flooring, and move in the household goods, which also still lie bundled on the grass at left. The most important piece of furniture, the wooden bedstead, waits at the right of the yurt. The whole process of raising the yurt takes about an hour.

was set cornerways in the crotch to give ample room for sitting with legs spread. (Problems of splitting one's seams in tight areas like this have led to the expression *bust a gusset*.) As a decorative touch, the tailor used a thick pale red yarn for the visible stitching; the dashed line of its course resembles the bright lane divider on a dark highway.

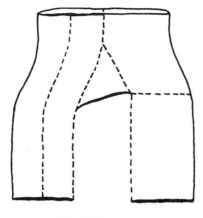

FIGURE 2.11

Pattern of purply-red-brown woolen pants from Cherchen, ca. 1000 B.C. Dashed lines indicate the positions of seams. The asymmetrically diamond-shaped gusset at the crotch was folded on the bias to give the cloth extra elasticity for freer movement.

No one knows when and where sleeves were first invented; people may well have thought them up independently several times. The Egyptians already had sleeved linen shirts in the First Dynasty, around 3000 B.C.; elegant early specimens are housed at the Petrie Museum of Egyptology in London. But sleeved clothing did not remain popular in Egypt, and the early Mesopotamians did not use sleeves at all, if we are to go by their depictions of themselves. The people of Europe and the steppes seem not to have picked up the notion until the early second millennium B.C., only a few centuries before someone made the sleeved shirt Cherchen Man wore to his grave. A second woolen shirt (white) and part of a third (purply-red-brown) have also survived, the latter piped with yellow and brown.

We drew nearer to an explanation for the mysterious purply-red-brown dye when we inspected the pants, partial shirt, and some other swatches of this strange fabric up close. Working in our makeshift study room with ten-power magnifiers and good light, Irene and I turned to each other simultaneously to ask, "Are you seeing what I'm seeing?" Both of us had learned long ago from books on textiles that you can't dye naturally pigmented wool, that only colorless (white) wool will absorb and hold a dye. But the dyers of Cherchen hadn't read those books. These purply-red-brown cloths apparently consisted of naturally brown wool tinted with a bright red dye, presumably the same chemical that, used on white wool, provided the contrastive red piping and the bright red felt of the man's leggings. The comparison of the brunette who adds red dye to her hair and gets a purplish highlight suddenly seemed especially apt.

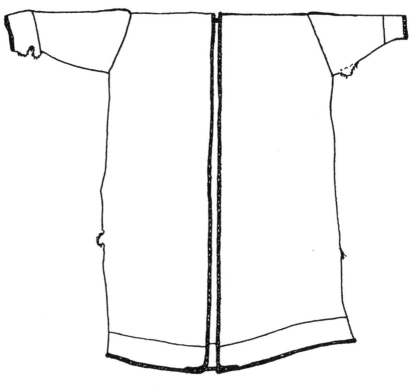

FIGURE 2.12

Pattern of Cherchen Man's overcoat, densely woven of dark brown wool with red cuffs and hem. The sleeves are slightly tapered, but the tailor couldn't bear to cut away any fabric and left the extra cloth inside. Fancy edgings plaited of red and brown yarns finished the front opening and bottom.

In Tibet today men still wear homespun woolen coats of a similar, if darker, purply-red-brown, achieved by dyeing naturally dark wool with a maroon dye.

Cherchen Man had other garments to keep him warm, in particular two remarkably heavy, long-sleeved overcoats, one of pale tan wool and the other very dark brown with red at the wrists and bottom (fig. 2.12). At first we felt puzzled by the mode of manufacture of the brown coat, for the line of weft, so heavy as to appear corded, seemed to dive at an angle into the decorative red bands at cuffs and hemline. In making normal plain weave, our wolf spider and her silken weft cord traversed the grass warp stems at right angles (fig. 2.4). Everything looks square in normal weaving. The funny angle in the overcoat cloth suggested that the coat had been cut and sewn on the *bias* (angleways to the warp and weft rather than square to them) and that the ends of the sleeves and bottom hem had been dipped into red dye *after* being woven and sewn up. Yet the line between the red and brown was too perfect for that. Finally the museum personnel took pity on our perplexity and opened the end of the huge wall case where the coat hung so we could squeeze inside for a closer look. Squatting in flattened pseudo-Egyptian poses, one in front of each side of the coat, we searched frantically for clues to the mystery, praying that our lungs would hold out long enough against the dust and naphtha.

"Look, the bottom edge is a selvedge!" (That's where our spider brought her silk web around the last grass blade as she turned to go back, thereby binding that stem to the others and preventing the cloth from unraveling.)

"Yes—and so is the front opening!" On the face of it, this didn't appear to make sense. We could now see two closed edges meeting at right angles and forming the structural borders of the coat. The threads inside had to run parallel to the selvedges, since they are what form those edges. This proved that the coat had been made on the straight of the cloth, not on the bias. (A cloth may be started on the loom by bending the warp threads—the grass stems—over a rod or cord. This creates a third closed edge or *starting selvedge* as the first edge, unusual in modern fabrics but a time-saver in handmade ones. See fig. 2.13a.)

"So what we took for the diagonal angle of the weft is an optical illusion!"

"How did they make it look diagonal, then?"

Our noses right up to the musty cloth now, we cough and wheeze as we hunt down rips in the fabric to use as peepholes into the structure.

"I can't believe this—it's like twill but with all the rules broken! Do you see what they've done?"

"Sort of. Where I'm looking, they've hopped the weft over *three* warps and then under two, and then packed the weft down hard to make the cloth so dense. That's how they get that low diagonal look that fooled us!"

"Yeah, your eye just slides from one row to the next interpreting it as all one row. So the wide red edge must be woven in as a stripe—"

"Look here: there's a warp broken where the color changes. You can see the red weft continuing underneath and coming up where your eye perceives it as a different row—but it isn't."

Twill weave differs from plain weave. In the usual sort of twill (fig. 2.13b), the spider with her silken weft alternately leaps over two stems and crawls under two, all the way across each row. But when she has crawled under the last two stems of a row and turns, she starts the next row by climbing over only *one* stem before continuing her routine of under two, over two. This offsets the pattern by one grass stem and creates the steep 45° diagonal we associate with twill. The pairing of the threads also allows them to nestle closely together to form a very dense and therefore warm fabric. That warmth accounts for why twill grew so popular in the frigid climes of Europe as soon as wool arrived from the Near East in the fourth millennium, largely replacing linen and plain

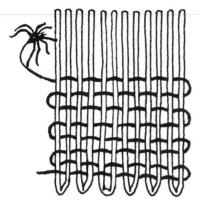

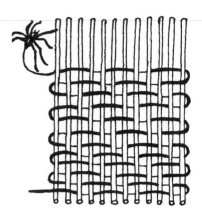

a) plain weave

b) 2/2 twill

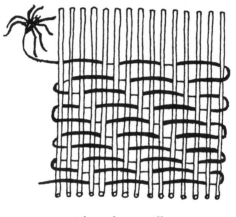

c) long-hop twill

FIGURE 2.13

(a) Starting selvedge, formed by wrapping the warp threads onto the loom in such a way as to form a closed starting edge, a third selvedge in addition to the 2 side selvedges. (b) Typical twill weave (2/2 twill), in which each thread passes over 2 then under 2 threads. In the next row the pairing of threads is offset by one, forming a diagonal pattern that runs at 45° to the threads of the cloth. The pairing, or *twinning* of the threads gives the weave its name *(twill)*. (c) The sort of *long-hop twill* found in many Cherchen textiles. Here, as in the man's overcoat, the weft hops over 3 warp threads, then under 2, offsetting by one thread in the next row. Because of the long hops, the diagonal pattern forms at a lower angle than with 2/2 twill.

weave. Cherchen Man too chose twill for his overcoat because of its warmth.

But in this Cherchen twill the spider took a running start and long-jumped over three warp stems at once, crawled under the next two, hopped over three more, and so on.[3] Coming back, as in normal twill, she offset her path by one thread (fig. 2.13c). But now the diagonal pattern climbs only one-in-three, not one-in-two, and has been tightly packed down, producing a diagonal at a much lower angle. We nicknamed the weave "long-hop" twill.

"The cuff's done the same way: the thread was dyed red, then woven in as a simple stripe, using this funny twill." Snorting and coughing, but with our mystery solved, we hastily made note of other interesting features (see fig. 2.12) and extracted ourselves from the case.

Originally the overcoat lay under a leather saddle in an upper layer of the tomb, well above where the man's body lay (fig. 2.14). It was therefore one of the first things out of the pit, and the gallery's designer had displayed it beside some enlarged photographs of the digging of the man's tomb.

One of the excavators at the Cherchen site was an Uyghur archaeologist, Dr. Dolkun Kamberi, who had done research in art and archaeology at the Ürümchi Museum and Xinjiang Institute of Archaeology for many years. When it finally became permissible for Uyghurs (a heavily controlled Turkic "minority" group) to leave China, he and his family had traveled to New York, where he spent five years getting a doctorate in Asian history at Columbia University. He returned, diploma in hand, the day after our little group arrived in Ürümchi. Kamberi no longer works there, but his return was heartwarming to behold. As news spread through the building that he was back, the guards and other workers came running to greet him with big grins, hugs, and even a few noogies. Clearly Kamberi had won the hearts of the people he had worked with.

During his time at the museum Kamberi and his archaeological colleagues had combed the southern edge of the great Taklamakan Desert for evidence of ancient towns, cemeteries, and rock carvings. At Cherchen, the only town of any size in the entire southeastern quadrant of the Tarim Basin (itself an oval 400 by 800 miles in diameter, mostly desert), they learned that locals had discovered an extensive antique cemetery on a plateau above the nearby hamlet of Zaghunluq. People often went to dig the salt present in concentrated patches on this plateau, nicknamed Tuzluqqash, Uyghur for "salt rock." In some places the salt occurred in such pure form that it could be used directly for cooking without further refinement. The ancient burial ground of several hundred graves

---

[3] In other pieces we saw, the weft hopped as many as five warp threads at a time, while still offsetting by one with each new row. As in the overcoat (over three, under two), the number of warp threads hopped over generally did not match the number climbed under.

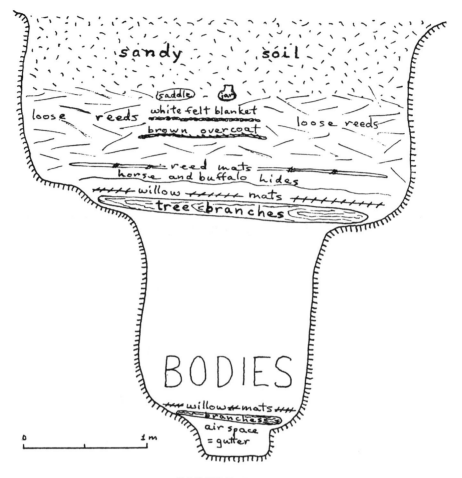

FIGURE 2.14

Diagram of construction levels in Tomb 2 at Cherchen, ca. 1000 B.C., showing a cross section across the narrowest part. Cherchen Man was found near the bottom (at "BOD-IES"), lying on mats and branches over a channel that promoted airflow. His brown overcoat and saddle blocked the tomb mouth higher up. (Vertical scale of filling not exact.) See fig. 3.1 for the horizontal layout of the bodies. (After Kamberi.)

stretched for three-quarters of a mile in length and roughly half a mile in width (1.1 by 0.75 km). Some of the tombs had already been looted. In trying to salvage the textiles that lay about at one spot where the village diggers had left them, the museum workers found the large intact tomb that held Cherchen Man and his family.

As seen in the gallery photograph, the main excavation pit looks wide but shallow at the top, more like the sand trap of an ant lion than like a vertical shaft; beyond and around it stretches barren desert, with a patch of green trees marking the village in the distance. Sandy soil naturally forms into a saucer-shaped trench, since vertical walls are impossible to maintain in sand. The sides, seeking their preferred angle of repose, will quickly slump into the hole and bury everything—the site and the archaeologists too, if one is not careful. With a dish shape you have to move more dirt, but you only have to move it once. To get to Cherchen Man's tomb, the Uyghur team first had to dig through half a yard of sandy soil and a one-foot layer of scattered reeds, over an area of ten by sixteen feet (fig. 2.14). Among the reeds they found two drinking horns (made from cattle horns) and a sheep's head. Just beyond the man's tomb, at the same level, the skull and front leg of a horse came to light. Under the reeds, blocking the tomb mouth, they found a pile consisting of the saddle and a black, round-bottomed clay jar lying on a white felt blanket, with the red-trimmed brown woolen coat underneath them. Immediately below this group the burial chamber was lidded with layer after layer of reed mats and skins of wild buffalo and horse, all resting on a roofing of thick branches.

The key picture shows the moment at which the excavators finally broke through this roof into the part of the grave with the mummies. Down in the middle of the pit two heads are visible, one of them blond, both apparently busy with something. Learning that the picture had been taken by Dolkun Kamberi, the only person we had seen at the museum who doesn't have black hair, Victor Mair inquired of Dolkun what other workman was blond. Dolkun speaks excellent English (and Chinese too, as well as his native Uyghur); even so, he seemed puzzled by the question. Then he burst out laughing.

"That head? That's not a workman," he exclaimed. "That's the head of the mummy himself—they're lifting him out!"

So close to alive do they appear in death.

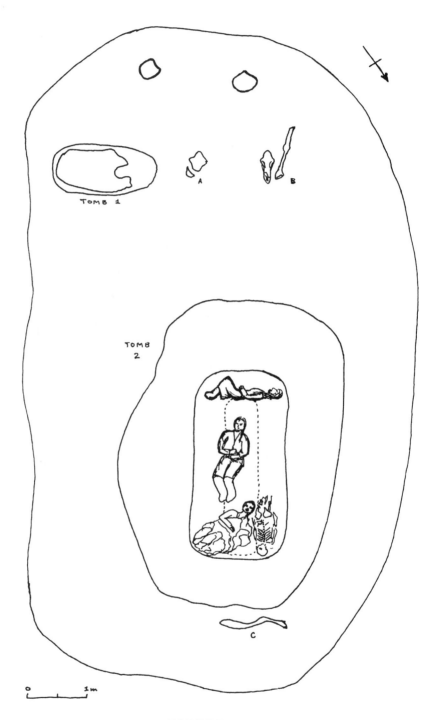

TOMB 1

A

B

TOMB
2

C

0   1m

FIGURE 3.1

3

Plus Three Women
and a Baby

CHERCHEN MAN was not alone down there in his grave: three adult women shared it with him (fig. 3.1). Two of their corpses had decayed to varying degrees, but the third remained in excellent condition, clothes and all.

The Cherchen Woman, as I shall call her, must also have been imposing in life, for she too stood well over six feet tall (1.9 meters; plate 2b). She lies in the gallery with her head propped up and her knees raised, hands held across her stomach by a wrist cord braided of two blue, two pink, and two red yarns. Her hair of light brown shot with white she wore braided into two long plaits, to which she had added two more artificial queues. One plait has a red woolen yarn braided in with one of its strands, while in two others the hairdresser had added red wool only for the last four inches, folding the thread so that half went into each of two strands. The tips of the completed braids were then plaited together and tied.

Like Cherchen Man, the woman wears a dark red chin strap, which, however, had failed in its task, leaving her mouth dried wide open, her desiccated tongue filling the gap. Paint half covers her face: golden yellow spirals across the bridge

Opposite page: Layout of intact tomb group at Cherchen, ca. 1000 B.C. Tomb 1: Grave of baby, covered by section of poplar trunk. Tomb 2: Grave of Cherchen Man, Cherchen Woman, and two other women, showing disposition of bodies at bottom of shaft. Dotted line indicates outline of channel under tomb floor (see fig. 2.14). (A) sheep's head; (B) horse's skull and horse foreleg stuffed with reeds; (C) large stick. (After Kamberi.)

of her nose and a large red triangle with more yellow spirals inside it on each cheek (plate 3a). She too has tufts of dark red yarn slipped through the lobes of her ears.

They match her dress: a calf-length robe of dark red, trimmed over the structural seams and around the neck with a slim pea green cord stitched down with little groups of alternating black and white threads. The material of her gown, densely woven in long-hop twill (fig. 2.13c), is of wool like all the other fabrics, yet with an extra sheen to it. Perhaps, Irene Good surmised, mohair or even crude silk had been mixed in with the sheep's wool. But as the woman's showcase remained sealed while we were there, we had no way of knowing. The sleeves, simple tubes sewn to the armholes in the body of the garment, reach down to the wearer's wrists, but the space under each armpit was left open to the breezes.[1] At the bottom of the dress, startlingly coarse stitches of brown yarn hold the hem in place. Below this, one can see the lady's knee-high boots of soft white deerskin and, here and there, glimpses of the felt padding inside them—yellowish woven felt with a bit of blue showing.

This woman had lain crosswise in the tomb, just beyond the man's head (fig. 3.1). At his feet lay two more women, one of whom time had reduced to little more than a skeleton. The other (plate 3b), although disintegrated in the middle like the Egyptian mummies, was still for the most part well preserved. One could still see her face, with high-bridged nose and mouth gaping wide, and she still wore tall white deerskin boots and a dark red dress with wrist-length sleeves like the first woman's. Over part of her lay a big cloth with bold red and white interlocking swirls looking like a dozen pinwheels set off all at once on the Fourth of July. Neither of these ladies resides in the public gallery, but a similar swirled cloth is on display (fig. 3.2). Originally it had been dyed a vivid turmeric yellow, faded now from sitting under the gallery window but still bright on the underside. After dyeing, the design of red and blue interlocking spirals had been *painted* onto the woven wool. Painting fabric is a rare technique in the ancient world and is another indicator of the versatility of the clothmakers of ancient Cherchen.

The spiral patterns on these cloths hold interesting clues because of their relationship to a major form of textile art found in Central Asia today. The

[1] A sleeved coat with similar openings under the arms was found in Egypt in a grave dating to the sixth or seventh century A.D., where it belonged to a Sassanian or Parthian (Iranian) riding outfit. Underarm openings seem also to have survived into this century in a number of folk costumes (ranging from Macedonia to Iran), all of which could lay claim to Iranian or Turkic influence or origin. In some cases the slit was demonstrably used as a way for the arm to bypass the sleeve sometimes—in hot weather or for special jobs.

FIGURE 3.2

Yellow woolen weft-faced cloth painted with red and blue spirals, from Tomb 2 at Cherchen, 1000 B.C. Compare cloth in plate 3b.

Cherchen spirals don't look like tidy little Aegean or Near Eastern spirals, which typically come in rows. Instead they sprawl all over the surface in waves, interlocking in all directions. They imply an origin in feltwork, even though the few ancient pieces of true felt we saw happened to be plain, and not from this quadruple burial.

The nomadic herders of Eurasia, as we said, have relied upon felt for the past several millennia as their most important construction material. William of Rubruck, a Franciscan monk from Flanders who set out on a Christian mission to the Mongols in 1253, observed this custom among his hosts: "With the coarse [wool] they make felt to cover their dwellings and coffers and also for making bedding. . . . From felt they make saddle pads, saddle cloths and rain cloaks, which means they use a great deal of wool." In addition, because nomadic herders move constantly, they carry few large objects. Whatever art they use to embellish their lives must ride piggyback on the necessities. Thus they have become masters at decoratively sewing their felt. In describing the

Mongol felt tents, or yurts, William of Rubruck says: "Before the doorway they also hang felt worked in multicoloured designs; they sew coloured felt onto the [piece that forms the basic hanging], making vines and trees, birds and animals."

Because of its matted structure, however, felt has a peculiar property: wherever you sew it along a straight line, the felt is likely to tear, just as a paper towel tears off along the line of perforation. The solution? Sew interlocking circles and spirals. Then the lines of sewing reinforce one another. So nomadic art of the steppes characteristically winds and curls (fig. 3.3) even when it has been transferred to wood carving, as on the base of the spindle found at Cherchen (fig. 3.4), or to appliqués on *woven* cloth (where the curls are unnecessary), which we saw everywhere in both Chinese and Russian Turkestan (fig. 3.5).

One of the most charming pieces of clothing from this tomb probably belonged to one of the three women: a cobalt blue shawl woven in a loose and gauzy plain weave with two slim cherry red stripes through it (plate 4a). Along the two sides the brown side selvedges have been turned and hemmed prettily with long white stitches, once again looking like the dashed white lines on a road. At both ends the weaver wove a handsome band ribbed with alternating bars of cherry and blue, then braided the blue warp ends into fringes tied off with overhand knots.[2] One could wear such a wrap to a soirée today without feeling ashamed.

Why were these three women buried with the man? The mind runs immediately to the ancient Indo-Iranian custom of suttee *(sati),* whereby the society required a man's wife to accompany him to the grave if he died before she did—a deed usually accomplished by her climbing onto his funeral pyre. But these bodies were not cremated, and no visible signs of violent death have survived the millennia. Of course they could have taken poison, but they might have died simultaneously by accident, for instance in an epidemic or other sudden catastrophe. (I recall noticing in Jacksonville, Oregon, an old tombstone of a family of five, all with the same date of death. It read: "Massacreed by the Modoc Indians." That sort of thing can happen.) New excavations in progress at Zaghunluq show that some later tombs were reopened many times to place more burials in the chamber, being constructed with an entry corridor for the purpose.

---

[2] The bars of alternating color, a favorite ancient pattern because it is so simple to weave, result from alternating rows of cherry and blue weft in plain weave. The weft is packed in so tightly that the warp and the weft below it can't be seen, producing a ribbed or corduroy-looking band in which the ribs stand out as alternating bars of color: one blue, the next cherry red, and so on. If we had a red and a blue spider weaving side by side, the red spider would *always* hop over the even warp stems (covering them with her red weft) and under the odd ones, whereas the blue spider would *always* do just the opposite, as they wove alternate rows. Thus even stems would get covered only with red and odd stems only with blue.

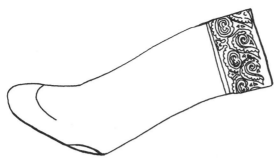

FIGURE 3.3

Appliquéd felt ornamentation on a felt boot from the burial in Kurgan 2 at Pazyryk, in the Altai Mountains north of Xinjiang, ca. 500 B.C. Textiles there were preserved by permafrost. Note the similarity of the spiral pattern in the felt to the painted spirals from Cherchen in fig. 3.2 and plate 3b. (After Rudenko.)

FIGURE 3.4

Wooden spindle found in Tomb 2 at Cherchen, with spirals carved on its whorl.

FIGURE 3.5

Inside a Kazakh yurt in the Nan Shan (Southern Mountains) south of Ürümchi, June 1995. Some of the hangings and both caps are covered with curly decoration typical of traditional feltwork, although these pieces have factory-made woven cloth as a base.

But such is not the case here. We will need to dig up many more graves of this early culture to discover whether simultaneous multiple burials were a habit or a random occurrence.

A FEW feet south of the mouth of the large tomb, near the horse head and foreleg (fig. 3.1, top left), the excavators found another grave, one added shortly after the principal burial. Because the little grave lay slightly above the mouth of the large tomb, the archaeologists had in fact found it first and named it Tomb 1, the grave of the four adults being Tomb 2. A smooth, curved slab of wood gave first notice of its presence. Underneath the slab, a small secondary pit held a tiny, perfectly preserved baby (plates 4b, 5a).

The infant, probably less than three months old, lay on a blanket of white felt, with a second, even whiter blanket of long-hop twill (fig. 2.13c) folded over some raw wool and placed like a pillow under its head. A pair of unusual gifts lay with the child: a small cow's horn cup and what may be the world's earliest preserved nursing bottle, fashioned, nipple and all, from the udder of a sheep (see plate 5a, to left). The baby could suck milk from the teat when the bag had been filled and tied shut at the other end. The curved plank of poplar wood (hollowed from a section of trunk) and a thick layer of reed mats covered the little burial in its shallow oval pit. Two feet away, in another hole, lay a sheep's head.

Two small bluish stones still close the infant's eyes, and a wee tuft of orange wool protrudes from each nostril (a means, known in other parts of the world, of wicking away any decomposition fluids that might come out through that orifice). Time and the desert have so perfectly preserved the face that its little ski-jump nose is intact, the tiny eyebrows still arch neatly above the blue eye-stones, and wisps of pale brown hair peek out onto the forehead from below the cap. Over the baby's head someone had carefully patted a bright blue bonnet of combed and barely felted wool with an edging of bright red in the same material to frame the face. This unique headgear earned the infant our nickname of the Blue Bonnet Baby, to distinguish it in the gallery from a much earlier child's mummy wrapped in beige and brown (see Chapter 4).

The rest of the infant's body was neatly wrapped in a purply-red-brown shroud or baby blanket identical in color to Cherchen Man's suit, the whole bound up by several turns of a twisted red and blue cord exactly like the one holding the man's hands in place. The cloth of the blanket, however, differed from that of Cherchen Man's suit by a subtle but handsome texture stripe. Both cloths consist entirely of plain-woven woolen thread of a single color and weight, but after each group of twenty-five to thirty rows, the maker of the baby's shroud added three or four rows of the same yarn that had, however, been overspun (fig. 3.6). The special yarn twisted into gnarls in the cloth, giv-

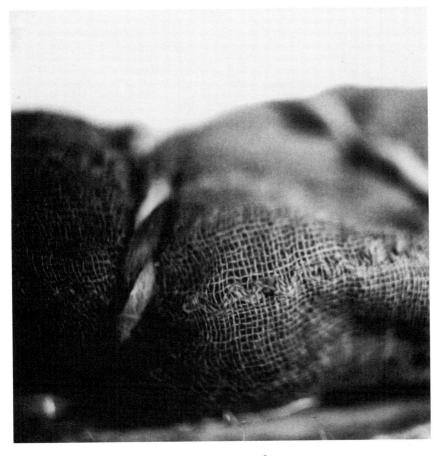

FIGURE 3.6

Detail of the Cherchen baby's shroud, showing narrow texture stripes of overspun yarn woven in at regular intervals. Overspun thread is made by twisting the fibers so much that the thread wriggles up into kinks when released, instead of lying flat.

ing a completely different texture to the thin stripes containing it. The trick is clever yet simple, making the most of very little—a trait we saw often among the mummies' possessions.

Not only is the dyed thread of the shroud identical to the man's clothing, but the bonnet appears to have been made from the same supplies of blue and red combed but unspun wool used for the man's leggings and the binding cords of both mummies. The similarities in these various materials make one suspect that the Blue Bonnet Baby was the man's own child, dressed from the same storehouse of supplies and dying soon after him. Indeed the whole group of finds suggests that one of the three women was the infant's mother and the nursing bottle a desperate but doomed stratagem by the survivors to keep the little fellow alive after her death. We take sterilized baby-formula and boilable glass bottles for granted today, but not so long ago, and in undeveloped countries even now, babies deprived of mother's milk routinely die from germs in the substitute milk supply unless milk is provided by a wet nurse, another lactating woman. (Well-wishers and avid marketers who provide powdered infant formula to such countries usually don't understand that the contaminated water used to mix with the powder dooms the child to a death probably more horrible and at least as certain as mere starvation.) The earnestness and inventive care of these prehistoric people still touch us across the millennia.

THE ÜRÜMCHI archaeologists worked on three other tombs at Cherchen, just a few among the hundreds in this ancient burial ground. None of the three graves was intact; the local salt diggers had come on them by accident and rummaged them thoroughly. The men later led Dolkun Kamberi and his associates to the site of their finds, a barren waste with little surface indication of the burials beneath. Nor had the bodies survived well in the disturbed graves. But some of the textiles had. With little else of human manufacture in the burials, these textiles yield the best clues we have just now to the local culture, contacts, and origins of the inhabitants of this far-flung place. So let's have a look at some of the fabrics and at what they tell us.

Tomb 3 produced two spectacular examples of a kind of cloth not seen before in ancient finds, though it proved to have interesting connections. Great lengths and widths of fabric had been made up laboriously by sewing together flat plaited bands, each only a centimeter wide—rather less than half an inch (plate 6, fig. 3.7). In one "patchwork" the best-preserved bands measured 143 cm long (roughly 5 1/2 feet), while in the second at least thirty-seven bands were sewn side by side. Some bands were monochrome, in bright shades of turmeric yellow, red, maroon, or blue; others contained multicolored patterns. Typically the cloths began with a few plain braids of different colors—say, yellow, red, yellow—then a patterned one, then several more plain ones of whatever colors the makers liked, another fancy one, and so on. The patterned ones took far more time to make, of course, so spreading out the "expensive" ones maximized their effect, as when people decorate their kitchens today with a few hand-painted tiles scattered among many plain ones. The designs included lozenges and triangles alternating in color like a harlequin's suit, some with decorative tufts at regular intervals where changing colors were tied on and off (fig. 3.7), and a particularly complex pattern that looked like little double axes laid end to end (fig. 3.8).

Huge cloths made up from narrow bands seemed, on the face of it, preposterously labor-intensive. That's like planting a lawn one seed at a time. Why not set up a single warp and then weave a lot of stripes on it, plain or fancy? But

FIGURE 3.7

Patterns on narrow plaited woolen bands found in Tomb 3 at Cherchen, 1st millennium B.C. In the lowest patterned band the ends of the different colored threads were left to hang out in little decorative tufts. (Photo I. Good.)

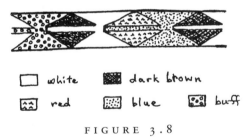

FIGURE 3.8

Design resembling double-bladed axes laid on their sides, from a plaited woolen band found at Cherchen, 1st millennium B.C.

as I thought about the culture as a whole, a different picture began to emerge.

These people made their textiles from sheep's wool. Someone had to tend those sheep, spending long and largely idle days and nights out in the meadows wandering about with them. Weaving on a loom requires many hours working in one place, and a large loom is too heavy and awkward to haul about easily, especially when a cloth is in progress. But band weaving is quite portable. Some cultures use a frame, but in most you just loop the far end of your long, skinny warp around a tree or your own big toe, pull back on the near end with your

FIGURE 3.9

Persian painting (19th century) of a young man wearing a coat of traditional striped silk that looks similar to the banded cloths of the early Tarim Basin (see fig. 3.8 and plate 6). (Courtesy of E. Ettinghausen.)

hand to create the necessary tension, and start weaving. If you have to stop and move, you just roll it up, unhitch the far end, and go. In short, anyone could weave or plait bands while herding sheep. Documentary films from 1985 show seminomadic women[3] in the highlands of Bosnia walking slowly among the boulders, great black sheepskin capes over their shoulders, singing at intervals

---

[3] Technically, transhumant. That is, they spend the winter in permanent houses in the lower valleys, with their sheep, then herd the flocks each summer up to the mountains, where they move from one temporary camp to another as the sheep graze.

in an ancient style that carries great distances. That way both sheep and family know where the shepherdesses are. All the while their hands keep busy, one woman spinning onto a spindle from a distaff full of wool, the other knitting socks with her ball of yarn tucked under her arm. One has a sense of glimpsing back into a lifestyle of the Bronze Age. The pace is slow, but nothing is wasted, including time.

So even though a cloth of plaited bands consumed more labor than a woven one, making it this way may have constituted the best overall use of time among herders. You spin and plait your wool while on the move most of the year, then quickly sew up the bands into larger cloths during the short sedentary season. That reasoning also suggests that herding was a *major* occupation among these people.

From a distance these banded cloths look remarkably like the typical striped silks seen in Persian paintings of millennia later (fig. 3.9) and still available today in the bazaars of Istanbul and Ankara. This elegant striped cloth, a favorite of both Turks and Persians, may well have developed out of the humble prehistoric band textiles of Central Asia.

Researching how the strips themselves were made, I found that the flat bands were created by a widespread method called *oblique plaiting* (fig. 3.10), related to simple three-strand braiding but done with many more threads. The bands of the plaitwork fabrics contained anywhere from ten to forty threads, sometimes laid in double, whereas some pieces of plain red plaiting from later sites in the Tarim Basin, nearer 500 B.C., measured six to eight inches wide and must

FIGURE 3.10

Design of plaited woolen band from Cherchen, with diagram showing oblique angle both of the pattern threads and of the hidden threads that bind them together.

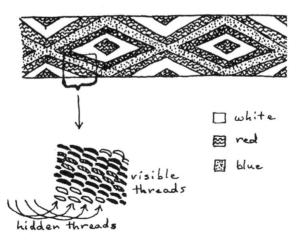

have required managing several hundred threads at once—probably *not* a job to do while herding sheep.[4]

I also kept an eye out for how Cherchen Man's peculiar round belt cord might have been produced—without luck until I happened to spend a weekend with a friend in Wales. Susan Wadlow and I met as children, and whenever I can, I visit her in the sheep-grazing borderlands above Shrewsbury, where the well-known medieval mystery series about Brother Cadfael is set. This area has specialized in textile production for at least a thousand years, and Susan knows much about aspects of cloth unfamiliar to me, such as lacemaking, which she teaches. Together we have solved a number of textile puzzles over the years.

My photographs of Cherchen Man's belt reminded Susan of a Japanese cord-making technique called *kumihimo,* and she fetched the stand she had made for herself when learning to produce it. A *kumihimo* stand (fig. 3.11) consists of a flat, tablelike wooden disk, about eight inches across, raised on four tall legs and with a two-inch circular hole in the middle. In use, it looks like a spaghetti-eating monster, with long strings all around disappearing into the circular mouth, for the cord forms down through the hole. A weight fastened to its starting end pulls the new cord ever downward, while the strings that go into its making radiate from the hole, cross the flat surface of the disk, and hang down over the outer edge. Each length of yarn to be used is wound around a spool-shaped weight to give countertension, making it easier to manage the whole process. Depending on the cord's pattern and how thick you want it to be, you may have anywhere from eight to a couple of dozen threads, each wound on its own spool weight. To form the new cord, you simply grab two weights that are opposite each other on the stand and interchange their places, and you keep doing this with the other pairs of weights until they have all shifted; then you start over. The process is easy—and mesmerizing. The number, positions, and colors of threads, the order in which you move the pairs of weights, and whether they pass to the right or left of each other, together determine the patterns.

Looking at the cord half formed on Susan's stand, I agreed with her: the basic structure matched the Cherchen belt cord. Only the pattern and thickness differed. We began to search through her *kumihimo* books, and eventually, at a craft fair in California, I located the right design. To obtain the sequence

---

[4] The patterns of alternating triangles proved to be a function of how the colored threads, moving across the plaitwork at an angle, would show on the surface for a ways, then turn a corner and run along completely hidden for an equal distance. By careful selection of the order and number of contrastively colored threads, the ancient artisans worked out a variety of geometric designs.

FIGURE 3.11

Wooden stand for making traditional Japanese *kumihimo* cords. The round cord forms down through the hole in the center, while the threads from which it is being made hang out over the outer rim of the stand, wound onto and weighted by heavy spools. Japanese spools are typically of wood with heavy metal cores; those in the photo are exact replicas of clay spool weights from prehistoric Greece, which weigh the same amount as the Japanese ones and were probably used similarly.

I had recorded for Cherchen Man's belt, I needed 24 threads in five colors.

Another detail struck me as I surveyed Susan's *kumihimo* stand: I had seen small, spool-shaped weights like that before. Not in Chinese Turkestan, for almost no early tools have been unearthed there yet. Virtually no grave gifts except cloth accompany the dead, and the archaeologists haven't begun to search out and excavate ancient house sites. I had seen them, I realized, in Greece, where spool-shaped objects turn up all over Bronze Age and even Neolithic sites.[5] Excavators in Greece had repeatedly asked me what the objects were for, since they occurred with other textile implements. It turns out they are just the right size and weight for doing this sort of plaiting.

Their presence suggests, then, that not only the early inhabitants of the Tarim Basin but also those of prehistoric Greece sat around plaiting something akin to *kumihimo*. It is frustrating that in Europe we have textile tools everywhere, but virtually no textiles preserved to prove the point, whereas in Central Asia we have loads of textiles but no tools! How can we compare data, then, to know who got what from whom?

And what about the Japanese? Did they receive the method from farther west long ago or invent it on their own? Certainly we have no evidence that anyone from so far east had trekked to Central Asia yet. The Japanese archipelago lies nearly three thousand miles from Cherchen and the Tarim Basin. Even the Chinese didn't get to Inner Asia for another millennium, and China lies directly between Japan and the Tarim. So if any influence in this matter traveled to or from Japan, it was later and headed east.

As for possible influence on plaiting methods between the Tarim Basin and Europe, again it must have moved from west to east, if it existed, because many of the Aegean sites with these spool weights go back long before 2000 B.C.—that is, well before anybody had settled in the Tarim Basin. The first permanent settlers in the desert basins appear to have arrived just about 2000 B.C. The Cherchen culture, which left us the round cords, didn't flourish until about 1000 B.C., a thousand years later.[6]

Tomb 4 produced at least thirteen cloths, mostly of unclear use. Some were simply swatches of plain dark red wool in gauzy plain weave, with and without denser stripes of the same color or with stripes in a much brighter red. Others, always dark red, had probably come from garments, since they retained the characteristic piping, although we could no longer say *what* garments. The tomb also contained a dark red onion dome hat (like that in fig. 2.7) done in spiral *nalbinding* and an open-fronted white jacket with one sleeve oddly several inches shorter than the other. Did the owner have a stunted left arm? In any case, someone had carefully mended some frayed threads on the sleeve by tying their loose ends together.

Tomb 4 also contained large banded cloths. One of these (plate 5b) had been

[5] In the Aegean the Bronze Age runs from 3000 to 1200 B.C., the Neolithic from about 6000 to 3000 B.C.

[6] Quite a number of different types of plaiting, not just *kumihimo* cords and obliquely plaited bands, survived from the Cherchen graves. A particularly common cord consisted of a thick yarn of white wool covered by a "skin" obliquely plaited from alternating pairs of fine red and blue, then red and yellow (or white) threads.

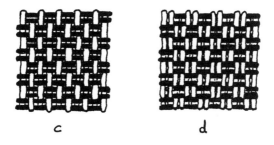

FIGURE 3.12

(a) Common (2/2) twill, in which weft goes over 2 warp threads, then under 2, offset-ting by 1 warp thread with each row. (b) *Half-basket twill*, in which 2 weft threads in-stead of 1 are laid into each row, otherwise following the usual twill pattern. (c) Plain *half-basket weave*, in which a doubled weft goes over and under single warp threads. (d) Plain *basket weave*, in which a doubled weft goes over and under doubled warp. Note that the plain basket weave and half-basket weave are just like plain weave except for the doubling. In these diagrams (unlike the previous ones with the spiders), the threads are shown close together, as they are in most fabrics. Fig. 3.12a is the same weave as 2.13b, but the diagonal effect of twill is much more striking when the threads are pushed up tight.

sewn together not of half-inch-wide plaiting like the others, but of seven-inch-wide strips of cloth woven in an unusual weave, half-basket twill (fig. 3.12b). Red and yellow stripes alternated, except where a short stretch of yellow had been added to a red one to fill out the needed length. Clearly the culture did not set a high value on symmetry. The piece must have formed the skirt of a large robe or dress, for the ends of the strips were sewn together into a circle over six feet (two meters) around, and near the top of what's left were marks where the material had been habitually gathered—presumably around the waist of the wearer. A thick plait of red, white, and blue edged the bottom.

We know little about the occupant of Tomb 4, not even his or her sex. Local

FIGURE 3.13

Twill tapestry of interlocked red and yellow spirals, from a disturbed tomb at Cherchen, early to mid-1st millennium B.C. (Photo I. Good.)

diggers had ransacked the tomb, destroying its structure and chucking things out in all directions. But the owner had good taste, for it also contained some far more intricate pieces of weaving than anything our team had seen up to this point—in particular, three elegant pieces of tapestry. One was a shred with interlocking red and yellow angular spirals (spirals again!), edged with a red, white, and blue braid (fig. 3.13). Another swatch, mainly white, had a band of zigzags colorfully executed in blue, light red, yellow, maroon, and peach.

The very fact of finding tapestry here startled us, since the Egyptians learned to negotiate this fancy technique only about 1500 B.C., after they had been weaving for three thousand years, importing the idea from their Syrian neighbors. How, we wondered, did tapestry get as far east as the eastern Tarim Basin so fast?

But maybe it wasn't quite so fast as it seemed at first glance. The radiocarbon dates of 1000 B.C. for the Cherchen burials were taken exclusively from the undisturbed tombs of Cherchen Man and his family, so this disturbed grave may have been later by several centuries, for all we know. New excavations of more than a hundred tombs at this graveyard done in late 1996, not yet published,

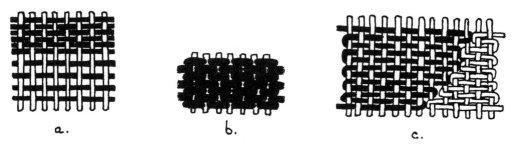

a.   b.   c.

FIGURE 3.14

In many fabrics there are about as many threads per centimeter in one direction as in the other *(balanced weave),* as in the lower part of diagram *a.* Without changing from plain weave, one can also pack the weft threads much closer together, as in the upper part of *a.* This produces a *weft-faced* weave, so called because we see mostly weft and not much warp. If one does this trick using a weft yarn that is much fatter than the warp yarn, as in *b,* the weft will virtually hide the warp. *Tapestry* uses this ability to hide the warp, so that different colors of weft alone can be manipulated to make designs, as in *c.*

show that the Cherchen cemetery up on the salt flat remained in use into the early centuries A.D. On internal grounds, a date of 500 B.C. for the tapestries would feel more comfortable to me. The presence of the peculiar purply-red-brown fabric, however, indicates that Tomb 4 belonged to a direct continuation and elaboration of Cherchen Man's culture. A strange detail of the tapestry confirms this continuity of tradition.

Tapestry depends upon tamping down the weft so tightly that it covers the warp (fig. 3.14b). That is, here our spider lays down plump rows of her silken weft so close together that you can't see the grass stems of the warp anymore. (The weave itself is normally just plain weave.) Since the warp doesn't show, changing the color of the weft alone during weaving will produce solid fields of color usable to produce designs—simple geometric ones, like the Cherchen pieces, or entire scenes of people, animals, landscapes, and so forth, as in the huge and famous Gobelin tapestries created for the French royalty. (Ironically, the famed Bayeux Tapestry depicting the Norman takeover of England in A.D. 1066 is *not* a true tapestry since the successive scenes are entirely embroidered onto the surface of plain cloth, rather than woven in.) The underlying technique of packing the weft to hide the warp, known as *weft-facing,* had probably been invented in the Near East as a response to trying to use wool for weaving, back around 4000 B.C. when woolly sheep first became available.[7] The same impetus had apparently led to the invention of twill in Anatolia about the same time.

[7] Although sheep had been among the first animals domesticated, around 8000 B.C. in the Near East, it took four thousand years of inbreeding to come up with usably woolly ones. Before that, sheep were kept for their meat. See Chapter 7.

Why these changes in weaves when wool arrived? The only fibers that people had before that—namely, plant stem fibers like linen and hemp (used since 25,000 B.C. at least)—don't stretch, whereas wool fibers can stretch tremendously (just like the hair from your own head: try pulling on both ends of one hair). When you pull tight the warp threads on the loom so you can weave the weft in around them, plant fibers stay put but wool keeps stretching. And it may eventually snap as you continue to punish it by beating the rows of weft thread in. Spacing the warp widely and then covering it, as in typical *weft-faced weaves* (fig. 3.14), protects the warp from wear; similarly the pairing of warp threads in twill (fig. 3.12a) cuts in half the strain during weaving. In short, both twill and tapestry developed in response to the peculiarities of sheep's wool, and all three—the two new weaves and the wool itself—developed far to the west of Central Asia and long before the graves of Cherchen.

The red and yellow spiral tapestry startled us, then, in not quite conforming to the way the rest of the world made tapestry. True, the weft covered the warp as it should, but looking closely, we saw that the weave wasn't the expected plain weave. These people had used their own peculiar long-hop twill (fig. 2.13c) to make their tapestry! Normal twill, which jumps only two threads, won't cover the warp, but by long-jumping over three and four warp threads at a time, as they had here, the weavers could easily make the weft cover the warp to produce a solid field of color. Such a substitution of technique suggests that these people had learned to make tapestry just by looking at pieces imported from the Near East, rather than by having been taught how to make it by other weavers. The weavers of Cherchen, like its tailors and hatmakers, were an inventive lot.

And nowhere more so than in the other tapestry piece from Tomb 4, a spectacular turquoise blue shirt or chemise with a stepped collar, broad and flat like that of a sailor suit, and a strip of polychrome tapestry setting off the bright red cuffs and hem (plate 7).

At a distance the collar seemed a lighter shade of turquoise than the body, although up close the weft seemed identical. We discovered that the makers had invented a weaver's equivalent of the old jeweler's trick of mounting tinfoil behind a gem to reflect the light through it more brightly. In this case, although the warp inside the main cloth was dark brown, within the collar it was peach pink, and despite the tight packing of the weft in the long-hop twill, the warp still peeked out from underneath just enough to alter the hue. This trick made the unique stepped shape of the broad collar stand out all the more.

The construction of the collar itself was not only inventive but a skillful tour de force. It lies flat across shoulders, chest, and back (woven with the warp running from one shoulder to the other), but its outer edge decreases by five square

Mummy of a 55-year-old male,
known as Cherchen Man, from
Tomb 2 at Cherchen, ca. 1000 B.C.,
in the southern Tarim Basin. He was
6'6" (2 m) tall, with light brown
hair; he wore white deerskin boots
and brightly colored woolen pants,
shirt, and felt leggings.
(Photo Jeffery Newbury/©1994.
Reprinted with permission of
Discover Magazine.)

PLATE I

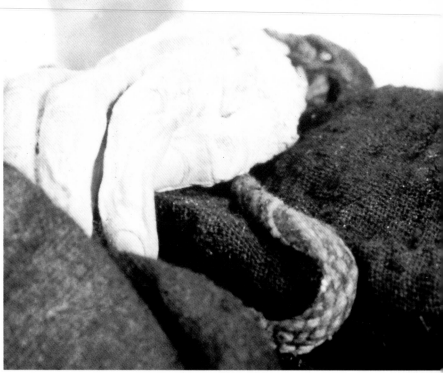

Cherchen Man's belt cord, plaited from yarns of five colors in a technique known among handcrafters today by the Japanese name *kumihimo*. (Photo I. Good.)

PLATE 2

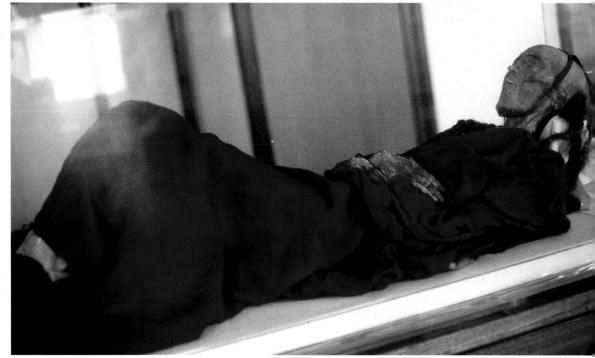

PLATE 2

Mummy of Cherchen Woman, best preserved of women in Tomb 2 at Cherchen (1000 B.C.). She stood over 6 feet tall (1.9 m) and wore a red dress and white deerskin boots.

Close-up of Cherchen Woman's face, with a chin strap that failed to hold her jaw shut, leaving her with a typical mummy gape. Note the face paint of a red triangle on her cheek, with yellow spirals both inside the triangle and climbing over the bridge of her nose.

PLATE 3A

PLATE 3B

Less well-preserved woman found to right of Cherchen Man's feet in Tomb 2; ca. 1000 B.C. The cloth visible on her left knee is decorated with red and white spirals typical of steppe art. (Photo D. Kamberi.)

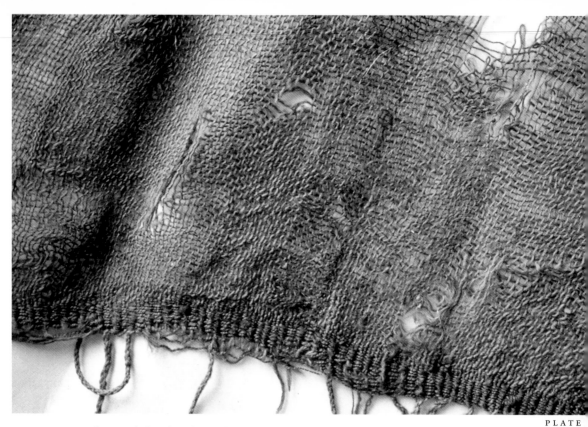

Blue wool shawl with 2 red stripes, 2 ribbed and bicolored end bands, and knotted fringes, from Tomb 2 at Cherchen, 1000 B.C. (Photo I. Good.)

Mummy of infant in a felt bonnet of blue wool with red edging; from Tomb 1 at Cherchen, 1000 B.C. Little blue stones cover the eyes, and tiny wisps of red wool fill the nostrils.

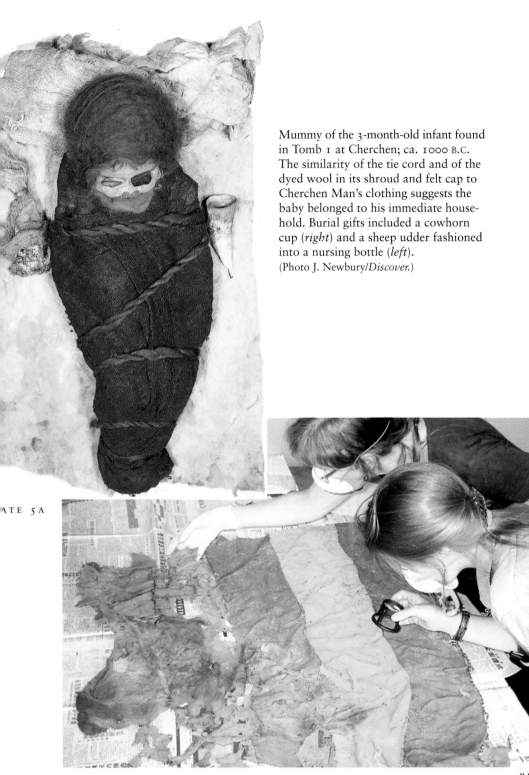

Mummy of the 3-month-old infant found in Tomb 1 at Cherchen; ca. 1000 B.C. The similarity of the tie cord and of the dyed wool in its shroud and felt cap to Cherchen Man's clothing suggests the baby belonged to his immediate household. Burial gifts included a cowhorn cup (*right*) and a sheep udder fashioned into a nursing bottle (*left*). (Photo J. Newbury/*Discover.*)

PLATE 5A

PLATE 5B

Irene Good (*foreground*) and the author studying a striped woolen skirt from Tomb 4, Cherchen, in a workroom at the Ürümchi Museum in 1994. Latex gloves protect the ancient fabrics from the oils in our skin, while dust masks protect our lungs. (Photo V. Mair.)

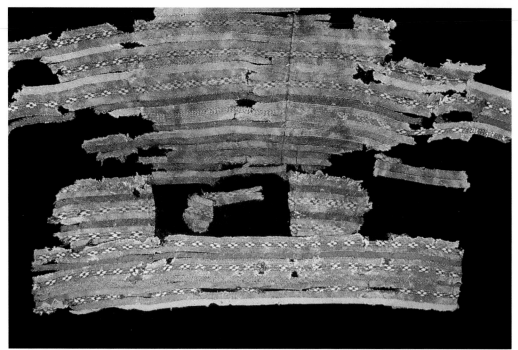

Cloth made up of many narrow bands plaited of wool and sewn together; from Cherchen, 1st millennium B.C. Note how the ornate bands are spaced out with plain ones. (Photo I. Good.)

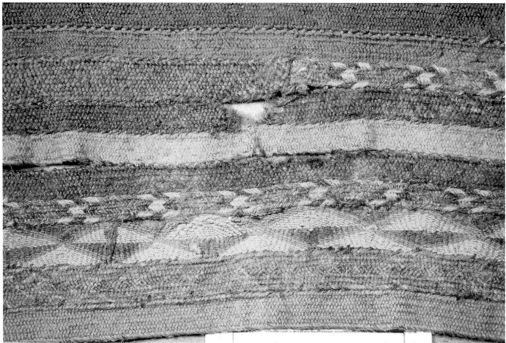

Detail of woolen cloth sewn together from narrow plaited bands, found in Tomb 3 at Cherchen. Symmetry was not an issue: a blue band ekes out the length of a fancy band in one row. (Photo I. Good.)

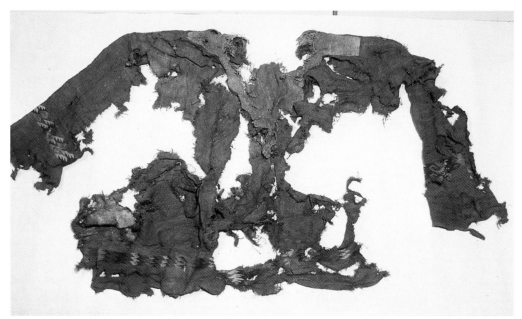

Turquoise blue woolen shirt from Cherchen, woven in long-hop twill, with tapestry in a 3-stepped jagged "lightning" pattern near the bottom, and spirals alternating with jagged "lightning" near the cuffs. The turquoise of the stepped collar is lighter than the body because its warp is peach pink rather than dark brown. 1st millennium B.C. (Photo I. Good.)

Detail of the turquoise shirt from Cherchen, showing red, brown, yellow, and blue tapestry design of spirals alternating with jagged "lightning" zigzags. (Photo I. Good.)

PLATE 8

Woolen brocade of Argali sheep standing on a red border below bicolored hourglass figures; from Tomb 4 at Cherchen, 1st millennium B.C. This is the only depiction of real life so far among all the Cherchen textiles.

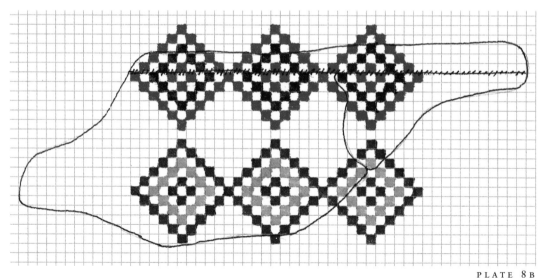

Drawing of a white woolen fragment brocaded with concentric lozenges, one stack of nested red and blue ones, the other of nested brown and tan ones. A seam line runs through the red and blue stack, to one side of middle, joining 2 closed selvedges so that the middles of the lozenges match up.

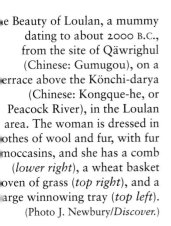

The Beauty of Loulan, a mummy dating to about 2000 B.C., from the site of Qäwrighul (Chinese: Gumugou), on a terrace above the Könchi-darya (Chinese: Kongque-he, or Peacock River), in the Loulan area. The woman is dressed in clothes of wool and fur, with fur moccasins, and she has a comb (*lower right*), a wheat basket woven of grass (*top right*), and a large winnowing tray (*top left*). (Photo J. Newbury/*Discover.*)

PLATE 9

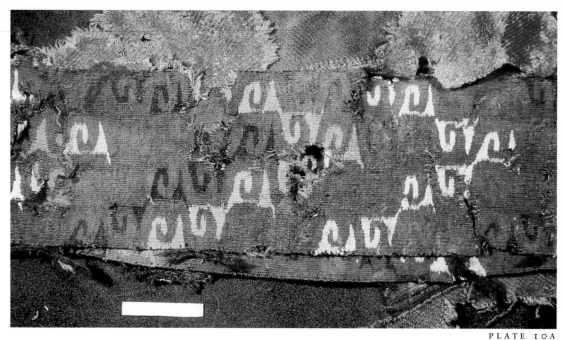

Woolen tapestry with tiny interlocked pattern of scrolls from a disturbed tomb at Cherchen, similar to some from a frozen burial in Kurgan 2 at Pazyryk in the Altai Mountains. The Pazyryk date of ca. 450 B.C. suggests a similar date for the Cherchen tapestry. (Photo I. Good.)

Mummy of a woman from Qäwrighul, near Loulan, ca. 1800 B.C., now housed at the Xinjiang Institute of Archaeology. She wears an oblong wrap woven of wool and a felt hood. (Photo J. Newbury/*Discover*.)

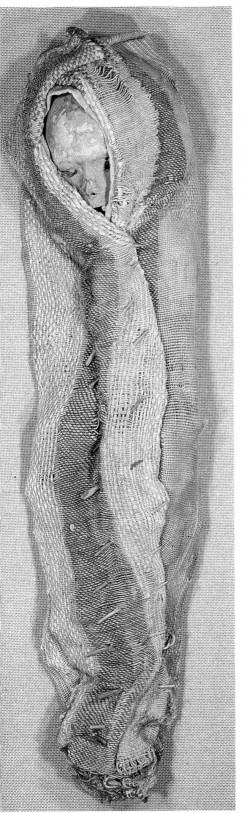

Mummy of 8-year-old child wrapped in a woven woolen shroud or blanket closed with wooden pegs; from Qäwrighul near Loulan, ca. 1800 B.C. (Photo J. Newbury/*Discover.*)

Textile folded over the top of the Qäwrighul child's head, showing the complicated pattern of the weave.

PLATE 12

Bicolor plaid woolen twills from the early Celtic salt mines at Hallstatt, Austria, dating to sometime between 1200 and 400 B.C.; woven in yellow and brown (above) and green and brown (below). The Hallstatt twills are remarkably similar to contemporary ones from Xinjiang, suggesting a common origin in weaving tradition. (Courtesy of Naturhistorisches Museum Wien; photos E. Barber.)

Plaid woolen twill from a burial at Qizilchoqa, near Hami, dating to sometime between 1200 and 700 B.C.; woven in light brown with light blue and white stripes. (Photo I. Good.)

Reproduction of 6-color plaid twill in garment from Qizilchoqa, near Hami (ca. 1200–700 B.C.). The garment was stitched together in light blue and fastened with a button also covered with light blue yarn. (Woven by R. Ashenden, after Wang L.)

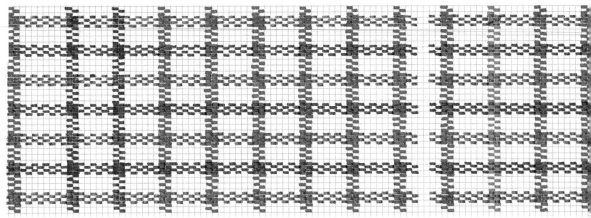

PLATE 14

Diagram of a typical red, white, and blue plaid cloth from the Qizilchoqa cemetery near Hami (ca. 1200–700 B.C.). Unlike the darker-ground plaids, which are twill, the several white-ground plaids like this one are woven in plain weave. The break denotes a section where the red and white stripes repeat many times.

PLATE 14

A Kazakh herders' camp of yurts (round felt tents) in the high grassy valleys of Nan Shan (Southern Mountains) south of Ürümchi. Horse riders are practicing for the annual races on the flat strip just above the yurts, while a modern minibus is parked between the yurts. The local stream from which the herders get their water has been channeled to run beside the modern paved roadway.

End of the Toyuq Gorge, where it opens out into the gravel desert of the Turfan
Depression. The red rock sides of the gorge are too steep to support life, but where
the river spreads out onto the flatland for a short way, the land is bright green with
the crops of the local people: grapes, melons, grain, and mulberry trees. The typical
oasis of Central Asia is of this sort.

Buddhist monastery caves at Bezeklik, in the Flaming Mountains near Turfan, 1st
millennium A.D. The barren red rocks of the mountains contrast sharply with the lush
green beside the small river at the bottom. The caves were once filled with religious
paintings, many of which were taken by the German explorer A. von LeCoq to Berlin
early this century (e.g., plate 16). Those that he left have been badly defaced by local
Muslims who believe that one should not depict humans. No restoration has been
carried out except of the walkway.

Detail of a painting from Cave 20 at Bezeklik (see plate 15a), near Turfan, ca. A.D. 900, showing Tokharian worthies donating trays of moneybags to a Buddhist saint. Note the reddish hair and pale eyes of the man at right, as well as the typically Caucasoid features of both (big nose, round eyes, heavy beard). The early mummies are of this same type, as are many of the current inhabitants of the region (see fig. 10.7).

steps as it goes, so that it forms a giant stepped cross. Another stepped patch
was sewn over the main cloth under each arm. Yet there are no raw or sewn
edges: the steps were sculpted on the loom—a tremendously time-consuming
task.[8]

The polychrome areas of tapestry, again in long-hop twill and differing between hem and cuff, were the work of experts. Near the bottom of the chemise
is a three-step jagged "lightning" pattern (of red, brown, yellow, and blue),
whereas near the cuff of the inset sleeve (plate 7b) we found spirals alternating
with jagged lightning shapes. People who don't have television and movies to
entertain them may have a lot of time on their hands to create ornate things.

My favorite textile of all depicts a row of sassy-looking Argali sheep with big
curving horns and large brown or bright blue eyes (plate 8a). Some of the sheep
are white, some tan, and some red-brown, on a dark brown background, all
perching above a red border and below a row of "hourglasses." They are done
in brocade technique—that is, by covering the basic weft (that holds the cloth
together) with extra weft threads in other colors to make the design. The Argali (commonly known by the Mongol word for "ram"; zoologists call it *Ovis
ammon*) is the wild sheep of the area and the largest of all wild sheep, standing
some four feet high at the shoulder and bearing impressive curly horns. I have
not been able to find that it ever has blue eyes, and I wonder whether the weaver
got that idea from the *people* of Cherchen. After all, someone had gone to the
trouble of finding blue stones—something of a rarity—to place over the infant's eyes, and a remarkable number of the non-Chinese people in the Tarim
Basin today have blue eyes.

This brocade was the only depiction of real life among all the Cherchen textiles, an attribute suggesting that it is a late piece. On the other hand, the simple brocade technique used is attested (in and around the Alps) as far back as
3000 B.C., the Late Stone Age.

Of the various remaining Cherchen textiles, three other pieces showed us
something completely new. One was a grungy, rumpled scrap of dark brown
twill with the remains of chain-stitched embroidery, the pattern of which was
not readily distinguishable. In the ancient Near East embroidery was relatively
late, developing only after millennia of decorating cloth with strictly woven designs. Apparently it was not an immediately obvious thing to do to cloth, al-

---

[8] The turquoise weft forms a closed selvedge at the bottom of each step as well as along the
slit of the neck hole, and the peach-colored warp turns back into the shed at the side of each
step—*at both ends.* But you can't weave thread into a shed that has already been closed! Unfortunately we did not have time to solve the riddle to our satisfaction, but my best guess is
that at the finishing end they had worked the warp ends back into the cloth with a needle,
doing it so carefully that you couldn't readily detect the difference.

though embroidery was starting to spread out of Mesopotamia and Syria by the time of Tutankhamon, ca. 1350 B.C. Embroidery seems to have started in China too by that time, chain stitch becoming a favorite Chinese stitch.

The second informative piece was a white cloth decorated with a simple but elegant pattern of little squares stacked and nested to make polychrome lozenges (plate 8b). At first glance it appeared to have an ancient mend, but the two edges joined by the stitching turned out to be closed selvedges, not torn edges. Someone had deliberately woven the pattern in such a way that the *interiors* of the lozenges would match up perfectly when seamed together—a feat that takes careful planning.

The third piece consisted of a strip of tapestry showing an interlocked scroll pattern in red, white, and blue that zigzags across the fabric (plate 10a). Its edge was sewn to a broad strip of red twill, with strips of green twill, brown plaiting, and dark yellow twill successively beyond that.

One detail in particular caught Irene Good's eye. A small section of the red scrolls in the tapestry consisted of a slightly paler and much silkier fiber than the rest. She eventually determined that it was cashmere, the fine hair of a type of goat named after its home in Kashmir, just north of India. This could account for the extra sheen Irene had noticed in the Cherchen Woman's handsome red dress. It also indicates that these people kept (or had access to) goats from the south as well as sheep from the west.

What caught *my* eye was its similarity, red twill sidebar and all, to some cloth found nearly seventy years ago at Pazyryk.

Pazyryk lies five hundred miles due north of Cherchen in the Altai Mountains, right where the steppe or grassland belt pinches to a narrow wasp waist between western Asia (Siberia) and eastern Asia (Mongolia) as the steppe zone passes through the one range of mountains that severely obstructs its east-west sweep (map 2.9). In a small Altaic side valley now called Pazyryk, nomadic herders of twenty-five hundred years ago laid their dead to rest in a group of kurgans, or burial mounds, some big and some small. Not long after, opportunists passing by noticed these conspicuous monuments, dug down into them from top center, and robbed the central burial chambers of whatever they viewed as valuable, objects of precious metal in particular.

High and northerly, however, Pazyryk lies in an area subject to subsurface permafrost. In some cases a few feet of groundwater had already seeped into the tombs and frozen so hard that the robbers could loot only the top half of the contents; the rest was stuck fast in the ice. And the conical holes that they dug funneled so much additional rain and snow straight into the interiors that everything else was soon encased in permanent ice as well.

Until 1929, when a Russian archaeologist named Sergei Rudenko came along with hot water. Opening first one, then another of the largest kurgans in the group, he loosened the contents a bit at a time with buckets of water heated over a campfire. Slow though it was, the work was well worth the effort, for the ice had preserved wood, leather, textiles, and even the ornately tattooed skins of the dead, lying in their hollowed log coffins.

The inner chamber of Kurgan 2, built up of notched logs like Abraham Lincoln's hut, had been hung with great lengths of cloth, presumably in imitation of the winter dwellings of the nomadic herders who built the tombs. (As in medieval castles of northern Europe, where huge tapestries adorned the walls, the hangings would trap the drafty breezes and keep the rooms a good deal warmer.) But this was one of the tombs already half filled with ice when the robbers dug in, and the bottoms of the hangings were already frozen several feet into the ice. Apparently the intruders viewed this heavy cloth as valuable, for they tore off as much as they could get at. The rest remained for us. It consists of wide strips of red woolen twill alternating with equal-sized strips of tapestry patterned in red, white, and blue interlocking scrolls. In short, it bears the same pattern as the Cherchen tapestry, with the difference that the little scrolls and the zigzagging of the color fields were woven at right angles to the way they lie in the Cherchen piece.

So great are the similarities (not just of the tapestries but also of sewing them to strips of plain twill) that one has to believe the two textiles belong to the same date as well as to the same tradition. Tree rings show that the five great kurgans of Pazyryk were built within fifty years of each other, probably between about 480 and 430 B.C. That suggests a similar date for the scrolled tapestry and the grave it came from at Cherchen. But exactly where these scroll-patterned tapestries originate is not yet known. There is much still to learn.

In all our days in Ürümchi we never glimpsed the inside of the storeroom, so I had no idea at the time what percentage of the Cherchen finds we looked at or whether our sample was representative. The armloads kept coming as long as we had time to work. Later Dolkun Kamberi told me that we had seen maybe a fifth of the Cherchen material and that he had tried to see to it that we could inspect representatives of all the most interesting types of cloth. Undoubtedly, therefore, much plain stuff was passed over, but even so, these ancient people clearly dressed in a remarkably colorful way. The reopening of the Cherchen excavations in 1996 apparently has brought many more boxloads of colorful cloth to the museum.

Beyond that, we had little context for most of what we saw. The labels read simply *85 Q Z*, meaning they had come from the 1985 excavations near the town of Cherchen—written *Qiemo* if you transliterate into Roman script the Chinese name of the place—at the little site called *Zaghunluq*. (I never asked

FIGURE 3.15

Ancient cemetery of the 1st millennium B.C. at Subeshi, near Turfan, in the Toyuq Gorge of the Flaming Mountains (Qizil-tagh; so named because everything is red-brown). The cemetery was originally flat, with no grave markers; the low mounds are debris and fill from graves beside them, dug up largely by local people.

why they used Roman letters on their labels when Uyghur has now reverted to the Arabic script and Chinese uses its ancient system of word characters.) Those that I have described as coming from particular graves had the additional indicator *M* (for *mù*, the Chinese word for a grave) plus the number assigned to the tomb, and often yet another number that normally indicates that this was the *n*th thing retrieved from that spot. So, for example, the textiles we saw from Tomb 4 all had *source* labels reading *85QZ M4*, but seven stopped there while others continued with the *find* numbers 6, 22 (three labeled "22"—all of similar but not identical red cloth), 50, 57, and 59. Remembering that the salt diggers had thoroughly ransacked Tomb 4, we can surmise that the pieces without find numbers lay about the surface, while the others came from more nearly their original positions in the burial. Even so, what we saw included only five of at least 59 numbered finds—not necessarily all or even mostly textiles, to judge by the mats, animal bones, etc. included in Cherchen Man's tomb.

Lack of context destroys much of the historical value of an object. Unscientific digging of archaeological sites has long been a problem worldwide, wherever the contents have been perceived as having value. (At Pazyryk intruders were robbing tombs by 400 B.C.; in Egypt the process had begun by 2500 B.C.) During our trip we visited a somewhat later cemetery site, dating to about 500 B.C., where nearby villagers had looted many of the remaining graves the minute the Ürümchi archaeologists left for the season. The place looked like the warren of a colony of ground squirrels: mounds and holes everywhere (fig. 3.15; map 10.2). And all about lay finger and leg bones, a jaw here, a pate there—old bones had no value to the robbers, so they chucked them everywhere. The archaeologist accompanying us, who had dug the site originally, climbed down eight feet into one of the pits where you could see more bones protruding and gently dug out the long hair and netted cap of the woman who had once occupied the grave. As he handed things up, we bagged them, and he told us that his team had found one gold earring and two gold beads in this cemetery, while excavating a dozen graves. On the strength of that, the locals had spaded up twenty or thirty more, and might have dug all the way to Ürümchi if they had found real treasure.

Whether they found any more gold, and whether they viewed anything else as valuable enough to keep or sell, we'll never know. Almost every site that archaeologists begin to dig, not just in China but the world over, runs the risk of being ransacked while the scientists aren't looking. But without the human cultural context, the central value of all the material—gold and bones alike—is lost forever. For understanding human history ultimately carries far more value than little bits of shiny metal. As Santayana said, those who do not know their past are condemned to relive it . . . unimproved.

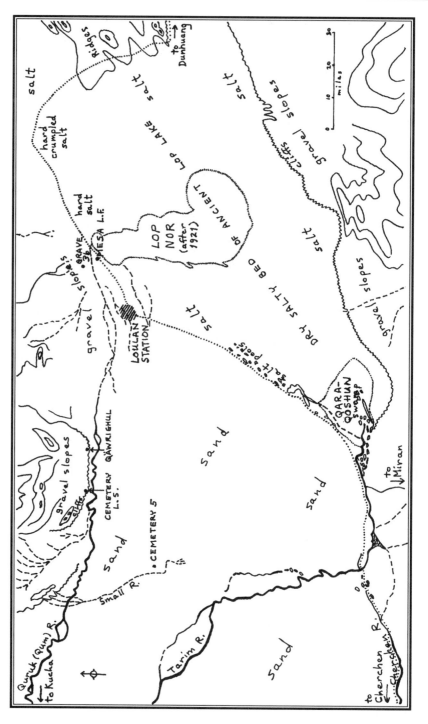

MAP 4.1

The
"Beauty of Loulan"

THE OLDEST mummies found so far in the Tarim Basin come not from
Cherchen in the south but from the area known in ancient Chinese annals as
Loulan, toward the east end of the egg-shaped Taklamakan Desert (maps 1.1,
4.1). They do not draw so much attention either in the museum gallery or in the
press, being less colorfully arrayed than the Cherchen folk. Instead they wear
only shades of natural brown and beige. But some of them are just as well preserved, and whereas the Cherchen Man's tomb dates to roughly 1000 B.C. (the
time of Saul and David in Jerusalem), some of the Loulan mummies seem to
have been buried as early as 2000 to 1800 B.C. (the era of Abraham and the pa-
triarchs).

The woman from Qäwrighul (Chinese: Gumugou), the so-called Peacock
River site northwest of Loulan Station, lies in state in the first case of the
mummy gallery, bundled up in a brown woolen wrap with her funerary gifts
around her (plate 9). Framed by auburn hair, her face looks so peaceful and

---

Opposite page: Detailed map of the Loulan and Lop Nor area. Dashed lines show beds
of intermittent rivers; dotted line from SW to NE shows Sir Aurel Stein's exploratory
route toward Dunhuang, approximating one early track of the Silk Road. Lop Nor—dry
when Stein passed through but wet when the ancient Chinese Loulan Station flourished
(ca. 100 B.C.–A.D. 330)—refilled with water in 1921, when the Quruk ("dry"—alias
Qum "sand[y]") River captured most of the water previously flowing south to the Qara-
Qoshun.

hauntingly beautiful that she has captured the imagination of the Turkic population of the whole province, who nicknamed her the Beauty of Loulan. A painting by a local artist of how she probably looked when alive now adorns wall posters and the CD covers of recordings by local Turkic musicians.

She is scarcely closer to "Turkic" in her anthropological type than she is to Han Chinese. The body and facial forms associated with Turks and Mongols began to appear in the Tarim cemeteries only in the first millennium B.C., fifteen hundred years after this woman lived.[1] But the Uyghurs do have a good reason to think of these mummies as among their ancestors, for a noticeable number of the non-Chinese people living in Xinjiang today have blue eyes and light brown or reddish hair, a legacy of old intermarriages with the ancient early arrivals from the west, who lost their linguistic and cultural—but not genetic—identity a thousand years ago in the rising tide of people entering from the north and east.

The artifacts around this woman tell us much (see frontispiece). Her crude ankle-high moccasins consist of leather with the fur on the outside, while her middy-length skirt, also leather, has the fur turned inward for warmth. Her knee-length overwrap, secured with a wooden pin, is woven of sheep's wool and constructed with extra weft forming thousands of long loops on the surface, loops intended to insulate the wearer. Provision against cold weather clearly concerned her: perhaps she died in the winter. She also wears a hoodlike woolen cap, rather like Little Red Riding Hood's, that could be tied snugly under the chin.

The hood alone tells many tales. To make it, the woman started by felting blond wool over two pieces of dark brown woven cloth. (Remember that felting can make a cap impervious to rain and wind; this was the Tilley Hat of its time.) We know the cloths came from two sources because on the left side both warp and weft have been spun the same direction, whereas half the threads in the right-hand cloth are spun the opposite way. Next she cut and sewed each half to shape it over the crown of the head and sewed the two halves together (fig. 4.2), clearly in that order because the thick plied thread of her stitches lies on top of the blond layer of added felting. To strengthen the center seam (running from the middle of the forehead to the nape of the neck) so that it wouldn't tear from the strain, she added three edging cords. One runs around the base of the neck and hangs out for use as a chin tie. Around the face, however, she whipped a plain brown cord to the edge of the cloth and then a second cord

---

[1] Even now, after many decades of ethnically Han Chinese people flooding into Xinjiang from central China as immigrants, most of the population outside Ürümchi is still Turkic, not Chinese.

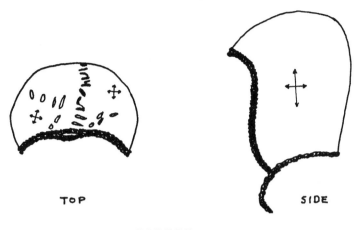

TOP   SIDE

FIGURE 4.2

Construction of the Beauty of Loulan's hood, 2000 B.C., sewn together from 2 pieces of felted, woven wool (crossed arrows show the straight of the fabric), which have been shaped at the crown by heavy stitches (left) and sewn together from the center of the forehead to the nape of the neck. An edge cord sewn around the bottom strengthens the seam at the back and hangs out for use as a chin tie. Two more cords strengthen the seam at the forehead and rim the face. The outermost of these is plaited of colored yarns.

plaited of red and probably blue yarns. This edging, despite the fading, gives us our one and only indicator that she and her people already knew how to dye wool.

She finished off her headgear by sticking into it a large, straight feather, which together with her blanket wrap gives her the air of an American child dressed up to play "Indians."

To counterbalance the impression that all these pieces could be deciphered as fully and subtly as the hood, I must mention that her blanket wrap caused us much headache and even hilarious embarrassment. Since the Qäwrighul lady's Plexiglas case remained closed, we had no opportunity to see the bottom side of anything or poke about among the folds of cloth. What you saw was what you got, and that did not include the answers to several puzzles. For one thing, we wanted to understand how she had woven the loops that formed the insulation, but the loops lay so densely on the surface that we couldn't see beneath to the structure. We noticed on the right side of her chest, however, a loopless section of cloth, a patch that looked the way one might expect the back of the cloth to appear if the loops had been woven in a fairly common way (fig. 4.3). But here the weaving was so dense that we couldn't see whether this piece had loops on its underside—that is, whether it was truly a swatch of the same cloth that had somehow gotten turned over. As Irene and I hunted for any place that might give us a clue, we also kept noticing torn regions where we could see a

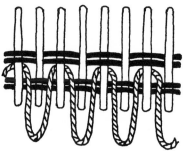

FIGURE 4.3

How the weft looping on the Beauty of Loulan's wrap was apparently done, with the regular weft doubled (giving half-basket weave) and an extra weft of thicker (S-plied) yarn forming loops between the double rows of regular weft.

netlike white cloth beneath, like surgical gauze only with mesh having quarter-inch-wide holes. Thoroughly intrigued as to what *that* was, since it looked more like plant fiber than wool, we finally asked Dolkun Kamberi, as he was passing through the gallery, whether he could find out anything about it for us.

"That white stuff?" he said, and then laughed. "Oh, that's just backing they added during conservation to keep the woolen cloak together!" So the mysterious white netting was modern cotton gauze, and its peculiar weave and unexpected fiber had to be erased from our archaeological notebooks.

If some things proved to be less than they seemed at first, others turned out to be more. With the woman lay part of a small comb (see plate 9, on right, and frontispiece).[2] Four of the coarse teeth of this comb remained, bound together at the top in a way showing that perhaps twice that many teeth had once existed. Visitors assume that she used it to comb her hair, but its form and coarseness closely resemble ancient combs found in the Near East, whose wear marks show they had been used over long periods of time to pack the weft in tightly during weaving. Perhaps she used her comb for both activities—a handy dual-purpose tool.

The four-thousand-year-old woman also possessed a neatly woven bag or soft basket. Inside it the archaeologists found some grains of wheat; and those who had laid her to rest had covered her head and chest with a large, flat basket in the form of a winnowing tray, used to clean wheat of its chaff. To winnow, you toss the wheat repeatedly into the air so that the wind blows the lightweight

---

[2] The comb is reconstructed in the frontispiece (low center, lying propped up on the basket) on the basis of several similar combs found by Folke Bergman in the Loulan area in the 1930s.

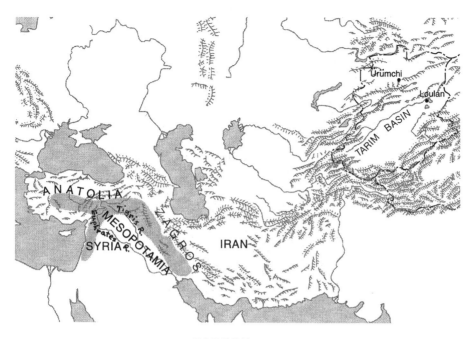

FIGURE 4.4

Map of the Fertile Crescent (shaded area around Mesopotamia), the foothill region of the Near East in which plants and animals were first domesticated in the early Neolithic (starting about 9000 B.C.). The idea of domestication gradually spread from Syria and the flanks of the Zagros Mountains into Anatolia (modern Turkey) and then to Mesopotamia (modern Iraq) in the 6th millennium B.C., finally reaching the Tarim Basin about 2000 B.C.

chaff (wheat husks) away to the side while the heavy, edible grains fall back down into a broad collection basket directly below (see frontispiece). Her being so well equipped for processing wheat suggests that this grain held a major place in her people's diet. This fact takes on more interest when paired with the observation that all the Central Asian textiles at this early period are made of sheep's wool, for both sheep and wheat were domesticated in the Near East, in the seminal area known as the Fertile Crescent (map 4.4). (The Fertile Crescent is a piedmont zone running from central Turkey and Syria past northern Mesopotamia and on south through the foothills of the Zagros Mountains, now the borderlands between Iraq and Iran. Here we find by far the earliest evidence for domestication of plants and animals, and here the wild varieties ancestral to domestic wheat, sheep, and several other early cultigens still live.)

The process of domesticating plants and animals began around 8000 B.C. or even earlier, leading gradually—and certainly by 4000 B.C.—to large-eared, large-grained varieties of wheat (such as emmer and einkorn) and to sheep that are woolly, as opposed to ones with hairy coats like a deer's (which is what the wild sheep have). The new and improved types of wheat, sheep, and other domesticates spread in an ever-increasing circle, of course; everyone wanted an easier life. Finally they reached eastward into the Tarim Basin, it seems, with this woman's tribe of people. Neither of these two cultigens could possibly have arrived from the east, from China, since neither of them existed there yet, nor were the wild ancestors of wheat or sheep indigenous to the Tarim Basin or to China. Each major early civilization has fed its masses on grain as an efficient food source, but each had to develop and domesticate what grew in its vicinity. Thus northern China, the heartland of budding Chinese civilization, thrived on millet (rice came in later from the south), whereas Central America began cultivating maize (corn), and Mesopotamia luxuriated in two domesticable grains, wheat and barley. The Qäwrighul woman's wheat basket and winnowing tray, like her woolen clothing and Caucasian features, demonstrate yet again the western origins of these early Central Asian cultures. Together they show that the migration had to postdate 4000 B.C., which is about when woolly sheep developed in the Near East from nonwoolly ones.

OUR BEAUTY is not alone with her wheat basket. The mummy of another woman dug up at Qäwrighul has a very similar basket by her head (plate 10b, peeking out to the right of her neck). This woman resided in 1995 not at the Ürümchi Museum but across town at the Xinjiang Institute of Archaeology (XIA), in its two-room viewing gallery. (*Xinjiang*, formerly spelled *Sinkiang* and pronounced approximately "shin-jahng," is the common Chinese name for the Uyghur Autonomous Region; it simply means "New Territory" in Chinese.) The XIA lady's lips have parted to reveal an even row of large white teeth, not the least decayed, and some wisps of red-brown hair show above her finely arched eyebrows. Like the first woman, she wears a hoodlike cap and an oblong woolen wrap. Her hood appears to be made of fiber felt, that is, nonwoven felt, the natural tan wool simply being matted together and then shaped with but a single seam from the pointy tip of the crown down the back of the head. The two ends of a tan plied cord sewn along the edge around the face served to tie it on under the chin, while the flaps beside her cheeks carry a simple ornament in the form of three parallel rows of tan stemstitch.

Given the extra work represented, tan decoration on tan seems superfluous, not to say dull. Maybe the threads had once been dyed but lost their color; learning to fix each different dye so it stays colorfast is not easy and must have required centuries of experimentation. We have seen that the Beauty's hood had a couple of colored threads, so dyeing was not unknown to the culture. Perhaps the same explanation holds for the decoration of the XIA woman's blanket wrap; its only adornment consists of some slightly paler and thicker threads that were twined in (as extra warp) from one edge of the cloth with considerable effort. If originally colored, they would have produced a very handsome effect.

In order to produce a wrap big enough to go around her with some overlap and also to reach from her shoulders to her shins, the ancient tailor—probably the woman herself—had to use two pieces of cloth, apparently the widest her loom could produce. The width of a farmer's furrow will tell you the size of the plow that made it, and the case was similar here. Not one piece of woven cloth that we saw from either Qäwrighul or Cherchen demonstrably exceeded two feet in width, although strips might be quite long. This tells us they used narrow looms. That narrowness, furthermore, dictated much about the forms of their clothing. A long, narrow, rectangular cloth coarsely woven of golden brown wool constituted the lower half of this wrap, and long whipping stitches attach it at waist level to a somewhat finer piece of the same color that clothes the XIA woman's upper body. Those who buried the woman pulled the fabric up high enough to cover her head (in the current display it is bunched around her neck to let us see her face), thereby exposing her ankles.

Once again, our analysis suffered from our not being able to look under anything, but glimpses here and there indicated that the cloths had *four* closed edges—selvedges—not just two, as in a modern factory-made cloth. (For example, at one corner the weaver had clearly incorporated the end of the heading cord into a simple side selvedge for a couple of inches.)

This tells us still more about the loom in use. Closed edges at both ends mean that the warp was *wound* around two transverse elements to achieve the necessary tension. These transverses could have been heavy cords tied firmly to the sides of some sort of rigid frame, or they could have been slim rods that would be slipped out and replaced by heavy cords when the cloth was finished. And we have already deduced that the loom was rather narrow, producing cloth no more than two feet wide.

From the fifth millennium B.C. when the Egyptians first learned to weave from their neighbors to the north, until about 1500 B.C. when they adopted a new loom from the same source, Egyptian weavers used a horizontal loom. It consisted of two beams pegged out on the ground with the warp wrapped around them and stretched in between (fig. 4.5 top). The design is simple and meets our requirement of a wrapped warp. One great advantage of this loom is that you can easily make your cloth as big as you like by pegging it out farther: six feet wide and fifty feet long presented no problem to the Egyptians.

The new loom that arrived in Egypt from Syria about 1500 B.C., however, was vertical (fig. 4.5 bottom), and it had the great advantage that one person could sit comfortably in front of it, instead of requiring two weavers to squat

FIGURE 4.5

The two types of loom used by the ancient Egyptians, as painted in their tombs. (After Davies.) *Top:* Horizontal ground loom (tomb of Khnumhotep, 19th c. B.C.). The warp is stretched between two beams pegged to the ground (3 of 4 pegs visible; perspective looks odd because warp is spread wider at back to prevent tangling; see fig. 7.7 for corner view). Two weavers (not painted to scale) squat on either side to pass the weft (probably in right weaver's right palm) back and forth between them. The sticks across the warp control the weave. *Bottom:* Vertical 2-beam loom (tomb of Neferronpet, 13th century B.C.). The warp is stretched between bars running across top and bottom of 2 vertical posts; 1 or 2 weavers sit in front of the loom to weave.

on either side. You could also see better what you were doing. That's why the Egyptians adopted it, since it came along with captive instructors in the art of making a new and intricately patterned cloth—namely, tapestry. (Before that the Egyptians wore plain white cloth and used their world-famous jewelry to dress up.)

This new loom, often known as the tapestry loom, consisted of a vertical frame with slim bars and cords across it to support and tension the warp. Because you have to insert the weft bobbin from first one edge and then the other to weave the cloth, you must either keep the cloth narrow so as to be able to reach or else use two weavers sitting side by side. (The Egyptians show both set-ups in their wall paintings.) Operated easily by a single weaver—all that's available in most small households—this loom too matches all the parameters we have deduced from the extant fabrics.

Other simple looms that meet our criteria exist, including the body-tensioned looms of Southeast Asia and the New World. But since both the horizontal and vertical two-beam looms existed well before 2000 B.C. in the Near East, where the other technology of the early Tarim people originated, these two are more likely candidates for the Qärwighul women's loom. Perhaps most likely of all is the very narrow and rudimentary two-beam loom still pegged out on the ground by Turkic nomads early in this century. Being so narrow (hence with few threads), the warp can be made very quickly, and the weaving proceeds along it very quickly—ideal for people who might be moving on next week.

THE THIRD and last mummy on display from this early period, also from Qäwrighul, corroborates all this reasoning in yet another way. The second Plexiglas case in the Ürümchi Museum, sandwiched between the Beauty and Cherchen Man, contains a small child perhaps eight years old, wrapped in a beige and brown blanket (plate 11). Long bone pins with simply carved heads, a dozen or so in number, pierce the layers of fabric to hold the bundle shut. When I looked at the available photographs of the Ürümchi mummies before going to China, I paid little attention to this blanket, it seemed so simple. But on close inspection it turned out to be one of the most complex (though not most difficult) pieces of weaving I saw there. Certainly its weaver would have benefited from using a loom that made the work easy to see.

Again the cloth is fairly narrow, with the width of the fabric running the length of the skinny little body and the tan warp going around it like the threads of a cocoon. One can pick out the simple brown cords that reinforce the side selvedges at the head and foot of the body and can also locate one end, presumably the tail of the cloth, lying folded back by the left cheek, where it signs off in a short but elaborate fringe. The fourth edge remains completely hidden just inside the bundle. All the "decoration" runs parallel to the child's spine and therefore was woven in as weft—the easy direction to do so.

Two wide stripes of natural brown wool near the ends of the largely tan cloth supply the most obvious adornment. Whoever wrapped the child used great care in folding the blanket so that these stripes framed the little face: a pale band closest to each cheek with the wide brown just beyond, like an oval picture frame in sepia. Here and there the edge of an inner cap of blond felt peeks out from under the cloth along the cheek and forehead. The preparer expended even more care in folding and pinning one edge of the cloth over the top of the child's head (plate 11b), for here is where the most elaborate decoration is found: a sort of checkerboard of natural red-brown and tan wools, together with some stripes of a thicker, whiter weft that sometimes defy the regular rows of the weaving.

The construction of the checkerboard is simple enough: the weaver paired the tan warp threads and wove a fat, three-ply, ruddy brown yarn across them.[3] Because the elements in both directions thus appear much wider than elsewhere, and because they contrast sharply with each other in color, they give the effect of a checked pattern, like a miniature French tablecloth. But the thick red-brown weft intrudes for only a few inches from the edge. Coming from the far border and meeting the brown along a rather uneven battle front at the child's right temple are thick white weft threads in a broad column traveling up all the way from the foot of the mummy. (At least *now* they are white, but the strange distribution of yarns and weaves makes me wonder whether they too, like the pattern threads in the XIA woman's clothing, might once have been dyed.)

This strange battle between zones of color and weave continues all the way around the baby's head. The broad brown stripe of plain weave that frames the face narrows considerably as it tries to sneak past the checkerboard, until a band of stout tan wefts launched from the opposite selvedge forces an uneven halt. Below that a new battalion of heavy pale weft threads in a slightly different weave surges up from the foot end of the mummy, only to be stopped cold at a second patch of red-brown checkerboard behind the ear, and so on. Finally everything gives way to plain weave as the center of the cloth disappears under the little mummy bundle, reemerging on the other side with a new battlefront at the level of the child's neck. The decor is not really symmetrical on any axis.

In fact it has the feel of a sampler, the sort of cloth a young woman makes when she first learns to weave, trying out a little patch here and a little patch there of each variation that occurs to her or that her mentor teaches. The transitions from one weave to the next look haphazard and inexperienced; but that is how one learns. Perhaps when her baby died, the mother wrapped the little body ever so carefully in her first piece of weaving, two valiant attempts laid gently into one grave.

THE GRAVES of Qäwrighul have a curious construction. The ancient gravediggers laid out the corpse, wrapped in its cloak or shroud, full length in a pit in the sandy ground with the head pointing east. Usually they used small boards to form a sort of coffin, often lidless and always bottomless—more like a low fence to hold back the restless sand long enough to lay the body in. After arranging a few gifts, such as a bag-shaped basket of wheat, a comb, or small bun-

[3]Technically a half-basket weave. See fig. 3.12c.

dles of ephedra twigs, the burial party covered the corpse against predators, sometimes stretching hides or a broad winnowing basket over the top or laying a row of small planks crossways. Then they filled the pit. Such graves generally contain neither pottery nor metal. What few implements the archaeologists have discovered consist of wood, bone, antler, fiber, and stone (some chipped in the Palaeolithic way, some ground to shape in the Neolithic manner).

With so few grave goods to go by, Wang Binghua and his fellow archaeologists from the Xinjiang Institute found it impossible, in 1979, to date the Qäwrighul cemetery by the old, standard method: comparing the objects they found to dated objects from elsewhere. So they sent a sample of organic carbon to Nanjing University for radiocarbon dating. The answer they received, that the graves dated to about 4500 B.C. (the Stone Age), astonished everyone. Granted no pottery or metal accompanied these burials; even so, no one had guessed them to be much older than 100 B.C. The tombs at Cherchen had not yet been found, and no one had ever used a method of absolute dating (see Chapter 5) on Tarim artifacts before. Beijing University then demanded a carbon sample; its tests produced a date of roughly 2000 B.C.: specifically 1880 B.C. ± 95 years. That still seemed awfully early, but less far afield than the first date, so this became the accepted one.

But this date too caused problems. Continuing excavation turned up a few bronze trinkets plus the marks left by metal tools used in shaping wood in other graves at the site. These ruled out the Stone Age for at least part of the cemetery, and Wang Binghua felt that all the graves belonged to at least roughly the same era. Since the Bronze Age began around 3000 B.C. in the Near East, a date of 2000 B.C. (but not 4500 B.C.) would tally nicely for a Bronze Age site by Western chronology. The trouble is, current archaeological evidence indicates that the Bronze Age in China didn't get under way until nearly 1500 B.C. If the use of bronze began centuries earlier in the Tarim Basin next door, it threw into doubt the doctrine that Chinese civilization grew up quite separately from Near Eastern innovations on all fronts, that the Chinese had invented such seminal crafts as metalworking and writing entirely independently.[4]

---

[4] Linguistic and archaeological researches since 1979 have only complicated the picture without entirely resolving it. It is clear now that the Chinese knew metals well before 1500 B.C. but also that at a very early date—second millennium B.C. at least—they borrowed Western terms for several cultural inventions (see Chapter 6). So early East-West contact truly existed. Whether the key contacts for China came through the Tarim Basin is another matter, but the date of 2000 B.C. for early immigrants from West Asia into Central Asia seems reasonable.

Note too that the paucity of evidence for metal at Qäwrighul may be skewed by cultural habits. It is just possible that these settlers had some sort of taboo against putting newfangled things like metals and pottery into their graves.

For a fuller discussion of the use and mechanism of radiocarbon dating, see Chapter 5.

Nonetheless this is the best date we have. And clearly the early settlers of the Loulan area eked out their existence with a largely Stone Age technology, with or without a few metal tools. The simple, though competent, level of their textile craft speaks to a similar early stage of development. Of course the fact that they brought with them woolly sheep from the West eliminates Nanjing University's date of 4500 B.C. Usably woolly sheep only came into being, through inbreeding in Mesopotamia, a little before 4000 B.C. But 2000 B.C. would be quite possible.

Only the digging and carbon dating of more such graves will provide final answers as to date. But the cemetery Wang excavated tells us yet other interesting things about the culture.

The Loulan people may have bestowed few goods on their dead before closing the grave, but they made up for it with elaborate formations of wooden "tombstones" afterward. Upon filling in the pit, these early folk all over the Loulan area marked the grave by erecting posts, so that their cemeteries came to look like small forests of poles. In fact modern archaeologists know they have happened upon an ancient cemetery when they see what look like the weathered underpinnings of a giant wharf marooned in the desert sands.

The most remarkable of these forests belong to a small series of strictly male graves (fig. 4.6), possibly a bit later than our three earliest mummies, since fragments of copper or bronze occur in these, but possibly just the graves of contemporary elites with more access to metallic wealth. Around these six male burials the mourners drove dozens of good-sized logs vertically into the ground in seven tight concentric circles. The posts sit so close together that one cannot walk between them; perhaps this ruse discouraged the local wolves and other carnivorous predators from disturbing the dead. More wooden posts, farther apart, stand in the ground in straight lines spreading out radially from the circle, like rays around a child's drawing of the sun. The pattern is so striking that the excavators would like to view them as actual sun symbols. Were these special men priests? Since these six burials were lowered much deeper into the ground than the others, the corpses did not dry out so quickly and hence deteriorated badly. (Not every Tarim grave contains a perfect mummy, just as not every oyster contains a pearl; the circumstances have to be just right for formation.) It would have been interesting to see if their clothes differed in special ways from the others.

The shallow, salty sand into which the bottomless graves of the commoner sort were dug, by contrast, sometimes sucked the moisture out of the inhumed bodies very quickly, thus mummifying and preserving many of them by completely natural means. After all, the area around Qäwrighul is desert today, spreading across the terraced hills north of Loulan Station and the intermit-

FIGURE 4.6

Part of the burial ground at Qäwrighul, early 2nd millennium B.C., where the Beauty of Loulan and other earliest mummies were found. The circles and radii of wooden posts set deep into the ground mark several of the male burials (2 visible in the background—center and right—as well as 1 foreground). What are apparently the remains of a curved log coffin can be seen at far right. Compare figures 5.3–5.6.

tently flowing river sometimes called the Qum-därya (Sand or Sandy River: map 4.1). The Turkic name of the range, Quruk-Tagh, says it well; it means "Dry Mountains."[5]

But the logs tell a different story. For how could the ancient dwellers of Loulan, nearly four thousand years ago, have found so many good-sized trees to fell if this had been total desert in their day? Did they really drag both their dead and hundreds of large logs over vast distances just to bury them in this salty sand? It seems unlikely. In addition to trees, there had to have been enough water nearby to produce natural grasslands on which to graze the sheep that gave the wool for their clothes, not to mention water for drinking and for raising the wheat that helped feed them. We know they kept cattle and horses too, species that need more copious grazing than sheep, and they hunted deer and caught fish. Fish need year-round water to live in.

Investigations into recorded Chinese history show that two thousand years ago a city thrived somewhere in the Loulan area, a vital link in the trade route from China to the Roman Empire—the so-called Silk Road across Central Asia

[5] Most of the local place-names are descriptive in this way. Because they give such a vivid impression of the landscape, I will not only give the translations but sometimes use them alternatively. The only such translation that is standardly employed in English, however, is "Yellow River" for *Huang He*.

(map 4.7). This city, known as Loulan Station, sat near the shore of a large, shallow lake, the Lop Nor, which received vast amounts of water from the Tarim River and its sometime tributary the Könchi-därya. Together these two rivers drain the meltwater from most of the mountain ranges that ring the Tarim Basin. Caravans coming from China passed westward through the Gansu Corridor to Dunhuang at the east edge of the Tarim and Turfan basins. There they passed into the desert through a part of the Chinese defense line called the Jade Gate, so named because much of the beautiful jade considered sacred in China since the Stone Age came from western provinces beyond this point. Next stop was the city of Loulan, a vital provisioner of water and food, whence the merchants could follow the Tarim River westward around the north side of the terrible Taklamakan Desert before crossing the mountains to Fergana and Samarkand and finally into the Roman Empire. At that time Loulan clearly had plenty of water.

But one dreadful day around A.D. 330 storms and flooding pushed the river's course far south across the flatlands, stranding the bustling city of Loulan and creating a new and smaller lake far away which came to be called the Qara-Qoshun (map 4.1). Its water gone, Loulan died, along with its trees and other vegetation, and the merchant caravans suffered much greater hardships than before, since the distance from Dunhuang to the next oases to the west was now roughly doubled from the already punishing journey of two weeks. Marco Polo knew of no lake in the northern zone in 1273, but only—as one scholar put it— "only the desert of Lop, in which he heard voices of ghosts speaking and out of whose depth there seemed to him to come the beating of drums—the howling of the sand-storms." And so matters stood when the first European explorers of modern times reached Central Asia.

At the beginning of this century ancient Chinese books and maps formed the principal source of information about the Tarim Basin. Consider the shock of the Europeans, then, when they arrived with their surveying instruments, to find that the lake of Lop was not where the Chinese maps traditionally located it but more than a hundred miles to the south. The Chinese maps are simply wrong, they said—off by one whole degree of latitude. It would be like finding that the Potomac ran through Philadelphia, not Washington (also over a hundred miles away). None dreamt that both river and lake could have moved so far.

None, that is, except the Swedish explorer Sven Hedin, who arrived in the Lop Nor desert in 1900 to map it. He reports:

> On the 28th of March I discovered in the northern part of the desert the ruins of the town of Lou-lan. As our meagre supply of water only allowed us a stay of twenty hours, we crossed the desert, in whose northern part I found nu-

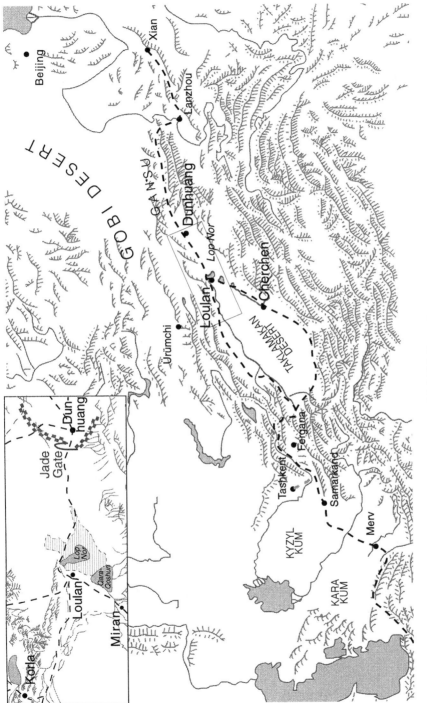

FIGURE 4.7

Map of the approximate course of the Silk Road around A.D. 300, running from Xian in China through the Gansu Corridor to Dunhuang and Loulan, thence through the Tarim Basin and over the Pamirs by several routes, and finally through the western oases to the Near East. The inset shows in more detail the area between Loulan and Dunhuang, where a protective extension of the Great Wall of China was pierced by the famed Jade Gate (*Yümen Guan*).

merous proofs of the existence of earlier basins of lakes, for many centuries dried up.

Since I saw that the discovery of the old town was of extraordinary importance—both geographically and historically—at the beginning of March, 1901, I returned there and unearthed in one of the houses about 150 manuscripts on wood and paper, many of which were provided with the date and revealed that the old town was called Lou-lan and was flourishing at about A.D. 260–270.

Although the land *looked* flat, Hedin took out his scientific instruments and carefully measured the altitude at various spots.

Against the levelled line the depression of the old basin of the lake showed itself with the greatest clearness. The . . . starting-point near Lou-lan was only a little over 2 metres higher than the surface of Kara-koshun [whither the lake had moved, farther south].

I now formulated the theory that, in a desert whose surface, practically speaking, is just as level as that of the sea, the flowing water must be extremely sensitive to even the most insignificant changes in the surface. The southern lake, Kara-koshun, whose mean depth, as I found, amounted to 0.81 metres [less than three feet], fills with mud which the Tarim carries with it, with decaying . . . matter, and with shifting sand, while the dried-up northern parts of the desert are hollowed out by the mighty force of the strong east-north-east storms and sink in the course of the centuries. Sooner or later this action will lead to the lake having to wander again into its northern basin. . . . Kara-koshun must dry up, and the lake of the Chinese maps in the northern part of the desert must fill with water again.

Returning to Central Asia in 1928, Hedin happened to learn from a local merchant friend that seven years before (1921) the Könchi-därya had abruptly moved over to the bed of the Qum-därya—the "Sand River," as the formerly dry course had been called. (It was also known as the Quruk-därya, the "Dry River"; see map 4.1.) Now the old northern lake basin had refilled, with the ancient site of Loulan near its shore, whereas the little fishing villages on the banks of the Kara-koshun (or Qara-Qoshun) had been stranded in their turn. The fish and the trees had died; the people and animals had moved away. Hedin thought wryly of his "long, laborious marches" in the dry sand bed of the Qum-därya nearly three decades earlier:

How well I remembered the broad, deep, dried-up river-bed with the dead forest on its banks! There stood the trunks like the gravestones of a churchyard, grey, split, dried, and as brittle as glass. Nothing living was to be found, nor a drop of water; a more God-forsaken region one could not imagine on the whole earth. More than fifteen hundred years ago a great stream had flowed through this furrow.

And now it did so again.

The "trunks like gravestones" sound eerily like those log circles of prehistoric cemeteries built two thousand years before the Chinese city of Loulan came into being, flourished, and dried up again. Perhaps still older dead forests, visible in prehistoric times, inspired these people to mark the land allocated to their own dead with similar memorials. How many times has the river swung back and forth during its history, like a giant pendulum with the lake as a huge knob flung about on its end? Where was it when the Loulan Beauty, the little child, and the lady at the Xinjiang Institute lived and died? These are questions that geologists, surveyors, and other scientific explorers can eventually answer—if they can get there.

Today the wandering lake wanders no more. There is virtually no water left to wander. A larger population upstream and increasingly rapid desiccation throughout the Tarim Basin have used it up. So here on the great wide salt flats the Chinese military test their A-bombs, assured of privacy in that "God-forsaken region." And the occasional archaeologist or geologist who wishes to wander about, whether local or foreign, is persona non grata, just as he often was a century ago.

But the consequences of traveling there in those days, despite resistance, were more personal than international, and a number of well-known people braved the risks. To those intrepid explorers we owe much of our information, and to them we must turn for answers.

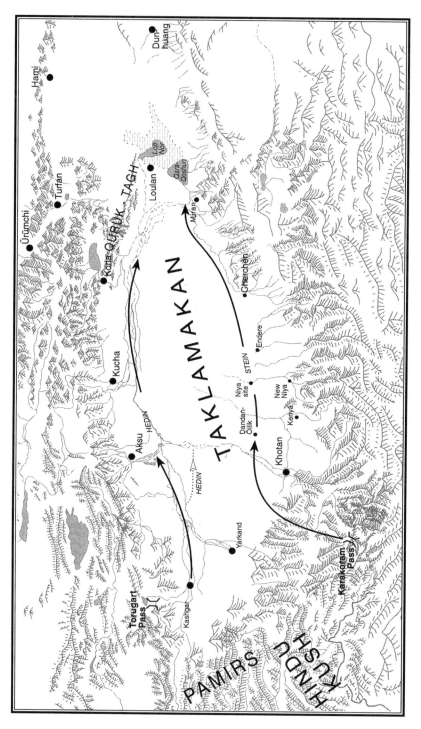

MAP 5.1

The Early Explorers

SVEN HEDIN first rediscovered the ancient site known as Loulan as he explored and mapped the wastes of the Lop desert in 1900. Among other things he was trying to track China's ancient route to the west, and the Chinese histories of early times mentioned Loulan as an important stop in the desert beyond Dunhuang (map 5.1). One must remember that when the Chinese station of Loulan died around A.D. 330, the Chinese had been literate for more than fifteen hundred years. (Chinese thus ranks as the longest-running written tradition in the world, by far, even if not the earliest.) Scavenging with a few men in the ruins of a large tract of houses, Hedin located third-century Chinese documents that, to his delight, repeatedly named the place as Loulan.

In December 1906 and again in 1914, another famous explorer followed Hedin to Loulan: Hungarian-born Marc Aurel Stein, later to become Sir Aurel Stein, who had a post in Calcutta under the Indian Educational Service of the British Empire. But while Hedin's great love was traversing and mapping new places, Stein's lay in collecting historical data.

Stein had confined his first trip into Chinese Turkestan, in 1900 and 1901, to exploring southern and western portions of the Tarim Basin, the areas closest

Opposite page: Map of the Tarim Basin showing 1st millennium A.D. sites explored by Stein and the general trajectories of Hedin and Stein in their early explorations (arrows), heading toward Loulan. The dotted line shows the path of Hedin's "Death March" in 1895.

to India, where he taught college. Between Calcutta and the Tarim stood the Himalaya and Kunlun ranges, pierced only by the Karakoram Pass, which is higher, at well over 18,500 feet, than most of the world's mountains. Undeterred, Stein trekked across this horrendous pass leading from the headwaters of the Indus into the Tarim Basin at its southwest corner (map 5.1). He sought to resolve a number of questions about the antiquities of the Khotan area, questions that had long troubled British scholars working on Indian literature and history.

For some years documents purporting to originate from the environs of Khotan had been straggling across the mountains into India and Europe. Many proved to be written in an Indic language called Prakrit, using an archaic Indic script called Kharoṣṭhī (fig. 6.2); other texts, nicknamed Khotanese, contained a hitherto unknown Iranian language. But one group, characterized by a strange sort of block printing, could not be deciphered at all. In fact top experts started to suspect these might be forgeries. Needing on-the-spot information, they helped Stein get the money and political backing he needed from the British government to make his expedition.

Over many months Stein dug up numerous texts and other antiquities in all the ruined desert sites he could hear of, but he found not a single block-printed inscription—not even at a site said to have yielded them. Gradually he realized just where to point the finger: at a wily Khotanese antique-seller named Islam Akhun. This man had abruptly moved to another town and set up as a "healer" when some of his other frauds had been discovered in Khotan. Confronted by Stein, Islam Akhun at first denied everything. Then he agreed, yes, he had sold some "old books" dug up in the desert by *others,* now conveniently fled or dead. (Ah, the pity of it, that they should have thus deceived him!) But when Stein read to him verbatim transcriptions of what the antique-seller had said while vending each and every manuscript years before, how he himself had dug up this one here and that one there, then Islam Akhun crumbled—though not without evident pride that his own words should have been immortalized in "Government Books"! Like Moriarty describing his plots to Holmes (the only one clever enough to appreciate their intricacies), the huckster then recounted to Stein exactly how he and his cronies had produced the forgeries, starting with handwritten texts in invented scripts on paper "antiqued" by dyeing and scorching, then moving to block printing when business got too brisk to keep up with a handwritten supply. Since the Europeans with the full purses clearly couldn't read even the genuine manuscripts, what did it matter if he and his friends made up their own?

The block print puzzle was solved, and this exploit plus Stein's other copious finds—published in the governmental *Preliminary Report,* the more popular

Sand-Buried Ruins of Khotan, and the remarkably interdisciplinary scientific work, *Ancient Khotan*—made Stein internationally famous.

In 1906, impatient to get back to his explorations, Stein returned to the Tarim Basin. This time he worked eastward from Khotan across the southern edge of the desert, stopping along the way to visit and excavate briefly at ancient centers of Buddhist culture, dating mostly from A.D. 500 to 1000. One by one he explored the oases of Dandan-Öilik, Keriyä, Niya, Endere, and Miran (map 5.1). In December 1906, when he could finally stock up on potable water for his men and animals by hacking blocks of surface ice from the salty pools around Lop Nor (the wandering lake), he headed north into the desert toward Loulan (map 4.1).[1] In *Ruins of Desert Cathay,* his thousand-page account of that trip, he writes: "Ever since my plans were first formed I had fixed my eyes on the ruined sites north of Lop-nor, discovered by Hedin on his memorable journey of 1900. After exploring their remains and whatever else of ruins we might trace in this region, I proposed to take my caravan right across the great desert north-eastwards to . . . Tun-huang [Dunhuang] by the ancient route which Marco Polo followed, and which has since been abandoned for centuries."

Stein did not undertake such an expedition lightly. The closest village to Loulan lay a hundred miles to the south, and everything necessary for weeks of survival, including every drop of water, had to be carried from there by people and pack animals at a rate of ten to twenty miles per day. Motorcars did not exist in Central Asia. He also had the example to ponder of Hedin, who, on his first trip in 1895, had not reckoned on a dishonest guide.

HEDIN HAD chosen to cross the west end of the Taklamakan directly, dunes and all, figuring that since his path would intersect the bed of the Khotan River at right angles, he couldn't miss his target (see map 5.1). The local guide, however, for all he bragged about knowing the way, greatly underestimated the distance across the Taklamakan; on top of that, he repeatedly drank deeply and on the sly from the reserve water, throwing off Hedin's reckoning of their precious supplies. Finally no water remained, and still no sign of the river. One by one the men and animals collapsed, the dishonest guide included. Unable to do anything for them—unless to reach water and bring it back—Hedin and those who could struggled on. At last only Hedin and one of the local men still moved, burying themselves in the cooler subsurface sand during the heat of the day and crawling onward at night, somehow refusing to give up. Reaching

---

[1] When salt water freezes, the salt separates out and only the water freezes. So the Tarim explorers, like those in the Arctic zones, could use winter ice as a source of nonsalty water.

some stands of dead, dried-up trees, then some live ones, they searched for water, but to no avail. Hedin's faithful foreman, Kasim, could go no farther. Still Hedin crawled on during the night, praying for water, stumbling through ever-denser thickets. Seven days and nights had now passed since the water gave out. Suddenly he heard the splash of a water bird landing nearby, and in a moment he stood beside a huge pool. Ever the curious explorer—how many people have the chance to observe their own bodies mummify and then revivify?—Hedin sat down and took his pulse ("forty-nine beats") and only then began to drink. He drank and drank.

"My dried-up body absorbed the moisture like a sponge. All my joints soft-ened, all my movements became easier. My skin, hard as parchment before, now became softened. My forehead grew moist. The pulse increased in strength; and after a few minutes it was fifty-six. The blood flowed more freely in my veins." He would live.

But how to carry water back to his dying companion? He took off his wa-terproof boots, filled them both, slung them by their bootstraps over the han-dle of his spade to balance on his shoulders, and set off in stocking feet to retrace his steps. At dawn he found Kasim, who felt sure he was breathing his very last. But Hedin's water revived him. Nearby shepherds gave Hedin bread and sheep's milk, and a couple of days later a caravan following the riverbed south to Khotan restored to Hedin the company of two of those left to die days earlier: the other foreman from his contingent, plus a camel. This local man, after collapsing for a day, had loaded the four remaining camels with what he knew to be Hedin's most precious instruments and records and, leaving the others dead where they lay, had struggled on. Reaching the poplars by the riverbed, he had unburdened the camels so they could graze on leaves, while he hunted for water—in vain. By the time the three kindly merchants found him lying in the sand and gave him water and food, all but one camel had either died or bolted. In all, only Hedin, the two local men, and two camels survived what Hedin sadly called his Death March. The pitiless desert gives no room for slack.

FORTUNATELY STEIN and his caravan found Loulan exactly where Hedin's map of 1900 plotted it. Several days of digging in the ruins produced not only more slips of wood bearing ancient Chinese writing but also Kharoṣṭhī tablets similar in language to those Stein had found at Niya. In these texts the name of the town was rendered as *Kroraina*, an indigenous form from which the mod-ern Chinese version, *Lou-lan*, has come via the more restrictive rules of Chinese phonology.

Kharoṣṭhī script (fig. 6.2) was used to write an Indic tongue called Prakrit, imported from India in the third century A.D. and serving for a short time thereafter as a common language for government functionaries all across the southern Tarim Basin. Prakrit, however, was not the original language of the area— or of the name Kroraina—any more than Chinese was, for the users of Prakrit governed a population speaking yet other languages. Remnants of those indigenous tongues show up as frequent loanwords in the Tarim inscriptions: a few from Iranian and many probably from Tokharian (see Chapter 6). But the rules for acceptable word shapes in Indic are more widely accommodating than those of Chinese, so *Kroraina* may be quite close to the original form, itself perhaps simply *Kroran*.

When the Chinese arrived sometime after 100 B.C. and set up their military station in the area, they had trouble saying the name. No distinction existed in Chinese between *r* and *l*. (Thus the Chinese today convert the Turkic names Ürümchi and Turfan into *Ulumuchi* and *Tulufan*. All languages do this sort of thing; we ourselves, being unaccustomed to the vowel *ü*, convert Ürümchi into *Urumchi*.) So the Chinese converted the name to a form something like **Glu-lan*—not really so very far from *Kro-ran-*. Next, as Chinese itself changed, it no longer permitted an initial group of consonants like *gl*, so the *g* was dropped (just as we drop the initial *p* when we say *psychology,* although the Greeks, from whom we got the word, didn't), arriving by stages at the form *Loulan*.

Stein viewed his eleven days of intensive but hurried excavation at Loulan/Kroraina as a major success. After withdrawing south for a month to replenish his stores, he marched toward Loulan Station a second time. Approaching now by a slightly different route, he found "rows of fallen dead trees" lining the banks of an ancient "southern branch of the Kuruk-darya, the 'Dry River', which had once carried water to the Lou-lan site." Following this dry riverbed northward, he made "abundant finds of stone implements, such as neolithic arrowheads and jade celts, picked up on eroded ground near by." In short, at some time well before the Chinese developed a garrison town here in the third century A.D., enough water regularly reached this area to support prehistoric peoples and a sizable number of trees—just what we had deduced from other considerations.

After more digging at the Chinese Loulan Station, Stein embarked on his next main task, tracing the ancient Silk Road to Dunhuang and its Jade Gate by hunting for archaeological remains toward the northeast (see maps 5.1, 7.1, and especially 4.1). He traced ruined forts and cemeteries for about fifteen miles in this direction, at which point he came upon

a small ruined fort . . . on the top of a precipitous Mesa [recorded on his maps as L.F.] fully a hundred feet high and commanding a distant view over the desolate waste around. The elevated position, together with the absolute aridity of the climate since ancient times, had assured here a truly remarkable state of conservation to the bodies of men and women found in graves outside what was evidently a look-out post occupied by indigenous Lou-lan people. Several of the bodies were wonderfully well conserved, together with their burial deposits (Figs. 66, 67 [fig. 5.2]). The peaked felt caps decorated with big feathers and other trophies of the chase, the arrow-shafts by their side, the coarse but strong woollen garments, the neatly woven small baskets holding the food for the dead, etc., all indicated a race of semi-nomadic herdsmen and hunters, just as the Han Annals describe the Lou-lan people when the Chinese found them on the first opening of the route through the desert.

It was a strange sensation to look down on figures which but for the parched skin seemed like those of men asleep. . . . The characteristics of the men's heads showed close affinity to that *Homo Alpinus* type which, as the anthropometrical materials collected by me have proved, still remains the prevailing element in the racial constitution of the present population of the Tarim basin.

(Measuring the height and breadth of people's skulls, alive or dead, in different parts of the world was viewed in Stein's day as a key scientific method for sorting out human dispersal around the globe.)

The distant view gained from this elevated point made it certain that we were here near the eastern extremity of the ground once reached by life-giving water from the river. Beyond to the east there lay the boundless expanse of shimmering salt, marking the dried-up Lop sea-bed.

Clearly Stein had come across people dressed just like the Beauty of Loulan (more properly, the Beauty of Kroraina?) and the woman at the institute, with their peaked and feathered felt caps, coarse woolen wraps, and neat little baskets of grain. A glance at his Fig. 67 (the original of fig. 5.2) confirms it. The man's face looks so European that Victor Mair, reprinting Stein's photograph in *Archaeology* in 1995, likens him to a "Bohemian burgher." Stein, in his fullest report, describes him as a youngish man with dark, wavy hair and a bad cut over his eye, whose "head and face suggested the *Homo Alpinus* type . . . familiar in the Hindukush and Pamirs."

The only new accoutrement listed is the set of arrows, but then Stein happened to find two *men* in the little cemetery on Mesa L.F., rather than two women and a child, as at Qäwrighul. If only he had mentioned whether the arrowheads were fashioned of stone, wood, or a metal! That might have given us a better fix on how developed these people were technically and hence on their date.

FIGURE 5.2

Prehistoric mummy of Caucasoid type found by Sir Aurel Stein on Mesa L.F., 15 miles northeast of Loulan Station. The young man, who probably died from the severe wound visible over his left eye, rests in a wooden coffin of two long curved boards once covered with short planks. What looks like a high-domed cap is a small basket (like the one by his right arm) that once lay over his face, on top of the woolen wrap that Stein pulled back for a photo. The plain-weave wrap, the two baskets, and the little globular packet of ephedra tied into its edge (beside the lower basket) show he belongs to the same culture as the Beauty of Loulan. (After Stein.)

He also remarks that one edge of the shroud had been formed into a pouch that held twigs of ephedra, a plant prized in both ancient and modern times for its stimulant properties. (Ephedra still provides an important asthma medicine, ephedrine. See Chapter 8.) Twigs of it also occurred in graves excavated in the 1980s at Qäwrighul.

The young man's cloak-wrapped body lay on the dirt in a bottomless coffin made from two poplar trunks hollowed out to form the sides, with a short board at each end. Seven short boards lay crossways over the top, while several cowhides covered the whole affair. What Stein describes as "a fence of closely set wooden planks rising about three feet above the present ground surface" surrounded the entire coffin, reminiscent of the circles of stakes surrounding the burials at Qäwrighul.

Seminomadic herders, said the Chinese annals. That much we deduced from the three Qäwrighul mummies in Ürümchi. They surely followed the pasturage needed by the sheep from which their woolen clothing came, yet they must have stayed put long enough to grow an annual crop of wheat. The arrows in the grave round out our information: hunting must have contributed significantly too. Hedin and others a century ago described wild boar, antelope, hares, ducks, geese, and swans that still teemed in the thickets around the rivers, where and when they flowed.

If Stein's mummies on Mesa L.F. are indeed contemporary with the fortress beside it (containing Chinese artifacts no earlier than the first Chinese takeover of the area ca. 100 B.C.), and if the radiocarbon dates of 2000–1800 B.C. for Qäwrighul are right, we must conclude that the people of Kroraina lived much the same style of life and death for fully two thousand years. Such extreme conservatism seems at first surprising, since the great cultures to either side—China to the east and Greece, Rome, and Mesopotamia to the west—were changing so rapidly.

The picture is all the more confusing because at a site he called L.S., located on a sandy terrace very close to Qäwrighul (map 4.1), Stein found several startlingly well-preserved Caucasoid mummies whose graves "revealed a method of burial identical with that observed at L.F." He deduced that "approximately the same period [i.e., early Chinese occupation] and origin may be attributed to them." One of Stein's graves contained a woman with a felt cap and a small grain basket to the left of her face, whose coffin had been covered by large, shallow winnowing baskets. All this sounds so much like the burials of the Qäwrighul women that a difference of two millennia is again hard to believe.

Stein's site as a whole offers still other close parallels to what now lies in the Ürümchi galleries. He described the scene as follows:

The graves were marked by rows of small posts placed close together and sticking out above the gravel surface, as seen in Fig. 336 [fig. 5.3]. They were

FIGURE 5.3

Grave marked by eroded circles of deep-set wooden posts, photographed by Aurel Stein at a site he named L.S., not far from Qäwrighul and clearly of the same culture. (After Stein.)

found in two small groups, at a distance of about 20 yards from each other. . . . The corroding force of wind-driven sand and gravel was strikingly illustrated by the abraded appearance of the rough wooden posts marking the individual graves. Their tops emerging only a few inches above the surface of the soil had the side facing to the north and east invariably scooped and splintered. . . . How high the posts had originally risen above the surface it was impossible to say. But like the wooden enclosures of the graves found at the Lou-lan fort L.F., which they at once recalled by their arrangement, they were probably once much higher.

Does that also mean they were much older than the less eroded ones on Mesa L.F.? To know that, we would need to know the relative rates of wind erosion at the two sites, but it is worth bearing in mind as a possible yardstick. Stein continues:

> The southern group comprised half a dozen graves. Of these the central grave attracted special attention by its sevenfold stockade of wooden posts neatly fixed in the ground to form an oval, 14 feet long from east to west and 10 feet across. The outer posts measured about 3 to 4 inches in diameter and the inner posts gradually diminished to the size of small tent-pegs. Straight rows of similar posts converged towards the oval from outside on the south and east.

In the middle of this oval he found only a few fragments of burned bones, considerable traces of fire, one piece of bronze tube, and the charred remains of a "narrow coffin-like enclosure" of the usual thick planks. No burnt burial has been reported from other graves of Kroraina. So this apparent cremation remains an enigma.

Unfortunately for us, Stein was a historian rather than a prehistorian, and although he carefully noted these and other prehistoric finds, he was unable to sort out their chronology fully. Still, he published enough material to whet the appetite of another scholar.

Folke Bergman, another Swede, joined Hedin's later expeditions in 1928.[2] Working with Hedin for several years, he concentrated principally on mapping prehistoric sites, investigating burials, and collecting objects. For example, in the Lop Nor area, according to Hedin's report, "eight sites belonging to prehistoric times were discovered and investigated. . . . In all 1,510 objects were found." By the time Bergman left Ürümchi for Stockholm in December 1928, he took with him "over 18,000 objects from nearly 150 sites."

Such a statement, far from delighting modern archaeologists, makes us shudder. Simply by removing those objects, Bergman was destroying masses of evidence. He is scarcely at fault, however; archaeology as a science was not yet well developed. As our skills at recovering the past have evolved, we have learned to ask far more detailed questions than archaeologists did seventy years ago. In Bergman's time only a few scholars, such as Sir W. M. F. Petrie working in Egypt and Sir Leonard Woolley in Mesopotamia, had come to understand that an artifact cannot be moved from its context without destroying records of human existence and therefore that we have a responsibility to society to record everything we possibly can about that context.

In addition, what we are able to recover and record has grown more and more complex over the decades. Petrie and Woolley recorded the exact positions of all visible objects with respect to one another and to absolute benchmarks before removing them. But now we collect the nearly invisible as well: tiny bits of bone and carbonized grain (what were people eating?), splinters of wood (what trees grew there?), samples of pollen (what was the total plant ecology, and hence the climate and even the season of deposition?), tiny fibers, feather barbs, and so forth. Bergman's collection of stone tools and potsherds ripped from their myriad contexts has only superficial value compared with the rich information that could be teased from one square foot of archaeological deposit today.

And then there is the matter of dating. Publishing his prehistoric Kroraina/Loulan material in 1941, Bergman admitted that he still had no idea how

---

[2] Hedin's expeditions of the 1920s and 1930s resulted in fifty-some volumes of scientific reports on Central Asia. They were funded largely by the Swedish royalty—traditionally a family of well-educated scholars—and by Alfred Nobel, who made his enormous fortune from the invention of dynamite and used that fortune to spur forward the acquisition of human knowledge.

to date anything not tied to Chinese artifacts of the historical period. So his Central Asian material falls basically into two categories: things cross-datable to Chinese artifacts (the Chinese arrived just before 100 B.C.) and things that are earlier. Hedin tended to call everything in the second category indiscriminately "Stone Age": a span of 150,000 years if we confine it to the era when modern *Homo sapiens sapiens* inhabited the world, and 2,500,000 years if we include all protohuman users of stone tools.

Again, this dilemma was not entirely Bergman's fault; he searched hard for clues and recorded enough data to fill a large book, *Archaeological Researches in Sinkiang* (1939). But much of his material came from wind-eroded slopes, where no stratigraphy remained to indicate what was older than what.[3]

ONE CAN see why the invention of an independent means of absolute dating caused such a revolution in archaeology. In the late 1940s an atomic physicist named Willard Libby saw that archaeologists could use the steady rate of decay of radioactive carbon in ancient objects of organic origin (wood, cloth, grain, etc.) to calculate how old they are.[4] To test his theory, Libby had to get ancient samples of known date, and fairly large samples at that, since isotope-counting techniques were still crude. It is said that visitors to New York's Metropolitan

---

[3] Archaeologists rely heavily on the same stratigraphic principle as geologists—namely, that what lies underneath had to have been laid down longer ago than what lies on top of it (just as the bottom sheet has to go onto the bed before the sheet and blankets that are to lie above it). This allows one to determine relative dating—what's older, what's younger—but not absolute dating—i.e., exactly how long ago either deposit was laid down. The principle is wonderfully simple in theory but fails to apply straightforwardly when everything has been moved around by wind or water, as on Bergman's eroded slopes, or by people digging holes such as garbage pits or graves. Then much careful observation and logic are required to interpret the record, and some information simply may not be retrievable.

[4] Cosmic rays constantly bombard the earth, sometimes creating from atmospheric nitrogen an unusual form of carbon, C^{14}. This carbon has an atomic weight of 14 rather than 12, having 6 protons (which make it chemically carbon) and an overload of 8 neutrons. (Nitrogen normally has 7 protons and 7 neutrons, giving it an atomic weight of 14. In other words, the cosmic ray turns a proton into a neutron in forming C^{14}.) The new form or isotope of carbon is radioactive—that is, it is unstable and may suddenly "decay" by ejecting a beta ray. The loss of the little beta ray turns the neutron it came out of back into a proton, however. So after decay the atom now has 7 neutrons and 7 protons again, reverting chemically to nitrogen.

While the C^{14} or radiocarbon is in the atmosphere, it attaches like any other carbon atom to oxygen as carbon dioxide (CO_2) and gets absorbed by plants, which animals eat, and so the C^{14} gets distributed evenly among all living things. Once the plant or animal dies, however, it ceases to ingest new carbon of any sort.

Over a period of roughly 5,700 years, half the radioactive carbon left in a particular sample decays. Knowing that, we have only to see what percentage of the radiocarbon in a dead organic sample has decayed in order to learn how long ago the organism died.

Or so the theory goes. Unfortunately we are now learning that the amount of radiocarbon in the atmosphere has not been entirely steady over the millennia. Scientists are gradually

Museum were startled one day to see a workman sawing a large plank off an ancient Egyptian funerary boat—the museum's generous contribution to scientific progress.

Although our estimate of the exact rate of decay has been refined and revised repeatedly, the method as a whole turned out to work extremely well within known limits, producing ballpark absolute dates of the form "550 B.C. plus or minus 30 years" or "2200 B.C. plus or minus 100 years." The slosh of plus or minus a few years is inherent in the statistical nature of radioactive decay rates. (Of course absolute dates include relative dating since something from 550 B.C. is more recent than something from 1000 B.C.) We now know that other radioactive isotopes can be used to date other substances, such as fired clay, bones, and lava flows.

An even more precise means of dating is currently being extended from the present backward—exact down to the year, without the plus or minus slosh factor.

When I wrote a description in 1985 of a log coffin burial found long since at Egtved, Denmark (map 7.4), I could only say that the girl and her woolen string skirt (fig. 5.4) had been laid into the grave mound toward the end of the second millennium B.C., maybe 1200. Relative dating plus the services of radiocarbon could box it in no better than that, and no written records existed in that area for another thousand years and then some. The Egyptians and Mesopotamians had been literate for two thousand years by that time, but they lived thousands of miles away, completely ignorant of northern Europe and its prehistory.

Time passed and science marched on. In 1991 I got off the train in Oxford and my archaeologist friends there greeted me with "Guess what? That Egtved girl was buried in the summer of 1370 B.C.!" Oddly, though the date was earlier than people had previously guessed, its very precision made the dead girl seem more recent to my mind. The source of this unexpectedly accurate date was dendrochronology, or tree ring dating, performed on the girl's log coffin.

---

charting these vicissitudes by calibrating samples against datable tree rings. Then too the problems of counting minuscule amounts of radioactive decay have been difficult to solve. But the technology of doing so is vastly improved. Today the sticking point is not so much equipment as the amount of money one has to spend on counting. (The longer you count, the more accurate the date.)

Since the process is statistical rather than absolute, it will always be expressed as a number plus or minus another number—e.g., 4200 BP (Before Present) plus or minus 100 years. Despite the "slosh" factor, a date of this sort can be a huge help for a place like the Tarim Basin in prehistoric times. But once, for example, the Chinese arrived in the basin and started dropping their coins (or the Romans reached Central Europe and started dropping coins there), the coins can be used to date an associated find to within a year or two—far better than radiocarbon dating can ever do. The C^{14} method must be used judiciously.

FIGURE 5·4

Hollowed-log coffin found at Egtved, Denmark, containing the burial of a young woman, 18 to 20 years old, lying on a hairy cowhide. (The wooden lid, cowhide, and cloth that covered her have been removed.) Her woolen clothes—blouse, sash (with bronze boss), and string skirt (wrapped twice around her)—are shown at right, as they looked during conservation. The string skirt is a traditional garment for women, made by hanging string or cords from a waistband; it is traceable in Europe back to 20,000 B.C. Tree rings indicate the oak for the coffin was cut down in 1370 B.C.; yarrow flowers in the burial show the girl was interred in summer.

Climate determines the amount of growth each tree manages during a growing season, as it builds a thin new layer of material all the way around its trunk (a tree ring). Outside the tropics these growing seasons are limited to one major season a year, producing distinguishable annual rings. But world climate is seriously (if temporarily) altered often enough to produce "hiccups"—especially thick or thin rings—in the sequence of growing seasons. Botanists noticed that those sequences of thicks and thins are sufficiently odd and unique to be recognizable from one tree to the next across vast distances. (Chief among the disturbances registered worldwide are volcanic eruptions that eject large ash clouds, such as Mount St. Helens in 1980 and Mount Pinatubo in 1991. Ash from both these outspewings circled the earth many miles high, blocking out much sunlight and turning sunsets a spectacular red for years afterward.)

Researchers began measuring the tree rings one year at a time, back from the present, and when the sequence from one usable tree would run out, they would search until they found another older tree with a provably overlapping sequence, so as to work their way yet further back in time. By 1991 they had worked out the tree ring sequence deep into the second millennium B.C. The log from which the Egtved coffin had been hewn matched the sequence of the early fourteenth century B.C. The tree itself had been felled in 1370, the year of its last growth ring.

Such accuracy, unhoped for even twenty-five years ago, is upending archaeology once again. The wonderful new information it is providing has forced a rethinking of large segments of ancient history. For example, we used to assume that all influence flowed from the splendid Near East to a backward Europe between 4000 and 1000 B.C. But now that we can prove that some of the important advances turn up much earlier in Europe than in the Near East, we'll have to rewrite parts of the history books.

BERGMAN HAD none of these tools, so the record of his work, like Stein's, is often frustrating—all the more so since Bergman too found mummies near Lop Nor that appear to belong to the ancient Krorainan indigenes. His discoveries, made in 1934, came from a place he labeled "Cemetery 5." It lay forty kilometers south of the main course of the (by then very wet) "Sand River" (which Bergman spells *Qum-darya*), just east of a newly refilled side branch that he nicknamed the Small River (map 4.1). Unfortunately the little hilltop cemetery had been partly destroyed by wind erosion and "native treasure-hunters" but was nonetheless

> still quite imposing. The top of the hill carries a "grove" of high poles or posts,
> probably erected to serve as funeral monuments, Pl. I [see fig. 5.5]. The ma-

FIGURE 5.5

Cemetery 5, found by Bergman in 1934, in sandy desert along the Small River west of the Loulan area. Tall carved wooden posts surrounding the prehistoric graves form a "forest" on top of the hill; fallen posts and coffins uncovered by wind erosion litter the slopes below. (After Bergman.)

jority of these poles are multilateral and they were once painted with red ochre. There are also some oar-shaped monuments of various sizes. . . . This site is most likely a clan-cemetery.

The dead rested in coffins of heavy curved boards fashioned after the size of the bodies, Pl. II:1 [see fig. 5.6]. The different members of the coffin were not joined by means of nails or any such medium but were kept together merely by a couple of ox-hides, placed on top of the lid and enveloping the upper part of the coffin. There were no bottoms. Due to the extraordinary aridity of the climate the corpses were mummified, the features in several cases being wonderfully well preserved. . . .

The dead were buried fully dressed and had been furnished with a few objects as funeral deposits. Such objects were small nicely plaited baskets, some long wooden pegs with two feather tufts, resembling arrow-shafts, Ephedra twigs, various bunches of grass, feathers and sinew, and, in some instances, some kind of indeterminable wooden objects which probably had some religious (shamanistic) function.

The dress . . . consists of the following articles: head-dress, mantle, loin-cloth, and shoes or moccasins.

The curve-sided coffins are clearly similar to the one pictured by Aurel Stein (fig. 5.2), who also mentions ephedra twigs, while the tidy baskets and feathers are familiar to us from Ürümchi. Pottery and metal are again conspicuously absent, but this time the vertical posts are taller than a person, instead of a few inches high (as at Qäwrighul and cemetery L.S.) or three feet high (as at Mesa L.F.).

FIGURE 5.6

Litter of curved wooden pieces of coffins on the wind-eroded slopes of Cemetery 5 on the Small River near Loulan; probably 1st millennium B.C. (After Bergman.)

Bergman's remarks, just quoted, come from a book by Vivi Sylwan, a Swedish textile scholar who analyzed the cloth and clothing that Bergman and Hedin brought back to Sweden. She called her book *Woollen Textiles of the Lou-lan People* (1941), and Bergman wrote a brief archaeological introduction. Sylwan describes in turn the "yarns, strings, and cords," the leather boots, the felt objects (principally caps), the plaited things, and finally the woven fabrics.

Of particular interest are the so-called loin-cloths which, with their long strings hanging down from a narrow waistband, look startlingly like the string skirts that I have traced in Europe from 20,000 B.C. to the present, the sort that the girl in the Egtved coffin of 1370 B.C. wore (fig. 5.4), though more crudely made. I had in fact encountered this publication many years ago, but because no date could be assigned to the finds other than "B.C."—"B.C." covers a lot of time—I could not fit them into the wider history of costume and left them aside.

Sylwan describes how the Kroraina/Loulan string skirts are made, some with a plaited band at the top, others with a woven one, and still others by simply suspending the strings from their middles by means of a lark's head knot over a slim, plaited cord (fig. 5.7). Bergman, for his part, describes how the garments were donned, and by whom: "The loin-cloths were worn under the mantle, and their fringes reached about half-way to the knees, in some cases down to the knees. The only difference noticed between the garments of the two sexes is that the loin-cloths of the women were broader than those of the men. . . . In a general way these fringed loin-cloths or fringe skirts resemble the well-known bronze-age girdle from Egtved in Denmark." The comparison to the Egtved girl's skirt is apt enough, but the summary description is somewhat misleading, as we shall see.

The European string skirt appears to have been worn only by adult women, and indeed as a badge of their childbearing ability (which is how it appears in the numerous European folk costumes in which it survives), yet at Loulan both sexes wore "fringed loin-cloths." In his own book two years earlier, however, Bergman makes it clear that the women's fringed loin drapings (fig. 5.7 left) had the same construction as the Stone and Bronze Age European ones—a horizontal band supporting strings or "fringes" hanging at right angles to the band—whereas the men's (fig. 5.7 right) consisted of a band or belt the *ends* of which terminated in a fringe, tied in front to hang down over the private parts. (In that sense the man's garment does appear narrower than the woman's when each is laid out on a table.)

Just as the European women from the Atlantic to the Urals had an age-old badge of their matured sexuality, so did the men—namely, a belt or sash. In many rural Slavic areas, for example, the boy received a red sash at puberty as a symbol of his virility, while the Celtic warrior of ancient times often wore only a belt. Both the male and female traditions can be traced backward from modern ethnography (recording the still-associated lore) through historical and archaeological data to the Bronze and Stone Ages in Europe. Once again our parallel data from the Tarim Basin point us westward.

In the same publications Bergman and Sylwan also discuss the material from a "Grave 36" that Hedin found on a tall mesa similar to the one described by Stein (Mesa L.F., quoted above). Bergman's practiced eye picks up many more of the details of interest to archaeology:

This single grave is situated on an imposing mesa, or clay hill, in the northern part of the delta of the Qum-darya. The coffin consisted of half a hollowed-out trunk, the ends of which were closed with semicircular boards and which had a cover of ox-hides. On top of the covering hides there was a small basket. The coffin contained the well preserved mummy of an old woman measuring only 1.52 m [five feet] in length. She was enveloped in a finely woven dark-brown mantle of soft wool with a yellow and red border (fig. 1 [fig. 5.8]). On the head she wore an outer and an inner cap. The former, of light-yellow felt, is pointed and the top is adorned with red cords and the split skin of an ermine. On the

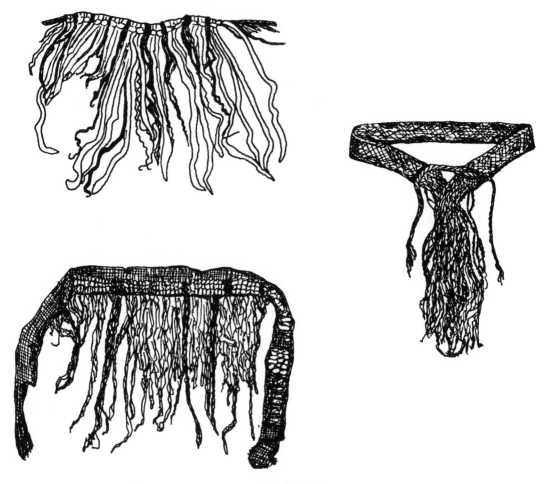

FIGURE 5.7

"Loincloths" found on mummies from the Loulan area. *Left:* Typical string skirts of women, with the fringe hanging at right angles to the band. The lady from Grave 36 (fig. 5.8) wore the top one, made by knotting 1 red followed by 2 white strands of woolen yarn successively to a belt band, using a lark's head knot. The lower skirt came from a woman's grave in Cemetery 5. *Right:* A man's belt band from Cemetery 5, with the fringe from the ends of the band used to cover the private parts. (After Sylwan, Bergman.)

left side there are two feathered pegs, rising boldly above the top. Both the caps are supplied with ear-flaps to be tied under the chin. . . .

Round the waist the woman wore a thin loin-cloth of woollen fringes, red and undyed, about 30 cm long. At a first glance it gives the impression of fur with long hairs.

The feet were stuck into a pair of raw-hide shoes of the same kind as those from Cemetery 5. They had a loose inner sole of lambskin.

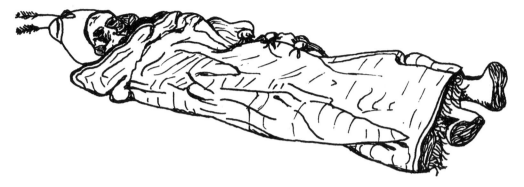

FIGURE 5.8

Mummy of an old woman, found by Bergman in a hollowed-log coffin in Grave 36 near Loulan. She was wrapped in a soft brown cloak with red and yellow border; she wore a red and natural-colored string skirt, rawhide moccasins, and a yellow felt cap decorated with red cords, ermine fur, and feathered pegs. Ephedra twigs had been tied into 3 little bundles formed from the edge of her cloak. (After Bergman.)

Six wooden and one bone pin apparently served to keep together the edges of the mantle. The wooden pins are carved of hard wood, three of them with several annular rows of triangular incisions.

A small wooden comb consisting of round pegs fastened in a transverse piece of tendon, a small doll made of rags, a small bundle of sinew-fibres and wool wrapped in a piece of red felt, and a lock of dark-brown hair kept together by a lashing were also found in the coffin.

Bergman summarizes his finds as follows:

It is quite evident that Grave 36 and Cemetery 5 belong to the same culture and the same people even though the general quality of the objects buried in Grave 36 is higher than the average of those from Cemetery 5. Neither contain[s] anything Chinese.

The only close parallels to these grave-finds are those reported by Sir Aurel Stein from the Lou-lan region.

The similarity of both these groups of finds to the three earliest mummies now in Ürümchi is also unmistakable: felt caps, oblong woven mantles, shoes, pins, combs, and the general layout. Sylwan's descriptions of the cloth bear out the resemblance: everything of wool, sometimes sorted into natural light and dark for color effects; a small amount of thread dyed red (and perhaps yellow); the warp at least sometimes closed at both ends, as on the mantle of the woman at the institute.

This array of clothes from the Kroraina/Loulan area is clearly much more primitive than the clothing from Cherchen dating to 1000 B.C. It shows neither the sophisticated array of patterns—no seams, no piping, no sleeves or pant legs—nor the skill at dyeing large amounts of wool into many bright colors (although a little dye was used). Does that mean that the Hedin-Stein-Bergman mummies from the area around Lop Nor (some or all of them) date to much earlier than these explorers thought—to the early second millennium B.C. like the three in Ürümchi? Or that Kroraina remained a cultural backwater, changing hardly at all from 2000 B.C. down to the time of the Chinese invasion shortly before 100 B.C.?

The latter is also a possibility; the ancient Chinese viewed the natives of the Kingdom of Loulan as "resembling birds and wild beasts." Stein and Hedin too, traveling before cars and roads reached the area, frequently remark that the "Lopliks" they encountered—the non-Chinese inhabitants of the few miserable fishing villages in the Lop Nor and Qara-Qoshun area—had scarcely progressed beyond a late Stone Age economy even then. Their flimsy reed huts, erected for a season or a few years near grazing grounds, also suggested to the explorers why they could not find habitation sites belonging to the equally simple folk who had lived there before the nomadic raiders and Chinese armies swept in during the second century B.C. Until they became the passageway between East and West, the people of Lop had nothing they needed to defend with strong walls, nothing anybody else wanted. The harshness of the climate had granted them no favors or riches.

Unlettered and unvisited, they left almost no trace in written history. So if we are to identify these forgotten people, we must use other means at our disposal.

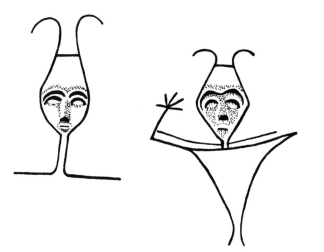

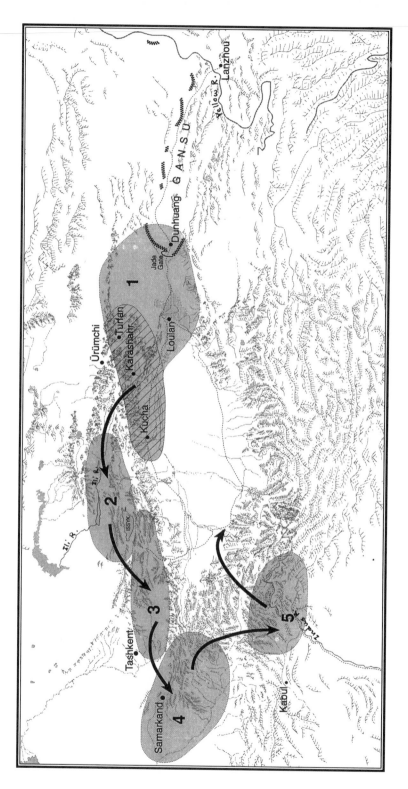

M A P 6 . I

6

Tokharians and Other
Hairy Barbarians

AMONG THE many texts brought back to Europe by early explorers, scholars noticed a group from the north side of the Tarim Basin that no one could read. These came largely from Kucha, Karashahr, and Turfan (map 6.1). The script looked reasonably familiar (fig. 6.2), largely resembling the well-known Brahmi scripts used for Sanskrit and Prakrit in India. (The Brahmi writing system best known to Westerners today is devanāgarī, in which the letter forms hang from the line like so much fresh laundry.) But the language was totally new. Fortunately many of the texts were translations of familiar Buddhist literature, so experts soon worked out the rudiments of grammar and vocabulary of this new tongue. Or rather, tongues, for the script hid not one but two closely related languages or dialects, nicknamed A and B. To everyone's surprise, these twin sisters represented an entirely new branch of the Indo-European family tree.

What is a language tree? It is a diagram showing how certain languages are related to one another. We can demonstrate the relatedness of some but not all

---

Opposite page: Map of Tokharian areas. Texts in Tokharian have been found principally at sites within the hatched area. The Yuezhi tribe, which probably spoke Tokharian, is said to have lived in Region 1 until chased out by the Xiongnu sometime before 150 B.C. The smaller half retreated to the hatched portion of 1; the larger half migrated to Region 2 (Ili River and Lake Issyk), then 3 (Fergana Valley), then 4 (Bactria, by 130 B.C.), and finally to 5 (Gandhara). Sections of the Great Wall of China, built to guard against the steppe horsemen, run from Dunhuang to east of Beijing.

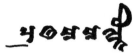

FIGURE 6.2

Left: Inscription on first sheet of Tokharian document written in a Brahmi script, saying (left to right) *pra-tha-ma ma-lto.* The first word means "first" in Indic; the second "first" or "head" in Tokharian. (After Sieg and Siegling.) *Right:* Heading of Prakrit document written in Kharoṣṭhī script on leather and found by Stein in rubbish heap at Niya, saying (right to left) *ma-ha-nu-a-va ma-ha-ra-ya li-ha-ti* ("His Highness the Maharaja orders"), a common opening in short texts. (The sign *ha* looks like our *2.)* (After Stein.)

languages. (Of course all languages may well be ultimately related, but that common ancestor would be so far back in prehistory that we can't know for sure. So if we say two languages aren't related, we mean only that we haven't enough data to *prove* a relationship.)

No one can listen to English very long without realizing that it comes in many varieties. Speakers from Boston and Los Angeles titter at each other's peculiarities of speech, while neither group can easily understand people from the Deep South, let alone from Yorkshire or the Australian outback. Yet all these dialects are changed later forms of "English" spoken in England before the New World was colonized. Travel then was slow and dangerous, so pronunciation changes and words for new things that developed in the colonies seldom made their way back to England. Nor did fashionable changes in the language as spoken in England make it out to the colonies; after all, language in the "mother" country kept changing too. The dialects diverged, in short, and now we *all* speak differently from the way we did in Shakespeare's day. (Who is "right"? None of us and all of us. We simply differ. All languages used by people who speak them natively keep changing, by their very nature and design.)

The relation between the worldwide dialects of English can be drawn in "tree" form—most conveniently with the twigs branching downward in time:

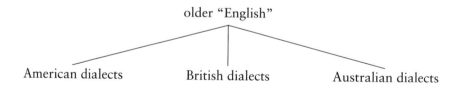

older "English"

American dialects   British dialects   Australian dialects

We could also add a tree for the continued development of U.S. dialects:

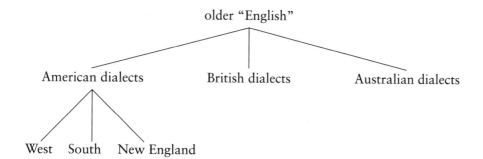

In the same way we can make trees that go further back in history. For instance, linguists can demonstrate that English, German, Dutch, and the Scandinavian languages are also simply changed later forms of a common ancestor language, spoken nearly two thousand years ago. We label this ancestor *proto-Germanic* (i.e., early Germanic) since we don't know what those preliterate people called themselves:

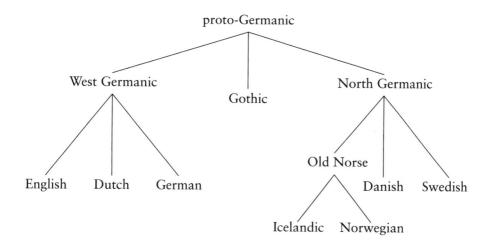

Likewise, several well-known modern languages descend from Latin as it was spoken in the Roman Empire around A.D. 400:

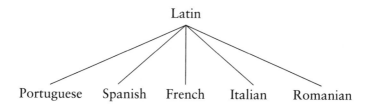

We even possess written documents across time and space that prove how each of these languages developed step by step from Latin. Thus the Romance (Roman-descended) languages and dialects have long provided an important laboratory for the study of language change and divergence.[1]

Back in 1786 Sir William Jones expressed the radical but insightful opinion that the Sanskrit texts of India (newly "discovered" by European scholars) bore to Classical Greek and Latin "a stronger affinity, both in the roots of verbs and in the forms of grammar, than could possibly have been produced by accident; so strong, indeed, that no philologer could examine them all three without believing them to have sprung from some common source, which, perhaps, no longer exists." He then added the Germanic and Celtic language families to his list of presumed kin. This was a major breakthrough, for Sir William had discovered the huge language family now called *Indo-European* (fig. 6.3). Why the name? Because this language family includes many (though not all) of the languages spoken in Europe, the Middle East and India, and because that was roughly their full extent before Columbus started the stampede to America.

What's more, Oriental Jones (as Sir William was called) had glimpsed a crucial notion: that the "original" language no longer exists as such. Just as with English, both the people who stayed home and those who moved away continued to change their language. Thus *everyone* ended up speaking changed later forms of a language that was no longer spoken. We no longer speak the English of the great English poet Chaucer, who lived less than a hundred years before Columbus. Just try reading his original text:

> Whanne that April with its shoures sote
> The droughte of March hath perced to the rote. . . .

(That is: "When April with its sweet showers/ Has pierced the drought of March to the root. . . .") The common ancestor of our Indo-European languages—nicknamed *proto-Indo-European* for lack of knowing what its speakers called themselves—was spoken around 3000 B.C., by our best estimate. But the earliest written texts in any Indo-European languages postdate 2000 B.C. So we are talking about prehistory again, and what we know of proto-Indo-European we

---

[1] Note that the distinction between "dialect" and "separate language" can be quite fuzzy among forms of speech derived from a common ancestor. How many differences have to accumulate before we stop saying "dialect" and start saying "language"? I personally find it easier to understand Italian on the basis of knowing Spanish than to understand Yorkshire English on the basis of speaking western American English, yet Yorkshire and American are treated as dialects of one language called English, whereas Spanish and Italian count as separate languages. There is no simple answer to this problem; it is a matter of degree, of what you wish to focus on, and of historical and political accident.

FIGURE 6.3

Simplified tree chart of languages in the greater Indo-European language family, which—before Columbus—extended from northwestern Europe to northern India. (It is now the dominant family of the New World as well.) The branches on this chart follow roughly *where* the daughter families ended up, west to east. Compare fig. 7.3, organized according to *when* the daughter families seem to have branched off. Not all descendants are listed; families marked with daggers have died out completely.

have had to reconstruct by regular principles from the daughter languages (see fig. 6.4).

The two languages, A and B, of the mysterious northern Tarim manuscripts were found to have the same sorts of nonaccidental relationships to other Indo-European languages that Sir William Jones saw among Greek, Latin, and Sanskrit. The twins belonged on the Indo-European tree—but where? Who were their nearest relatives? What were these new tongues called? How and when did they get out to the wilds of Chinese Turkestan when all their relatives flourished far to the west? And is this the language that our Western-looking mummies once spoke?

Clearly these language relationships have a strong bearing on interpreting the early migrations into Chinese Turkestan from the West. The language questions, moreover, closely parallel the textile problems, a fact that becomes more apparent as we look further into Languages A and B.

Linguistically these twins show features lumping them most closely with the *westernmost* Indo-European languages: Celtic and Italic, and to some extent

ENGLISH	LATIN	GREEK	SANSKRIT	TOKHARIAN (A/B)	Older Form:
mother	māter	mētér-	mātár-	mācar	< *mēter-
me	mē	me	mā		< *mĕ
moon/month	men-sis	mēn		mañ/meñe	< *men-
six	sex	hex-	şaş	şāk	< *seks
seven	septem	heptá	saptá	špät	< *septm̥
sew	su-	hu-			< *su-
nine	novem	e-nnéa	náva	ñu	< *newn̥
name	nomen	ó-noma	nắma	ñom/ñem	< *nomn-
night	noct-	nukt-	nákt-	noktim	< *nokʷt-
nee-dle	ne-	nē-	s-nā-		< *(s)nē-
weave		huph-	ubh-	waw-/wap-	< *uB-
wool	lāna/vellus	lênos/oulos	ū́rṇā		< *Hwln-

TABLE 6.4

Table showing cognates of a few words in various Indo-European languages from different subfamilies. (See fig. 6.3 for the subfamilies.) Note that although sounds differ from one language to the next, they show *regularity* in their variation. Thus, for example, what is word-initial *s-* in most of the languages always shows up as *h-* in Greek, and the vowels *e* and *o* always turn up as *a* in Sanskrit. The regularity is more real than apparent sometimes since the interactions between neighboring sounds can get quite complex while still being quite regular. To keep the reconstructed forms at right somewhat intelligible to nonlinguists, the transcriptions have been simplified; capital letters indicate sounds for which there are no Latin letters.

Germanic. But they are not particularly similar to their nearest geographical neighbors, Indo-Iranian and Balto-Slavic (see fig. 6.3). This is all the more surprising because other Tarim Basin people in the first millennium A.D. were writing and speaking Indic and Iranian languages. And indeed, the twins have many loanwords from these neighbors. But their basic structure is neither Indic nor Iranian, nor that of any other Indo-European daughter group. The pair forms a separate branch of the tree and, on the face of it, one that originally hobnobbed with the most westerly branches. We will come back to this problem presently.

As with proto-Germanic and proto-Indo-European, no one knew what the writers of these inscriptions called themselves or their language, and scholars began to fret over how to label the new dialects. Some sidestepped the issue by using geographical adjectives. At the oases of Turfan and Karashahr (map 6.1), explorers had found documents in both Language A and Language B, whereas at Kucha they had found only B. So Language B could be called Kuchean, and the less widespread one (A) Turfanian. On the other hand, B clearly functioned as the local vernacular, whereas A appeared to be more archaic, perhaps a liturgical language like Latin today—a written form used only in church and schoolroom, no one's native language anymore.

One manuscript found near Turfan provided grist for a mill that has been grinding ever since. A Buddhist text, like most of the others, it was written in Uyghur, still the dominant Turkic language in the Uyghur Autonomous Region today, and quite readable. (Turkic is not Indo-European; it belongs to the Altaic language family. See fig. 9.7.) The colophon or capsule description on the document stated, moreover, that this text, a drama, had been translated into Turkic from a language called *twghry*. Interestingly all other known versions of this drama are written either in Uyghur, like this one, or in Turfanian—that is, Language A. The experts pounced: *twghry* must be the name of Language A at least, if not of both dialects.

It so happens that the people who did most to spread Buddhism into the Tarim Basin lived in northern India, having recently emigrated there from Bactria (map 6.1, Region 4). Before that, Greek historians tell us, this same group had moved into Bactria from Fergana (Region 3) in the second century B.C. (The Fergana Valley lies immediately west of the Tarim Basin across the Pamir Mountains. It is so rich that today a fantastically gerrymandered border divides it into unequal thirds among Uzbekistan, Tajikistan, and Kyrgyzstan; no one wishes to give up an inch of its soil. The Greeks had become acquainted with this whole area in 329 B.C. while following Alexander the Great to India and back; see map 10.7.) Thus in a short time these wanderers had moved from Fergana to Bactria to northern India (today northern Pakistan), where they eventually converted to Buddhism. They are known to Greek history as the *Tókharoi* and to Sanskrit documents as *Tukhāra*.

On the basis of the similarity of the word *twghry* to these names, and in view of the strong Buddhist connection, two scholars in 1908 declared that the new language(s) must have been called Tokharian. And so the twins are labeled to this day, Tokharian A and B, even though we have no further proof the equation is right. Whatever we call them—and I'll use "Tokharian" from now on as a convenient label—we do know that the languages descended from proto-Indo-European.

Whereas Tokharian A and B—Turfanian and Kuchean—were spoken in the northern Tarim Basin, ghostly shadows of a third related dialect have survived in numerous loanwords found in administrative documents of the southern Tarim. These latter were written in Prakrit, an Indic and hence (also) Indo-European language, using the Kharoṣṭhī script of India. We have mentioned that these Kharoṣṭhī tablets used the form *Kroraina* to refer to the town and kingdom that the Chinese, with their more restrictive sound system, reduced to *Loulan*.[2] Hence this third dialect goes under the label *Krorainic,* although we do not know for certain that it was the chief language of the Kroraina kingdom. The Prakrit documents with Krorainic loans come from an area considerably south of Kroraina/Loulan, and from documents of the third century A.D., several hundred years earlier than the main body of Tokharian texts. The earliness of Krorainic thus gives it special importance in tracing Tokharian linguistic prehistory, even though we have so little of it. On the other hand, the Tokharian A and B texts, all from areas north of Kroraina/Loulan, date principally from the sixth to ninth centuries A.D. Shortly after the last such texts the Tokharian language died out. New immigrants speaking other languages (such as Uyghur, the dominant Turkic language there today) moved into the Tarim Basin during the ninth and tenth centuries and soon overwhelmed the speakers of Tokharian.

As Indo-Europeans the Tokharians must originally have come into the Tarim Basin from much farther west. The same goes for the tall, hirsute, wheat-raising, sheepherding people represented by our mummies. The obvious question is: were some or all of our mummy people ancestors of the Tokharians?

Physically they could have been. The frescoes that the later Tokharians drew of themselves, piously donating bags of money to their local Buddhist monasteries or posing in a row wearing fine knightly attire, show great handlebar mustaches and full beards only half hiding pale cheeks (plate 16). Some men have dark hair and eyes, but others have light brown or even red hair and bright blue eyes. And all have high-bridged noses. In short, they look far more like the man from Cherchen or the "Bohemian burgher" of Loulan than like the Chinese, Mongol, or even Turkic peoples. We can no longer discern the eye color of our desiccated mummies, but unusual blue stones covered the Cherchen baby's eyes and blue eyes were brocaded onto the Argali sheep, both inspired, perhaps, by blue-eyed people.

When the Chinese began to have regular contact in the second century B.C. with the inhabitants of Central Asia, the easternmost of whom they called the *Yue-zhi,* what amazed the Han Chinese most about these Yuezhi (besides their "barbarian" and "backward" ways) was how hairy the men were. Clearly men with heavy beards contrasted with the Chinese males, whose facial hair is restricted to upper lip and tip of chin. A modern Chinese scholar explains that the Han Dynasty Chinese came to use the name *Hú* for anyone with "deep eye sockets, prominent noses, and beards" and that this term *Hú* was applied to

---

[2] This linguistic process was described in Chapter 5.

the Yuezhi, among others, though not to the (Mongoloid) Qiang among whom the "Lesser Yuezhi" lived. Other Chinese sources characterized the "Greater Yuezhi" as having "white" or "reddish white" skin, another typically Caucasoid feature.

So things seem to point to our mummies as being early Tokharians. The historical Tokharians had the same European physical features as the mummies, they spoke an Indo-European language that had to have come in from the West, and they and the Iranians were the only Indo-European speakers we have record of ever dwelling in the Tarim Basin.

But not so fast. People can change their language at will, without altering a single gene or freckle. The Tokharians of our documents lived and spoke in the first millennium A.D., whereas our mummies lived and talked between 2000 and 1000 B.C. We have a gap of over a thousand years to bridge to get from the mummies to the documented Tokharians and only a bit less to the Yuezhi and Krorainic. We also haven't demonstrated whether the early people of Loulan, Cherchen, and other Tarim areas spoke languages from the same family as each other. At that early date all were illiterate like everyone else close by, so no direct records exist. Other groups speaking other languages (Indo-European or not) could well have wandered in from the west around 2000 B.C. and then died out completely, being replaced later by Tokharians. How would we know? In the course of time thousands of ancient languages all over the world must have dropped off their language trees without trace, like overripe plums. Until the Sumerians invented writing in Mesopotamia around 3500 B.C. or so, no permanent linguistic records existed, and none existed in East Asia until the Chinese developed their script about 1500 B.C. Yet humans had been speaking for a hundred thousand years or more when writing was invented, and even today not every culture is literate. Much has gotten lost.

Dead mummies speak not. As James Mallory, a well-known archaeologist of Indo-European cultures, has quipped, "the mummies don't come with letters in their pockets" either. Making matches between languages and material culture is arguably the most difficult task prehistorians attempt. So how *do* we match unwritten ancient languages with tattered archaeological remains?

First, we must wring every possible drop of information, linguistic and otherwise, from literate neighbors; then—more difficult—we must wring out of our reconstructions of unwritten ancient languages any concrete cultural information that can be matched up unmistakably with the material remains.

In the case of the early Central Asian people, the nearest literate folk were the Chinese. The Chinese began probing to the west late in the first millennium B.C. through the Gansu (Kansu) Corridor, a long, narrow valley that led between the mountain ranges from the fertile provinces of northern China westward to the edge of the Tarim Basin (see map 6.1). From the westernmost bend of the Yellow River, or Huang-he—named for the nutrient-rich yellow silt that it carries—to the eastern end of the Tarim Basin is a distance of nearly eight hundred miles, the length of California. A modern traveler flying over the broad zone of parched orange mountains between Beijing and Ürümchi can sometimes glimpse the Gansu Corridor running parallel to the flight path on the south side. With its intermittent watercourses, this long rift is only slightly less arid than the dusty mountains that flank it to north and south. But even a little water made Gansu a lesser evil for the ancient wayfarer.

The vast difference between China's rich agricultural valleys and the scrubby deserts and grasslands of Inner Asia gave rise, in fact, to the very problem that the Han Chinese of two thousand years ago needed to solve. All too often, horse-riding barbarian warriors swooped out of the western mountains into the lush Chinese farmlands, pillaging the settlements, killing the men, and carrying off grain, women, and silks. In vain the emperors bribed the barbarians to stay away, sending huge loads of silken textiles and even occasional royal princesses. With somewhat greater success the Chinese laborers built great stretches of wall across the mountains to keep the riders out of China and to give early warning of their approach. Around 220 B.C. the powerful Qin Dynasty emperor Shi Huangdi (literally "First Emperor") ordered many sections of previously built wall to be joined together into what the world knows today as the Great Wall of China (fig. 6.5)—roughly fourteen hundred miles long with twenty-five thousand watchtowers.[3]

But the mounted attacks continued, particularly by the ferocious *Xiong-nu* (pronounced roughly "shung-noo"), who were probably the ancestors of the equally savage Huns of Western fame. The only recourse left to China was somehow to weaken the barbarians internally.

Bit by bit the Chinese forced a passageway through the forbidding Gansu Valley to Dunhuang at its west end (map 4.7), famous later for its Buddhist caves and the Jade Gate leading to the desert beyond. Other people already lived in the Gansu Corridor—namely, those hairy barbarians the Chinese called Yuezhi—but no sooner had the Chinese arrived than the Xiongnu swooped

---

[3] A newscast a couple of years ago announced that the Chinese had just discovered a long-lost two-hundred-mile section of wall. How can you lose something two hundred miles long? (Contrary to popular legend, the Great Wall is *not* visible from space.) The fact that such a thing could happen bears witness to the desolation of this countryside in western China.

Although short-ruling, the powerful Qin (pronounced "chin") Dynasty that hooked up so many pieces of the wall apparently gave us our name for the country, China. Emperor Shi Huangdi is also famed today as the man who caused thousands of life-sized terra-cotta warriors to be set up to guard his tomb—still unopened because of its enormous size and the number of booby traps built into it.

FIGURE 6.5

A restored section of the Great Wall of China, as it looks today near Beijing. The road-way connecting the watchtowers was protected on the enemy side by a crenellated shield wall.

down from the north, chasing the Yuezhi westward out of Gansu and blocking the way again. A description from that time reported: "Formerly they [the Yuezhi] were very powerful and despised the Xiongnu, but later, when Maodun [Modun] became leader of the Xiongnu nation, he attacked and defeated the Yuezhi. Some time afterwards his son . . . killed the king of the Yuezhi and made his skull into a drinking cup." The emperor Wudi (one of the great Han Dynasty rulers) then sent an ambassador named Zhang Qian (pronounced roughly "chian") to persuade the disgruntled and dispossessed Yuezhi to attack the Xiongnu from their new position in the west while the Chinese beset them from the east—a classic squeeze.

Zhang Qian was a palace attendant when the emperor called for a volunteer capable of carrying out this difficult and dangerous mission. Accompanied by a hundred men and guided by a former slave of the Xiongnu, named Ganfu, he set out westward through enemy territory soon after 140 B.C. The Xiongnu captured them, however, and took them to their king, the Shanyu, who had no intention of letting a Chinese envoy get through to his far flank. The Shanyu did not kill his captives, however, but married Zhang Qian off to a Xiongnu woman, with whom he had a son. After ten years, being less closely watched than before, the emperor's envoy finally managed to sneak away to the west, apparently taking his new family and Ganfu with him.

A month of travel brought the fugitives to the kingdom of Dayuan (modern Fergana). Its ruler had heard report of the wealth of Han Dynasty China and was delighted to make direct contact at last. He entertained the Chinese emissary and sent him on his way, with guides and interpreters, to the Yuezhi now living in the area that the Chinese envoy called Daxia but that Alexander and his Greeks had called Bactria when they conquered it exactly two hundred years earlier.

There, however, the mission fared less well. It seems that the son of the unfortunate king who had been made into a drinking cup had moved with his people some fifteen hundred miles westward to a valley "rich and fertile and seldom troubled by invaders." Comfortably settled at last, he had no wish to scare up trouble again, let alone reencounter the bloodthirsty Xiongnu. After a year Zhang Qian gave up talking and headed home toward China—only to fall once again into the hands of the Xiongnu. But luck eventually wandered by again. A year later the Shanyu died and civil war broke out among the Xiongnu over the succession. Amid the turmoil Zhang Qian, his wife, and Ganfu finally made it back to China. The year was 126 B.C., thirteen years since the envoys had left.

Although Zhang Qian had failed in his ostensible mission, he had gathered much valuable information about the people and areas beyond the Xiongnu, and the wise emperor honored him for it. We benefit also. To begin with, we learn that "the Yuezhi originally lived in the area between Qilian or Heavenly Mountains and Dunhuang." Today the name Qilian refers only to the mountain range lining the south side of the Gansu Corridor, also known as the Richthofen range; whereas the mountains continuing the same line farther west, dividing the Tarim Basin from the Dzungarian Basin, are known now as the Tien Shan or Tängri Tagh, literally the "Heavenly Mountains" in both Chinese and Uyghur (respectively). It appears from various bits of evidence, including Zhang Qian's description, that the early Chinese called any of this line of mountains out in the wild west by both names—Heavenly Mountains and Qilian—indiscriminately. Note that Dunhuang is only a few miles north of the Richthofen range, hardly enough space for the sizable nation described as living out there. The area between Dunhuang and today's Tien Shan, however, is the space of several hundred miles around Kroraina/Loulan and Kucha, a territory that would give the Yuezhi considerable room to live.

The imperial envoy continues: ". . . but after they were defeated by the Xiongnu they moved far away to the west, beyond Dayuan [Fergana], where they attacked and conquered the people of Daxia [Bactria] and set up the court of their king on the northern bank of the Gui [Oxus, or Amu] River. A small number of their people who were unable to make the journey west sought refuge among the Qiang barbarians in the Southern Mountains, where they are known as the Lesser Yuezhi." In short, the Yuezhi split up early in the second century B.C. (Stage 1: see map 6.1). The larger group traveled west-northwest past what is now Ürümchi to the vicinity of the Ili River and Lake Issyk (in modern Kyrgyzstan; Stage 2), and thence southwest to Fergana (Stage 3) and then Bactria (Stage 4). The smaller group, however, remained in the Tarim Basin, just up into the mountains from where they had been before (if our analysis of the mountain names is right). When he traveled through, said Zhang Qian, "the Loulan and Gushi peoples live[d] in fortified cities along the Salt Swamp." *Gushi* equates linguistically with *Kucha,* while the Salt Swamp is of course the Lop Nor area. (Note that he distinguishes the Gushi from the Krorainians, but whether he means this linguistically or politically or both is unclear.) All these details correlate closely with what we learned of the Tókharoi from the Greeks, who also mentioned Stages 3 and 4 of the migration.

(We can also use Zhang Qian's report to fill in more on our map of the Tarim Basin itself. Just west of the stay-behinds lived some people the envoy called the Yumi, then came the Yutian, and beyond the Yutian came the watershed we call the Pamirs, for "west of Yutian, all the rivers flow west and empty into the Western Sea, but east of there they flow eastward into the Salt Swamp." Yutian thus can only be the west end of the Tarim Basin.)

We know that people in Kucha later spoke Tokharian, because that is where so many Tokharian B texts were found. Does that entitle us to assume the same for the Gushi folk in the second century B.C., half a millennium earlier? Were they among the remnants of the Lesser Yuezhi? And what did the Yuezhi speak anyhow? Can we show that *it* was Tokharian?

For some decades arguments roiled around this point. Since the Yuezhi themselves left no texts, the answer was sought in Chinese sources again. Of course the ancient Chinese historians don't just come out and say, "The Yuezhi speak Language X." So the focus of work had to shift to word histories.

As it happens, quite a few words attested in Old Chinese have turned out to have Indo-European etymologies. For example, a whole cluster of Chinese words to do with wheels, wheel spokes, axles, and chariots—all objects first invented in west-central Eurasia—has proved to be Indo-European in origin. Some of the terms can't be assigned specifically to one Indo-European language or another; others seem to go back to Iranian forms. But several words belonging specifically to the Yuezhi—borrowed directly into Chinese or otherwise noted by ancient historians—have demonstrably Tokharian etymologies, starting with the names for the mountains where envoy Zhang Qian said the Yuezhi "originally" lived. The names of both the Qilian and Kunlun Mountains evidently came from a Tokharian word for "holy, heavenly" (A: *klyom,* B: *klyomo*—probably cognate with the Latin *caelum* ["sky, heaven"], from which we get the English *cel-estial*). Furthermore, the Chinese had recorded these names of those mountains several dynasties before the Yuezhi were chased out and the emperor's envoy traveled through. Still today the mountain range rimming the north side of the Tarim Basin is called the Celestial or Heavenly Mountains (since that is what Chinese *Tien Shan* and Uyghur *Tängri Tagh* mean), and the southern mountain rim is called the Kunlun.

On the strength of such linguistic fossils, the identification of the Yuezhi as speakers of Tokharian has gained fairly wide acceptance.

The geography matches well too. The last stages of the semicircular trajectory of the Greater Yuezhi, moving from the eastern Tarim Basin to Fergana to Bactria (Stages 1–4 by way of Regions 1–4 in map 6.1), exactly coincide, dates and all, with the Greek chronicles mentioning the arrival of the Tókharoi from Fergana into Bactria. These Tókharoi then progressed through another half circle. First they moved to the northernmost corner of the Indian subcontinent (Stage and Region 5), where they became known to the Sanskrit writers as Tukhāra and where they took up Buddhism. Then they carried their newfound religion north across the Himalayas and Kunlun, right back into the Tarim Basin where they had left their cousins behind six hundred years earlier. (Did they know that? Is that why they climbed over whole mountain ranges to share their philosophical good fortune with their northern neighbors?) Maybe the archaic, churchy-sounding Tokharian A was the changed later language of the far-traveling Greater Yuezhi, now acting as Buddhist missionaries, while Tokharian B was the dialect developed by the stay-at-home descendants of the Lesser Yuezhi, perhaps that of the "Gushi" people. A manuscript of the late first millennium A.D., found at Dunhuang, says that a small state between Turfan and Kucha still had the name Yuezhi. It seems as though every signpost we trip over points to this one area.

So inch by inch we have fought our way to the precious information that Tokharian speakers had ensconced themselves in parts of the Tarim Basin, especially in the east, well before the Xiongnu started shoving people around in the second century B.C. We have also learned some of the value of old place-names.

The natural languages we know of are always changed later forms of older languages (hence the family trees we looked at), and among the most common types of change is word borrowing. People constantly borrow words for interesting new items that they encounter, including names for new places. The Chinese, as we saw, borrowed local Tokharian names for mountain ranges flanking the Tarim Basin. American settlers did the same thing, borrowing Amerindian names by the thousands: Allegheny, Adirondack, Massachusetts, Narraganset, Chappaquiddick, Potomac, etc. It is usually easier to borrow geographical names from the locals than to make up new ones, especially names of key geological features, such as mountains and bodies of water. Old settlements too, like London or Kroraina/Loulan, may hang on to their names for millennia; London's name was established in England long before Germanic speakers or even the Romans (still earlier) reached Britain. On the other hand, new settlements receive names from the language (or familiar name repertoire) of the founding people: New Haven, Walnut Creek, Grants Pass, New London.

When wave after wave of new people passes through, each group speaking a different language, the layers of old language accumulate like lines of seaweed on the sand behind the tide, each marking the extent of a former incursion of the flood. Thus in addition to sorting out which language is which, linguists can map the regions anciently inhabited by people long gone, by tracking the origins of the place-names. For example, Athens—or *Athēnai,* as the Greeks call it—has been a principal city of the Greek-speaking world for thirty-five hundred years or more, but the name itself belongs to yet earlier non-Greek inhabitants, as do the names of several hills in the vicinity, such as Hymettos and Lykabettos. These form part of a large group of names ending in *-ttos* or *-ssos* that can be traced to the Minoans and that had their maximum extent just before 2000 B.C. Similar tracking of place-names has shown that the Baltic branch of Indo-European, now confined to two pocket countries along the shores of the Baltic Sea, Latvia and Lithuania, once stretched eastward past Moscow almost to the Urals, a huge area curtailed many centuries ago by the expansion of the Slavs. The locations of the seaweed piles of old names tell the story.

In Xinjiang we can do the same. As we've said, the word *Xinjiang* itself (a slightly newer form of *Sinkiang*) is simply the Chinese for "New Territory." That tells you something about history right there. Most of the local place-names are not Chinese but transparently Turkic—Qum-därya (Sand River), Quruk-därya (Dry River), Quruk–tagh (Dry Mountain), Kara-Shahr (or Qara–shähär, Black Town), Qara-qash (Black Jade), Qizil (Red), Yangi-bulaq (New Spring)—or Chinese renditions of same (e.g., *Kezi'er* for Qizil). Sometimes the Chinese versions lead to comic effects, as when the Turkic river name Könchi became the Kongque He, which means "Peacock River" (*hé* is "river" in Chinese), although no peacock—a forest bird from far to the south—could live in the dry wastes through which this river flows. Other names predate the Turkic layer, going back to Tokharian (Qilian, Kunlun), or to . . . to what? Plenty of names still remain to be explicated, old names like Kroraina, Cherchen, and Lop.[4] As in Greece, we may have a residue unassignable to any

---

[4] Two groups have laid claim to *nor,* the second half of *Lop Nor. Nor* is Mongol for "lake" and occurs as part of many lake names in Xinjiang and other parts of Central Asia, while *nur* is Uyghur for "bright" (as in the white of the salt flats). Mongol probably wins this one. But *lop* is opaque in both languages and in Chinese too, a fact suggesting that the name goes back to a time before Turks, Mongols, or Chinese had entered the territory.

known language, possibly the last shadows of ancient languages that died out in prehistoric times. If one of these residues known from a cohesive group of place names spreads over exactly the same territory as one of the prehistoric cultural areas known from archaeological digging (as was the case with the -*ssos/-ttos* names in the Aegean area), then we have strong evidence that the people of that early material culture spoke that language.

Thus, in various ways, the study of place-names—toponyms—can be very profitable for mapping where speakers of bygone languages lived at one time. It has yet to be done systematically for the Tarim Basin—a lengthy job—but clearly it will yield interesting information.

Place-names are not the only kinds of words that go on loan. People also borrow words for new objects and ideas. Again, it's generally easier to borrow the words right along with the new items than to think up brand-new vocabulary. Consider, for example, all the words for foods that we've borrowed into English: *pizza, spaghetti,* and *ravioli* from Italian; *hamburgers, wiener, pretzel,* and *sauerkraut* from German; and all of *gourmet cuisine*—from *soup* to *salad* and *sauce,* from *entrée* to *dessert*—comes from French. It's easier just to adopt the term *filet mignon* than to say "a steak cut crossways from that tender muscle that runs down next to the spine." Because of the Norman French invasion of England, French left the largest "seaweed piles" of borrowed words in English—some 60 percent of our vocabulary. We even borrowed words like *beef, pullet,* and *venison* for culinary purposes although we already had the native words *cow, hen,* and *deer*—words now, but not originally, limited to the live animals.

It is by digging through this sort of borrowed vocabulary, to deduce who got what from whom, and when and why, that we have a chance of extracting letter fragments out of the pockets of our prehistoric mummies. We can do this difficult trick if we can locate a group of *borrowed* words corresponding to *new* elements in a craft for which we have material remains. Then we can equate the lenders of the new technology with the lending language.

For example, we have noted that the Chinese borrowed a sizable cluster of words to do with wheels and chariots; they encountered a new and highly useful technology among their neighbors and borrowed both the technology and the words connected with it. We know from linguistics that those words came from Indo-European sources, and we know from archaeology that the peculiar art of making spoked wheels (and with them a chariot light enough to be drawn by fleet-footed horses) was developed at the western end of Asia, in the vicinity of the southern Urals, during the third and early second millennia. We know too that this wave of technology entered China in the mid-second millennium

B.C. Such information indicates that the Chinese learned chariotry from speakers of Indo-European languages.[5]

That's China; but what about the Tarim? We know nothing yet of how these early people lived, almost nothing of their houses or implements. Words to do with architecture and transportation therefore can't help us, and the people put little into their graves except the clothes they wore.

But textiles and clothing can tell many tales. Our English words for basic textile activities like *weave* and *sew* are very ancient, coming straight down to us from proto-Indo-European (fig. 6.4), whereas terms like *felt, crochet, mantle,* and *sombrero* we borrowed from various sources along the way. Ancient Greek inherited from proto-Indo-European the simple terms for weaving on the most primitive of all looms, the narrow band loom, but borrowed the entire vocabulary needed for weaving on the large loom of early Europe, the warp-weighted loom. Such stratification is as clear as any on a good archaeological dig.

The early folk of Loulan seem to have *introduced* weaving into the Tarim Basin. Since useful technology tends to run downhill like water, from the more developed practitioners "down" to the less developed, anyone ignorant of weaving who came into the Tarim later than the Loulan folk would soon learn the craft from them, words and all. By the same token, later local weavers ignorant of how to produce a skillful newcomer's attractive fabrics and styles would likely borrow the new methods, words and all. Clothes in particular constitute our oldest material signs of social status and identity.

Fragments of whatever language the early Loulan settlers brought into the Tarim along with the first weaving technology could therefore show up in the textile vocabulary of other languages attested there later. Likewise, the improvements we noticed at Cherchen may have left linguistic marks. Thus if Tokharian speakers carried into Central Asia the first knowledge of weaving, or brought later the more sophisticated techniques of weaving and dyeing that we saw at Cherchen, then Tokharian textile words expressing these innovations should turn up in the "seaweed piles" of borrowed textile terms in the languages

---

[5] Much of this method's power comes from the existence of *many* words associated with one another in meaning—the more the better. Working out etymologies is so fraught with interlocking difficulties that a linguist, no matter how diligent, may happen to be wrong about single words. Some unreconstructable chance event may have knocked one form askew. But linguistic reconstruction works on the basis of sets of regular *correspondences* (see fig. 6.4), so the more words we have at our disposal, the harder it is to get fooled about the whole group. We may not wish to stake our lives that, for example, Chinese *guĭ* "wheel axle end" came from Indo-European, though it probably did. But there is no doubt whatsoever that a sizable chunk of ancient Chinese vocabulary came from Indo-European—not just to do with chariotry, but also in architecture, divination, healing, and other matters.

that we know came in still later, such as Turkic (especially Uyghur) and Chinese. Conversely, if piles of borrowed textile words indeed turn up but aren't Tokharian, then we can surmise that the early inhabitants spoke other languages.

On the other hand, the words for felt and feltmaking should show a different history. Nomadic herders in the steppe zone north of the Tarim Basin specialized in making felt, not in weaving, and they used their felt for everything from house walls and flooring to dinner plates and clothing. Only when something had to have tensile strength (like straps) or softness (like undershirts) did they sometimes turn to weaving. Better yet, they often bought the woven material from their neighbors to make up as needed.

As on the steppes, the early textiles of the Tarim consisted of wool. Yet after analyzing the ancient cloth brought back to Sweden by Hedin's expeditions, Vivi Sylwan remarked that for all their skill at weaving wool the prehistoric Loulan people made pretty indifferent felt—not at all like true nomads. So of the two ways of making cloth, weaving was apparently the older and more comfortable technology among these people when they entered Central Asia from the west. Parallel to this, the Indo-European languages as a whole share their basic word for weaving (see fig. 6.4), but only a few of the Indo-European subfamilies acquired words for felt and they seem to have done so after the proto-Indo-European community broke apart.[6] Such correlations make some form of Indo-European look increasingly probable for the earliest Tarim settlers, though not yet proven.

We may not have enough of the particular textile words we need to do such a study on Tokharian. Our Tokharian manuscripts consist mainly of random scraps of translated Buddhist literature and shreds of local business dealings— not a good cross section of the total vocabulary. But we do have a few relevant terms, including a clearly Indo-European word for "weaver" (*wawāttsa* or *wapāttsa*, cognate with English *weave, web*—see fig. 6.4). So we know the Tokharians came to the Tarim Basin with an ancient knowledge of weaving. Indeed, Tokharian itself may show interesting loans, telling us something of where its speakers had wandered and who taught them.

Of all the waves of cloth technology that swept into the Tarim Basin, however, none carries more intriguing mysteries than the textiles worn by a group of mummies from near Hami (Qumul), three hundred miles northeast of Loulan. Although these graves are roughly contemporary with the Cherchen

[6] The picture is confused by the fact that Greek, Latin, and Germanic seem to have borrowed many textile words (including the ancestor of English *felt*) from a common source. As a parallel, the term *Coca-Cola* is found in almost every language of the world today, but in every case it's only a recent borrowing from a common source, *not* a word inherited in common from a tongue spoken in the Stone Age.

group (if we may believe the present dating), time and weather have abused the bodies rather more. But the cloth has survived quite well enough to show an uncanny resemblance to a series of textiles of the same age from central Europe, woven by ancestors of the Celts—fellow Indo-Europeans from the other end of Eurasia. To these textiles and their implications we will turn next.

NIYA XV

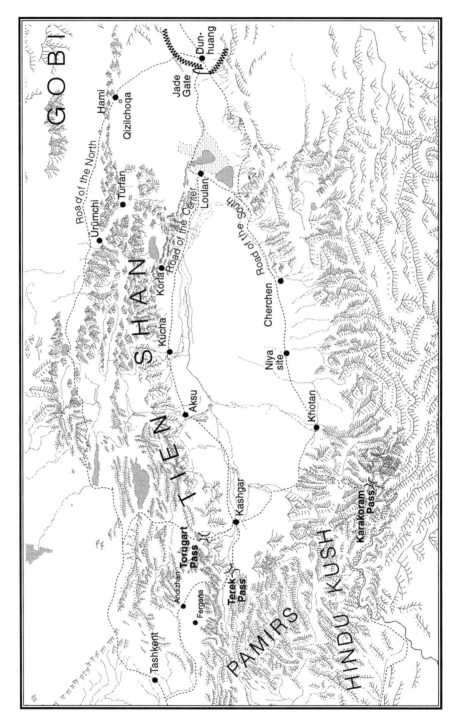

MAP 7.1

7

Hami and Hallstatt

THE TOWN of Hami, as the Chinese call it (the Uyghur is Qumul), lies at the northeast corner of the greater Turfan Basin, itself sandwiched between the much larger Tarim Basin to the southwest and the huge Gobi Desert to the northeast (map 7.1). Three hundred miles east of Ürümchi and two hundred miles northwest of Dunhuang, Hami has long been a major oasis in the desert.

When Chinese merchants traveled the Silk Road through the heart of Asia two thousand years ago, they had three choices after they trudged out of the Jade Gate through the Chinese defense wall just beyond Dunhuang (map 7.1). They could take the *Road of the South,* trekking hundreds of miles over the grueling salt flats of Lop Nor to Loulan and Cherchen and then around the south side of the Taklamakan Desert to Niya and Khotan. From there they could either finish the circuit of the Tarim Basin by heading north to Kashgar and west over the Pamirs (where the lowest pass, the Torugart, at 12,000 feet tops Mount Hood by a thousand feet), or climb directly south to the lung-defying 18,500-

---

Opposite page: Map of Tarim Basin showing the three principal routes making up the Silk Road in early times, starting from the Jade Gate through the Chinese defensive wall just west of Dunhuang. The northernmost route, although the providing the least harsh climate, was most subject to attacks from horse-riding nomads to the north. The site of Qizilchoqa, near Hami (Qumul), has produced many mummified remains from roughly 1200–700 B.C.

foot Karakoram Pass (nearly 4,000 feet higher than the tip of the Matterhorn) and over it to the Indus River valley, gateway to India.

A second possible route, the *Road of the Center,* again started across the salt desert to Loulan, but from there it skirted the north side of the Taklamakan, passing through the oases of Kucha and Aksu before meeting the Road of the South at Kashgar and traversing the Pamirs to western Turkestan.

As a third possibility, travelers could choose the *Road of the North,* crossing the stony desert northwest from Dunhuang via Hami and the Turfan Depression to the relative cool of Ürümchi, on the north side of Tien Shan range. Thence they continued via much lower and greener valleys to the Ili River and western Turkestan (just as the Greater Yuezhi had done; see Chapter 6 and map 6.1).

Geographically the Road of the North held all the advantages of easier travel. Unfortunately, over much of the last twenty-five hundred years the horse-riding "barbarians" of the steppes have made this easier route unsafe, as we learn from Chinese historians. The bandits often swept down from the northern grasslands onto helpless caravans, killing the merchants and couriers and carrying off all the valuable goods. Nonetheless Hami continued to flourish as an important oasis town; any place blessed with year-round water remained critical to life in the Central Asian desert zone.

Not far from Hami, at a place called Qizilchoqa (Red Hillock), archaeologists in 1979 found an ancient cemetery. Wang Binghua, of the Xinjiang Institute of Archaeology in Ürümchi, had systematically searched the old watercourses in that region, looking for ancient remains and questioning the locals—always a useful ploy, since many pairs of eyes are better than just your own. One day an elderly peasant led him to a low, sandy hill near the village of Wupu, where old bones kept turning up around the local brickworks of Qizilchoqa. Slight hollows in the sand divulged the burial places—a couple of hundred of them at least. The bodies at Qizilchoqa, entombed with their knees up, in low rectangles of mud brick covered with logs, matting, and then sand, had not withstood the millennia as well as the best-preserved mummies of Loulan and Cherchen (fig. 7.2). But the remains leave no doubt as to the appearance of these people in life. According to Hadingham's report in *Discover,* "the men generally have light brown or blond hair, while the women have long braids; one girl has blue tattoo marks on her wrist." Like the other early mummies, they had Caucasoid features and wore multicolored woolen clothing.

Their cloth, however, had a look all its own (plates 13, 14a), radically different from that of Cherchen and Loulan. At these two sites we found mostly variations on plain weave, and at Cherchen the peculiar long-hop twill (fig. 2.13c), some of it in tapestry. At Qizilchoqa the dominant weave proved to be

FIGURE 7.2

Mummy from Qizilchoqa (Wupu), near the city of Hami. Although this cemetery, like that at Cherchen, dates to ca. 1000 B.C., the bodies are not so fully preserved. (After Mair.)

normal diagonal twill (figs. 2.13b, 3.12a) and the chief decoration was plaid— that is, wide and narrow color stripes in both warp and weft, as in the woolen twill material of a Scottish kilt.

And there lay the big surprise. The Gaelic-speaking Scots, along with the Irish, Welsh, and Bretons, belong to the Celtic branch of Indo-European; and the Indo-European family tree, when organized by dialect similarity (fig. 7.3) rather than modern geography (fig. 6.3), shows Tokharian on the branch next to Celtic. For Tokharian shares more linguistic features with Celtic than with any other branch. Since the similarity extends to textile technology too, the case warrants careful investigation. In fact it was this puzzle that had drawn me to Chinese Turkestan in the first place.

Let's begin with Celts and tartans. The tartans we associate with Scotland are not particularly old. During periods of intense nationalism in the seventeenth and eighteenth centuries the Scottish clans formalized the plaid designs, or setts, used in weaving their twill cloth, certain patterns becoming associated with certain clans. Today one can order a woolen kilt or scarf in any one of the tartans ("dress," "hunting," and so forth) of Macdonald, Campbell, Gordon, Gunn, or many another clan. Because this formalization took place not long ago and for known reasons, and because few old textiles survive, many historians

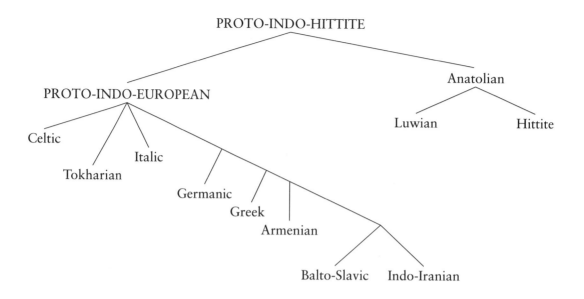

FIGURE 7.3

Suggested tree of Indo-European languages organized according to the relative time at which the various subgroups seem to have wandered away or otherwise ceased to partake of common changes. (Not all branches are listed.)

have assumed that the idea of plaids was relatively new to Scotland in the seventeenth century.

Archaeology tells a different story. The Celts have been weaving plaid twills for three thousand years at least.

The Celts did not originate in Britain but began to reach the British Isles only in the fourth century B.C., as they fanned out rather abruptly from Central Europe (map 7.4). Some of their tribes had already overrun northern Italy, breaking Etruscan power there and sacking Rome in 390 B.C.; others advanced down the Danube River, terrorizing the northern Balkans. These were not the small, dark-haired, white-skinned people we associate with Ireland and Brittany today. Rather, they were huge blond warriors with pale blue-gray eyes and prominent noses, to go by the descriptions and sculptures left by the Greeks and Romans.[1] Fierce as they were large, the Celts soon conquered today's northern

[1] One of the most beautiful and poignant of these sculptures is a Hellenistic marble statue of a defeated young Gaul (Celt) of splendid physique; he is stabbing himself after killing his wife, who hangs limp on his arm, so they would not have to endure slavery. This statue, now housed in Rome, is (justly) reproduced in most basic books on Greek sculpture.

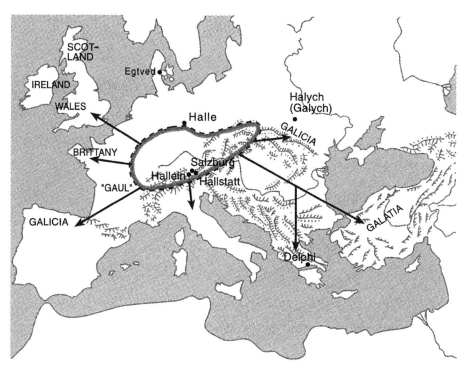

FIGURE 7.4

Map showing the central area of the proto-Celtic Hallstatt culture in about the 5th century B.C., just prior to Celtic expansion after 400 B.C. (arrows). Plaid twills (plate 12) similar to those from Hami were found in the salt mines at Hallstatt and Hallein, in the Alps above Salzburg. Ancient salt-mining sites often have the word element *hal(l)-* in them; areas in which the Celts once lived often have names with *Gal-*.

Italy and France, Julius Caesar's Gallia or "Gaul" (so named after a Celtic group), then northern Spain, Belgium (named after another Celtic tribe), and Britain (likewise a Celtic name). Much of Caesar's fame and power, in the first century B.C., came from subduing Gaul and southern Britain and annexing them to the Roman Empire. (He was crossing the river Rubicon, the boundary between Roman Italy and the North Italian province of Gaul, when he uttered the famous statement "The die is cast!") Caesar opened his noted account of these campaigns with the words that every student of Latin learns: *Gallia est omnis divisa in partis tris*—"All Gaul is divided into three parts."

The Celts (or Gauls) who headed east were slower to reach the notice of the literate Mediterranean countries, but they too did well. A group of marauding Celts even attempted to sack the Greek holy of holies, the sanctuary of Apollo perched on the precipitous slopes at Delphi, in 279 B.C. Driven off—in part, legend says, by the god himself shaking rocks down the mountain at them—they wandered up to Bulgaria, where vestiges of plaids remain in some of the local folk costumes. Eventually these eastward-moving Celts fetched up in central Turkey in what came to be called Galatia, where the apostle Paul visited later.

For nearly a millennium before their expansion, the early Celts had lived in present-day western Hungary, Austria, and southern Germany (map 7.4: central zone), an area they had entered from the east apparently in search of metals to mine. In central Austria, however, a group of them found something equally lucrative to dig for: salt. Compared with normal rocks, salt weighs little. Laid down in thick layers eons ago by ancient seas drying up (as around Lop Nor today), then overlaid by other sediments, salt tends to rise in great bubbles through the mass of other rocks during geological upheavals. Whole mountains of it poke up among the Austrian Alps above Salzburg (German for "salt city"). Rock and soil, even entire forests have long covered these Alpine salt domes, so that they look like everything around them. In early times only those in the habit of digging deep shafts—miners—would be likely to discover the strange treasure beneath.

And treasure it was. In addition to being an essential nutrient, salt provided the best-known preservative of food, especially meat, in a time before refrigeration or canning. Gold may glitter enticingly, but you can't eat it. During the first millennium B.C., Celtic communities grew rich exporting salt and salted meat to the growing civilizations of Greece and Rome just south of them, importing wine and other luxuries in return. In fact many of the finest Greek vessels have turned up at Celtic sites. Rich Celtic families, it seems, liked to carry on their drinking bouts in style.

About 400 B.C., as Celts began to expand swiftly across Europe, the miners of central Austria figured out a new way to mine salt: by flushing it out as brine and then boiling off the excess water. Before that, during the period from about 1300 to 400 B.C., they had dug mine shafts deep into the salt mountains, broken up the rock salt with pickaxes, and hauled the chunks out in backpacks. More recent miners, who have worked the beds anew since A.D. 1311, still encounter these prehistoric tunnels—nicknamed heathen rock, or *Heidengebirge*—inside the great salt mines of Hallstatt and Hallein. As groundwater moves through the mass, the salt continually dissolves and recrystallizes, gradually closing the old shafts and preserving everything, even delicate organic matter, in a saline tomb. The ancient shafts thus appear as patches of dirty salt full of strange objects. The artifacts include axes, picks, and other tools; cloth rags preserved color and all; pieces of leather backpacks; and ends of thin wooden splints used by the ancient miners as torches to light their work. This culture of Central European miners takes its archaeological name from the salt-mining site of Hallstatt, high above Salzburg.

Hallstatt, Hallein: the similarity of name is no coincidence. Just as Salzburg got its name from its powerful salt monopoly among the German-speaking peoples, and the river that it sits on, the Salzach ("salt water"), got a German name referring to its slightly salty taste, so the great salt-mining sites took their names still earlier from what seems to be an old Celtic form denoting salt, *hal(l)-*. It appears again in the East German city name *Halle,* which sits on a vast underground salt bed, and possibly in the name of a salt-mining city and province that has shuttled between Polish and Ukrainian control, *Halych* or *Galych,* known in English as Galicia.[2]

Between 1959 and 1974, the German specialist Hans-Jürgen Hundt described thread by thread the 117 pieces of cloth then available from the Hallstatt-period mines in Austria, roughly 1300 to 400 B.C. (Hundt, who died recently in his eighties, was a pioneer in borrowing for archaeology the methods developed by crime laboratories to identify bits of degraded fiber and their dyes.) We know from local records that yet more prehistoric cloth had been found in earlier centuries—and discarded. The chronicle of 1573 tells of a man's body with flesh and hair intact, still fully clothed and shod, found together with his wooden pick; and in 1734 the annals mention the garb of a partially clothed skeleton. The salt mine fabrics are uniquely important in two ways: alone among prehistoric European textiles their colors are preserved, and they are almost the only textiles that survived in Europe from the period between 2500 and 500 B.C. (The other major group comes from Denmark—including the Egtved string skirt in fig. 5.4—scattered over the centuries from perhaps 1800 B.C. down to Roman times, and with little to no color left.)

Very few pieces large enough to be recognizable as garments have survived from the mines, but those few tell interesting tales. Inside the seams of a woolen vest, Hundt found a multitude of mummified lice eggs, or nits, showing that those little varmints plagued the ancient salt miners. Albert von LeCoq, a German explorer traveling in Chinese Turkestan at the same time as Hedin and Stein, recounts similar problems. The lice got so bad that he would spread mer-

---

[2] Another area called Galicia and long inhabited by Celts exists in northwestern Spain (map 7.4). Like Galatia, the name of the Classical province in central Turkey where the Celts who overran Anatolia in the third century B.C. ended up, this name probably came from an ethnic name for the Celts found in *Gaul/Gallic* and *Wales/Welsh.* It is not clear which of the two—"salt" or "Gaelic"—is the source for Slavic Galicia/Halych.

There are many other, less well-known continental salt sites with *hal(l)-* in their names: Hall in the Austrian Tyrol, Reichenhall in Bavaria, Schwäbisch Hall in central Germany, and so on.

cury ointment on a sheet of paper, press another sheet on top, cut the sandwich into strips, and have all those in the group place the strips in the pockets of their infested garments. As they traveled in the hot sun, the mercury (which of course is deadly toxic) would vaporize through the clothing and kill all the lice and their nits—highly effective, but not exactly healthful for the person either. The ancient miners had neither the benefits nor the side effects of such poisons.

Among the rags these Hallstatt miners dropped, only about twenty show no decoration at all. Fully seventy-five are woven in twill patterns (sixty-five show simple diagonal twill, like the Hami pieces, and ten something still fancier, built up from zigzagging the diagonals: fig. 7.5), and many of these plus some of the plain weave fragments show plaid patterning (plate 12). Like the Scottish tartans and the Hami twills, the Hallstatt plaids contain a rhythmic mixture of wide and very narrow stripes—not what one would call checkered. The Hallstatt plaid twills also have the peculiar distinction that the zigzags *never* fall in phase with the color stripes. The favorite colors included dark brown, yellow, and pea green, with occasional deep blue, copper red, and white.

If the Bronze and Iron Age ancestors of the historic Celts wove woolen plaid twills so similar to modern ones, clearly the prenationalist Scots in the intervening centuries wove this sort of thing too. The historians were thrown off by the problem that European textiles just don't survive well from *any* period, what with a yearly climate of wet and dry, wet and dry. Such fluctuations destroy fibers faster than anything other than fire or moths. So we have as little Scottish cloth from A.D. 1500 as from 100 B.C. But the overall similarities between Hallstatt plaid twills and recent Scottish ones, right down to the typical weight of the cloth, strongly indicate continuity of tradition. The chief difference is that the Hallstatt plaids contain no more than two colors (although a few three-color cloths turned up that were not plaid), whereas the Scottish tartans are generally multicolored.

Some of the plaids from Qizilchoqa contain more than two colors also. When Victor Mair visited the excavation site with Wang Binghua, the excavator, in 1991, Wang stuffed a fragment of a plaid into Victor's pocket and told him to take it home and study it (plate 13a). That plaid, a typical diagonal twill that Irene Good analyzed, consists mostly of a milk-chocolate–colored ground with narrow stripes of light blue and white breaking up the surface into a very attractive plaid. The Chinese archaeologists found much cloth like Victor's swatch; large pieces appear in museums elsewhere in the Uyghur Autonomous Region. Not only does this woolen plaid twill look like Scottish tartans, but it also has the same weight, feel, and initial thickness as kilt cloth and as the Hallstatt materials. I say "initial" because Scottish kilts intended for daily wear on the chilly moors usually got a thorough felting after weaving, to shrink up and

FIGURE 7.5

Diagram of 2/2 twill in which the direction of offset has been reversed after several rows, producing a zigzag instead of a straight diagonal pattern (as in plain 2/2 twill—figs. 2.13, 3.12).

fill any little holes that might let wind and weather through. To the extent that the woolen cloth shrinks, it becomes thicker than when initially woven.

Another small fragment of plaid twill of the same weight, this one in the museum in Ürümchi, has only two colors, red and pale blue-gray, distributed in a way that reminds me of Scottish-style plaid skirts that served for schoolgirl uniforms in my childhood. Unlike the Hallstatt plaids, some of those from Qizilchoqa approach a checked pattern, thanks to the regular width of the stripes. The museum in Aksu has large swatches of such a plaid twill, in red and blue with a bit of white.

Wang Binghua's wife, Wang Luli, also published a piece of plaid twill: a large portion of some sort of vest. Her photograph shows broad stripes of purply-brown thread with the plaid formed by pinstripes in no fewer than five other colors: light and dark blue, red, white, and black (see plate 13b). To make the vest, the tailor joined pieces of this stuff together with pale blue yarn, edged the vest with two narrow plaited cords, and added a pair of buttons covered with the same pale blue yarn. Very stylish.

So Hami plaids might have as many as six colors, therein resembling the modern Scottish rather than the ancient Hallstatt way of doing things. Of course how many colors one uses has to do with the available dyes as well as with taste.

Are these resemblances between the Hami and Hallstatt cloths an accident or not?

Stripes are easy to think up, and weaving stripes both horizontally and vertically to get checkers or even plaids isn't hard either. That much similarity might be pure accident. And once you have wool, changing to twill structure forms a natural, though not obligatory, step (to make a denser cloth and to keep the warp from breaking). But the regular combination of plaids and twills in the same cloth and the similar play of wides and narrows in the plaids move us into a border zone where it's harder to imagine the sum total as accidental. Especially when we combine all these traits with a similar weight of cloth—quite unlike that from Cherchen or Loulan, or prehistoric Denmark either for that matter. Of course differences exist too. First, the Hami plaids contain three to six colors, whereas the Hallstatt ones are strictly bicolor. Second, no early cloth of plant fiber occurs in the Tarim Basin, unlike in Europe (see below), but that difference may be simply a matter of what cultigens the early Central Asian immigrants succeeded in bringing with them, rather than of what they knew when they started out.

Yet none of this settles the matter. To demonstrate a shared ancestry, we need some shared trait that is totally off the wall, such as the bizarre Hallstatt rule about not letting plaid stripes coincide with the zigzag stripes of the twill weave. If the two sets of weavers shared that, or something equally arbitrary, then we would know in our hearts that they came out of the same tradition.

Unfortunately, almost nothing has been published in the fifteen-plus years since most of the Hami material was dug up, and we could learn only that great quantities of colorful cloth came out of the excavations, just as at Cherchen. So we must move on, for now, without this material.[3] Luckily, scientific reasoning can provide many routes to the truth.

Yet another class of plaids from Qizilchoqa look quite different from the typical Scottish ones: predominantly white cloth crossed at short and regular intervals by pinstripes of blue and red threads (plate 14a).[4] The brightness of the white caught my eye. Were these made of plant fiber rather than wool? In fact they turned out to be wool—but not twill. The weaver had used plain weave for a change, rare at Qizilchoqa.

---

[3] From what I did see, both in Ürümchi and among some Xinjiang textile fragments that Chinese merchants have unfortunately set afloat in the antiquities "black market," I can add that the Hami and Hallstatt cultures each produced a cloth in which the 2/2 twill abruptly turns into basket weave (Hallstatt) or half-basket weave (Hami; see fig. 3.12 for weaves). But nowhere did I see the characteristic Hallstatt disregard of counting threads in the weft direction. The Central Asian weavers counted their weft rows, the Central European weavers eyeballed them. And nowhere did I see the characteristic diagonal of the twill switch to the opposite slope to create zigzags. Would looking at a hundred more fragments turn up exceptions? If so, we could then ask whether the plaids and zigzags were in or out of phase. If not, we could suspect that the two twill traditions (if they had a common source) branched off before Westerners thought of making zigzags.

[4] To be exact, one piece had red, red-brown, and dark blue lines of paired threads in one direction and red, turquoise blue, and dark blue lines the other way. Another had pairs of red threads at intervals in one direction, while in the other direction the spaced-out pairs of colored threads alternated between red and gray-blue.

Fabrics of remarkable similarity come from Hallein, a huge salt mine in the next valley over from Hallstatt. In the Hallstatt-era shafts at Hallein, modern miners have found several white woolen cloths with pinstripes of blue and red.[5] As in the Hami swatches, the weavers produced precisely these fabrics in plain weave, not twill, and made the colored stripes two threads wide. Even the choice of colors is the same, and the bands are placed with a kind of regularity not seen in the darker-ground plaid twills. They differ chiefly in that only the warp is striped at Hallein, not the weft too.

The peculiar similarity of the white-ground cloths, added to all the likenesses in the dark-ground plaid twills and the similarity in dating, moves us so far from chance that I have to conclude the Hami and Hallstatt traditions are directly related. The next question then becomes: *How* are they related? Our best shot at this problem comes from looking at the origin of twill itself.

Although people in the Near East had been weaving since 7000 B.C. at least, our first evidence for twill weave comes from shortly before 3000 B.C. At Al-ishar, a site in central Turkey (map 7.6), several fragments of twill cloth still clung to a jawbone and to pieces of animal skin in a child's burial. Another scrap of twill, specified as woolen, comes from Martkopi in Georgia, on the south slope of the Caucasus Mountains, from some time in the third millennium. About the same time, weavers in the famed city of Troy set up a warp-weighted loom specifically to weave twill patterns; the loom's remains were preserved for us when the city burned to the ground around 2600 B.C.[6] There in northwestern Turkey these early Trojans already had great sophistication in their textile manufacture, because the tiny gold beads found by the dozens in the fill around the loom weights must also have adorned the cloth that burned unfinished on the loom. Soon after, the Minoans of Crete began modifying their warp-weighted looms to accommodate twill, and they depict themselves wearing twills, pinstripes, and plaids, among many other fancy designs, over the next few centuries. After that come the twills from Hallstatt and Hami, around 1000 B.C.

Twill weave itself most likely began as a way of handling wool on a loom, but usable wool became available only around 4000 B.C. in Mesopotamia, after long inbreeding of sheep. The original wild sheep were hairy rather than woolly and had been domesticated for their meat, not for the wool they didn't have yet. But as inbreeding proceeded between those animals docile enough to survive under domestic conditions, the peculiar genetic makeup of sheep also caused

---

[5] More exactly, light or dark blue and red or red-brown, just as in the Hami pieces.
[6] This destruction, affecting what archaeologists call Level II at the site of Troy, occurred some thirteen hundred years before the Trojan War described by Homer, which is equated with the violent destruction of Level VIIa.

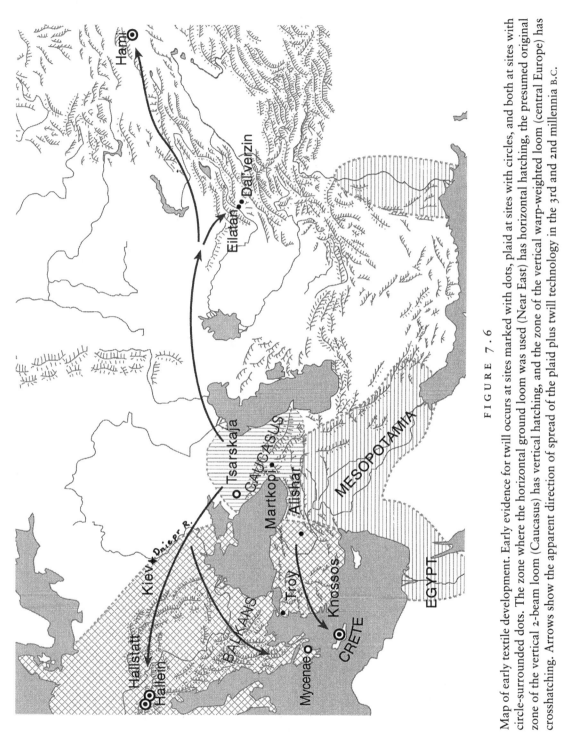

FIGURE 7.6

Map of early textile development. Early evidence for twill occurs at sites marked with dots, plaid at sites with circles, and both at sites with circle-surrounded dots. The zone where the horizontal ground loom was used (Near East) has horizontal hatching, the presumed original zone of the vertical 2-beam loom (Caucasus) has vertical hatching, and the zone of the vertical warp-weighted loom (central Europe) has crosshatching. Arrows show the apparent direction of spread of the plaid plus twill technology in the 3rd and 2nd millennia B.C.

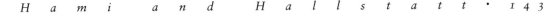

FIGURE 7.7

Three principal kinds of loom used in early Europe and the Near East, as depicted in ancient monuments. *Left:* Horizontal ground loom of Egypt and Mesopotamia. *Center:* Nearly vertical warp-weighted loom of Europe. *Right:* Vertical 2-beam loom of Syria and later Egypt, possibly originally from the Caucasus.

woollier fleeces to develop—a process undoubtedly helped along by farmers once they got the idea of selective breeding. A radical change about 4000 B.C. in the pattern of slaughtering domestic sheep (killing them old to maximize the wool and milk harvested, instead of killing them as yearlings to minimize the care needed to reap one feast and one hide) signals the development of sheep with usable wool on their backs. By 3500 B.C. these woolly sheep had reached places as far away as the Balkans, a thousand miles from Mesopotamia. Now, the Mesopotamians, who, like the Egyptians, used a horizontal ground loom (fig. 7.7 left), responded to the problems of weaving wool by going over to weft-faced fabrics. Twill, on the other hand, was the initial response of those using the warp-weighted loom (in western Turkey and Europe; fig. 7.7 center) and . . . and what? What did the people of the Caucasus use? If it had been the warp-weighted loom, we should have found the weights, the one nonperishable part of any ancient loom and therefore the easiest to track archaeologically. But the eastern edge of the zone where loom weights occur runs north through central Turkey (where Alishar is) and on up to around Kiev in the Ukrainian steppes (for map, see fig. 9.9). If the Caucasus peoples used the Mesopotamian ground loom, on the other hand, we would expect them to have taken the Mesopotamian solution to using the new fiber they received from Mesopotamia. So perhaps they used a third type of loom, the vertical two-beam loom (fig. 7.7 right), which soon turns up in literate zones just south of there.

Wool entailed other innovations too, because unlike the plant stem fibers, it came in a wide range of natural colors and was easy to dye. Evidence of exploiting this new virtue turns up first in the Caucasus again—on the north slope of that great range, at Tsarskaja (map 7.6).[7] The undergarment of a chieftain in-humed there in the mid-third millennium consisted of white, linenlike cloth ornamented with purple thread and red tassels, while the garment over that consisted of a fuzzy yellow and black plaid cloth, almost certainly woolen.

So both plaid and twill first turn up in northern Anatolia and the Caucasus region, to the best of our scanty knowledge.

That information indicates some useful approaches to our bigger problems. It suggests, first, that the two groups of twill weavers moved outward from a central spot, rather than half of them traversing the entire cross-continental distance (in either direction). Starting from the general vicinity of the Caucasus, one group went west, the other east (map 7.6) sometime after rudimentary knowledge of woolly sheep, simple diagonal twill, and plaid coloring had developed there.[8] They carried that knowledge with them. This scenario also matches the most widely held theory as to where the proto-Indo-Europeans started from, around 3000 B.C., when they began spreading out toward their current positions—namely, the patch of steppe just north of the Black Sea, Caucasus, and Caspian Sea.

Does this mean that our two groups of weavers had to be Indo-Europeans? No: today the Caucasus zone buzzes with many languages, some Indo-European (like Russian, Ossetic, and Armenian) and some not (like Georgian and Chechen). So on that evidence our immigrants *might* have spoken anything.

But we do know, first, that the Hallstatt folk must have been proto-Celts and thus Indo-European, since their culture developed directly into the La Tène culture, which the Romans encountered and recorded as linguistically Celtic. Second, the striking similarities between the plaid twills of Hami and Hallstatt greatly strengthen the case for the Celtic and Hami weavers arising from the same ancestral tradition. Though lying four thousand miles apart, they parallel each other too closely for sheer chance. The history of weaving, moreover, suggests that the common source of this tradition lay somewhere near the Caucasus around 3000 B.C., just about where the fountainhead of the Indo-European language family apparently sat. Third, linguists have figured out that the language features tying Tokharian so closely to Celtic (and also somewhat to Italic) are *archaisms,* not innovations. That is, neither group was still close by when the new linguistic habits spread through the central community. What

---

[7] Tsarskaja, meaning "of the Czar," was the name of the place when excavated in 1898; the revolutionaries felt called upon to rename it, of course, so on today's maps it appears as Novosvobodnaja, meaning "New Freedom."

[8] By this time too, apparently, a double tradition of dark-ground bicolor plaid twills and white-ground plain weave with red and blue pinstripes had evolved, which came to be elaborated in somewhat different ways by the two branches of emigrants.

Tokharian and Celtic shared was being first out of the cannon, as it were—being the earliest groups to start trekking away from the homeland, and for that reason, perhaps, carrying the same technology.[9] Fourth we may add the striking physical similarity of the Celts or Gauls observed by the Greeks and Romans with some of our tall, blondish, and probably blue-eyed mummies, a somewhat unusual type in the genetics of Eurasia.

The case looks good for the mummies from Hami, at least, having been Tokharians and erstwhile neighbors of the Celts. But the sticking point comes, once again, with trying to equate the Tokharians, a linguistic group, with *any* of the prehistoric and thus illiterate peoples of the Tarim. We must find yet other evidence if we are to progress further toward identifying the ancient mummies now lying in Ürümchi.

[9] If the Celts indeed came into Central Europe as miners seeking metal ores, might the Tokharians have left the Caucasus area at the same time for the same reason? Might they too show evidence of having once been miners searching for ores, but in the opposite direction? Is linguistic evidence of metalworking embedded in what we have of the language? How might the excavated remains of metalwork stack up against both linguistic fossils to do with metal and the Celtic and Caucasian techniques of metalworking? (Although the early Loulan people left almost no metal, the later sites contain quite a bit, with some clear ties to the northwest.) There must be twenty potential thesis and book topics in this and the previous chapter.

Appendix to Chapter 7: Looms

WE CAN deduce a good deal about early looms in the Tarim Basin from the material we have at hand. Like those from Cherchen and Loulan, the cloths from Qizilchoqa come in narrow widths of about half a yard, so the loom was consistently narrow. Furthermore, mistakes in the shedding run both the entire width and length of the fabric. With heddle bars, the mistakes get mechanized along with the rest of the task. (Interestingly, the museum workers I "talked" with, through an array of translators, hand waving, and diagrams, expressed great dismay when I pointed out mistakes in the weaving—until I got across to them that the mistakes allow us to reconstruct details about the loom. Then scientific curiosity gained the upper hand over cultural chavinism.)

So the early Central Asian loom was both fairly narrow and mechanized with shed and heddle bars. Because the Tarim fabrics sometimes have four selvedges (see Chapter 4), we can also deduce that at least one local type of loom had two parallel beams instead of weights to provide the tension.

All in all, the simplest hypothesis is that these people used a sort of glorified band loom with the warp spread on a bar at each end, but spread no farther than could be managed easily by a single weaver. With such a simple loom, whether the warp was set vertically or horizontally or something in between may have been a matter of momentary convenience, confounding our modern categories. Turkic nomads in Central Asia still use looms of this sort, pegging out both ends on the ground or tying one end to a handy tree and pegging the other end. The shedding mechanism hangs from a little arrangement of sticks that can be shoved along the warp as weaving progresses. (The proto-Indo-European vocabulary could encompass such a loom.)

What about the Hallstatt loom? Excavations at villages of the Hallstatt culture have turned up plenty of evidence for warp-weighted looms (the common loom of prehistoric Central Europe), and a Hallstatt potter left us a drawing of a woman weaving on a warp-weighted loom. The depiction even shows the shed and heddle bars. A second Hallstatt urn, however, shows what appears to be a two-beam loom with a checked fabric on it. In other words, the Hallstatt people may have brought this loom with them and then gradually dropped it in favor of the locally better-developed warp-weighted loom. Either of these types of loom can easily produce fabric of any width up to about six feet, with four feet being normal for the warp-weighted loom. Unfortunately the Hallstatt cloth fragments are not big enough for us to measure the width from selvedge to selvedge, to get an idea of standard width.

Thus we find that the evidence for type of loom is still too inconclusive to help us pinpoint origins, although the data do not contradict our hypothesis that the Hami and Hallstatt weaving traditions are related.

TURKIC
WEAVER, 1916

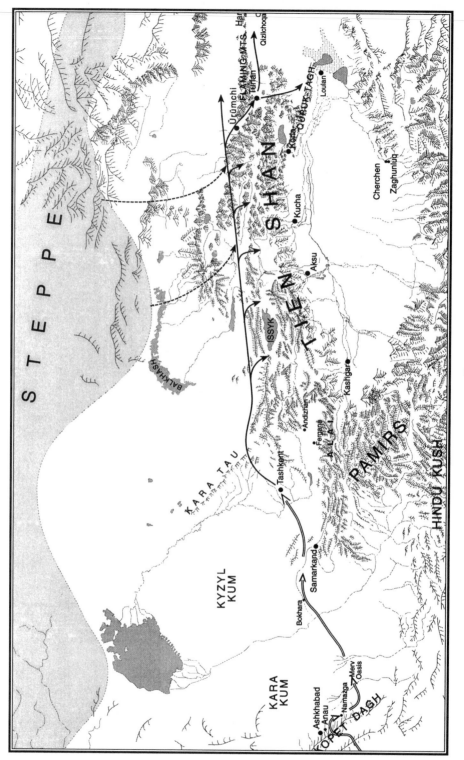

MAP 8.1

The Oasis Hoppers
and Their Kin

WHAT CAUSED those first settlers, so splendidly mummified in Ürümchi, to come to Innermost Asia anyway—to move to such a desperately difficult ecological zone? The fully nomadic horsemen of the next three millennia never wanted to live there: they only dropped in long enough to raid and plunder, then rode away again. Neither the rugged mountains nor the desert-dry flatlands at their feet could provide enough fodder for those huge domestic herds that they viewed as their chief wealth.

The Chinese didn't want to live there either—at least not until the formidable population pressures of this century began to make the Tarim Basin look better than nothing. Until then the Chinese viewed Turkestan as only a buffer against nomads and a passageway to rich markets in the West. It rated no better than a hell-hot equivalent of Russia's ice-cold Siberia due north of it; it was here that China's government sent you in banishment without quite killing you outright. Instead the exiles were handed the dangerous and thankless job of keeping Chinese law and order for the sake of the Chinese merchants and en-

---

Opposite page: Map showing the eastward path of the early herder-farmers, who came over the Kopet Dagh from the Iranian plateau with Near Eastern ideas by 4000 B.C. and began spreading east from one oasis to the next a bit before 2000 B.C. (hollow arrows). Some of them may have continued east along the north side of the Tien Shan (solid arrow), while steppe herders may have moved down into this same corridor (broken arrows).

voys who had to pass through. Hedin, Stein, Roerich, and the other Europeans who visited the area early in this century make this Chinese dislike of the area quite clear in story after story, as do the Chinese chronicles of earlier times.

The first deliberate settlers came into the Tarim Basin about 2000 B.C., to the best of our knowledge, long before the Chinese and well before the nomadic herders of the steppes. They came from somewhere to the west. Only around 1000 B.C. did the nomads develop to a peak the relatively free and easy way of life that depended on managing huge herds by riding horses. (Chariots, let alone carts, just aren't swift enough.) But the Tarim settlers of the early second millennium B.C. largely preceded the horse-nomad era, depending for a living on small-time agriculture and on herding small flocks.

Making a life this way in the scattered oases of the desert (see plate 15a) is not easy. To begin with, the Tarim oases often lie far apart, a ten to fifteen days' trek through desert so dry that not a weed can grow—no fodder for one's animals, no water for man nor beast. Furthermore, the first humans to reach an oasis find a jungle, a massive thicket of reeds, tamarisk, and poplars wherever water rushing down from the rugged mountains reaches the flatland. Here lies the usable and desirable soil, the rich silt washed down each year that has been caught and held by the roots of countless plants. But taming such a jungle requires hard-won knowledge.

Recent excavation and research have revealed an area where we can see such knowledge arise—in the next desert to the west, stretching from the Caspian Sea to the Pamir range, the lofty divider between Chinese Turkestan to the east and Russian Turkestan to the west (map 8.1, 8.2).

Until the Soviets embarked on perestroika, American archaeologists could not visit most of the archaeological sites dug by their Soviet counterparts, let alone excavate alongside them. Obtaining excavation reports proved almost as difficult. American libraries saw no reason to stock Russian-language publications since so few Americans could read Slavic languages, and the Russians were leery of trafficking with Americans as individuals. Gradually through the 1980s it became possible to visit Soviet sites and local museums, to bring Soviet archaeologists to our country and our scientific conferences to talk with us, and to attend their conferences as well. Glasnost in turn abruptly opened the way to work side by side with Soviet archaeologists. Fredrik Hiebert, then a graduate student at Harvard, recognized a huge opportunity, dived into learning Russian, and headed off in 1989 as part of a Russian team excavating at the oasis site of Gonur Depe in ancient Margiana, in today's Turkmenistan (map 8.2). Leading the dig was the veteran Soviet archaeologist Viktor Sarianidi, who had been studying Bronze Age sites all over Russian Turkestan for thirty years.

The road to knowledge contained chuckholes, however. Even when Americans could get Russian excavation reports, the literature produced as much frustration as satisfaction. Soviet theories of social progress led their scientists to look for and record different things from those a Western archaeologist would, and differing methods of dating led to widely divergent assignments of dates to sites that seemed to have the same culture. The gaps sometimes amounted to five hundred or a thousand years. All this made it hard for Western scholars to pursue answers to problems from ancient Mesopotamia or prehistoric Europe across Soviet borders. Especially difficult were problems like the origins of farming practices, whose solutions depend on identifying such things as ancient pollen and the weed seeds characteristic of cultivated crops, not on house walls and pottery. The Soviets found it just as trying to work with our reports, which didn't supply much data for the formation of the state or the rise of the proletariat.

Arriving at Sarianidi's camp, Hiebert found that the Russian strategy consisted of mapping the locations of the oasis settlements, then laying bare the top layer of an entire settlement with all it contained. Certainly interesting in itself, and thoroughgoing in its way. But Hiebert wanted to track origins. He needed a vertical section, not a horizontal one. Finally Sarianidi let Hiebert go off to one side of the main settlement and dig straight down as far as he wished in one small area, a mere six feet by six, collecting samples of the *succession* of pottery styles, tools, and shreds of organic matter all the way to the bottom. Nothing points up the difference in approach so clearly as an aerial photograph showing the huge, flat oblong of the fortified settlement cleared off by the Russian team, and over to one side a little black spot, the small but very deep pit where Hiebert charted the stratificational sequence.

Each approach contributes valuable information, of course. Combining the material from both demonstrated that people of a single Early Bronze Age culture had begun to spread across the oases of Russian Turkestan two or three centuries before 2000 B.C., moving from southwest to northeast—that is, headed directly toward the Pamir and Tien Shan ranges and (if one could get over those huge hurdles) the Tarim Basin. Hiebert turned his attention southwest, looking for the fountainhead of this expansion.

The most reasonable place to look lay in the foothills of the Kopet Dagh (map 8.2), a tall but narrow screen of mountains separating the deserts and oases of Russian Turkestan from the great Iranian plateau and, beyond it to the west, Mesopotamia and the early Near Eastern centers of technological advancement.

Considerable literature on the archaeology of the north side of the Kopet Dagh already existed before the Iron Curtain lowered. In 1904 an American ge-

FIGURE 8.2

Map of "Russian Turkestan," an area of desert and oases lying between the Caspian Sea and the Pamir Mountains. The ancient towns along the Kopet Dagh were founded by New Stone Age farmers from farther west, who began to expand eastward from one oasis to the next a little before 2000 B.C. (the Early Bronze Age).

ologist named Raphael Pumpelly[1] had excavated at the great double mound called Anau, seven miles south of Ashkhabad (the modern capital of Turkmenistan), while the Russians dug the important nearby site of Namazga Depe and several other mounds, all of them initially Neolithic settlements. Each early town lay on a small watercourse, carefully positioned to enjoy year-round use of the life-sustaining water that gushed out of the mountains above, but high

---

[1] Pronounced *Pum-'pell-y.*

enough up into the foothills that its people could carry on the simple agriculture typical of the Stone Age Near East, dry farming. (Dry farming does not use irrigation canals but relies on rain and groundwater to moisten the crops as they grow.) Anau seemed to represent one culture, whereas Namazga, Altyn Depe, and the other towns, strung like beads along a two-hundred-mile stretch of the Kopet range, represented a slightly different culture to which Namazga has given its name.

Hiebert knew the Anau material well from Pumpelly's collection at the Peabody Museum in Harvard. So next he joined the Harvard-Russian collaborative team reopening the excavations at Anau to reassess it by modern methods, including current dating techniques.

I too had once studied the Peabody's Anau collection, in pursuit of some oddly shaped hollow spindle whorls that apparently had climbed over the Kopet Dagh from Iran in the early fourth millennium B.C. A spindle whorl is a little flywheel that you add to your spindle to make the stick rotate more evenly and with greater momentum, through its inertia, when you're spinning thread onto the spindle (see fig. 3.4). A simple ball or disk of clay, wood, or stone—even an onion or an apple—will do the job just fine. So going to the extra trouble of molding the clay whorl into a hollow nose cone shape, as the people of Anau had, bespoke a special *cultural* tradition. The relative imperishability of the clay whorls, moreover, made it possible to trace the movements of their makers.

Oddly, of all the early sites along the Kopet Dagh, only Anau had these strange whorls, yet there they occurred by the hundreds. Obviously these folk had come to Anau with a flourishing textile industry—maybe (but here I could not find the data I needed) as the bringers of the newly woolly Mesopotamian sheep (see Chapter 7). How else to account for such an emphasis on spinning yarn?

The new work so far has shed less light on where the people of Anau and Namazga came from than on where they went. But that story is highly illuminating to us. These foothill farmers became so successful that they could no longer support their teeming populations. There simply wasn't enough water. Behind them lay the mountains they had climbed over and the vast Caspian Sea. Before them to the east, beyond the thickets where their precious rivers disappeared into the sand, lay two great deserts, the Kara Kum (Black Sand) and the Kyzyl Kum (Red Sand). But if one skirted the south end of the Kara Kum, one came to the Murgab River and then to the Amu-darya, which drained the north slopes of the mountains of Afghanistan and the Hindu Kush (map 8.1). The Amu-darya manages to flow all the way north to the salty Aral Sea, whereas the Murgab spreads out, forming the Merv (or Mary) oasis as it disappears northward into the sands of the Kara Kum. Along their banks both rivers support the dense thickets and jungles typical of Central Asian desert oases.

Undoubtedly the foothill farmers of the Kopet Dagh had learned much about the taming of these thickets from their own home territory: how to clear off the tangles of plants, how to catch the game living in them, how to replace the wild with the sown. So when contingents from these towns swarmed out eastward somewhat before 2000 B.C. to find new lands, they had the know-how to manage the project.

But just barely. For, as archaeologists began to recognize from the finds, the first colonists still made a living much as their ancestors had in the Kopet foothills, planting crops where the water flowed rather than bringing the water to the crops. Within a generation or two, however, the survivors had learned to build systems of dams, irrigation canals, and levees to channel the water through the fields—much more efficient ways of dealing with the harsh but fertile oasis environment.

Then began the series of tightly organized, fortified oasis settlements that the Russians had been excavating. The size of the fort (a sort of sprawling, multifamily manor house and shrine, enclosed by ramparts) and the distance to the next fort resulted from a complex interplay of how far from the living quarters one could still work the land effectively, how many people that much land would support, and how long it took to get to the next settlement. As in Alsace and other European provinces where the farmers lived in walled villages for protection and trudged out to their fields every day, the little settlements grew up two to three kilometers (a couple of miles) apart in a great network. In fact, once Sarianidi and his colleagues understood the regularity of this pattern, they could locate previously unnoticed sites rather easily.

After the settlers had conquered the techniques of making a good living in the desert oases, nothing stopped them from moving on. Beyond the Amu-darya flowed the Zeravshan (which in wetter years reached the Amu and in drier ones ended short of it in the sand) and the Syr-darya, which drained the rich Fergana Valley and the west slopes of the Pamirs westward into the Aral Sea (map 8.1). The country between these oases, unlike the Taklamakan, does not lack vegetation entirely, so it does not form a complete barrier to movement. Merv, Samarkand, Tashkent—hop by hop the great and fabled oasis settlements were founded. Part of the impetus for moving on was undoubtedly political, for as one geographer of Asia put it, "any expansion of crop acreage is tied up with reorganization of the water supply." Where water is scarce (as in California and the Near East), water rights give rise to physical and/or legal battles, conquests, and refugees, starting with the ancient Sumerians, whose vengeful wars over water rights probably lie behind the biblical story of being driven from the Garden of Eden.

The climate of the Tarim Basin is more extreme even than that of the Iranian plateau, so severe that Stein and Hedin had to avoid the searing summer heat entirely and do most of their work in the winter, when they could find a source of water in the form of ice encrusting the salt ponds. Even then the photographs show them each bundled in so many fur coats they could hardly waddle, and they each recorded temperatures so low that the ink they were trying to write with in their "warmed" tents was freezing in the pen. Such extremes suggest that only the highly skilled oasis hoppers from the west could have found the Tarim Basin a viable place in which to settle and make a living. The persistently eastward movement of the oasis settlers too shows that they could well have spread all the way to the Tarim. The timing is about right, for they hopped their way across Russian Turkestan around 2000 B.C., and our first clear finds of settlers in the Tarim, around Loulan, have been dated roughly to 2000–1700 B.C.

As the crow flies, more than a thousand miles separate Loulan from Tashkent and the eastern edges of the Kyzyl Kum, and that crow would have to fly over some pretty high mountains along the way. So how would these ancient settlers have *found* the Tarim Basin?

The shortest route from Russian Turkestan, according to modern maps, heads up the Fergana Valley to Andizhan, then over the 14,000-foot Terek Pass through the northern Pamirs, dropping down the other side to Kashgar at the west end of the Tarim (maps 7.1, 8.1). Kashgar can also be reached from the west via a somewhat lower pass of 12,000 feet, the Torugart, on a road that heads south over the mountains from Lake Issyk in the next east-west valley north of Fergana. But shortest isn't necessarily best or easiest, especially when we know that the early settlers brought domestic animals with them. The Kirghiz nomads who wander these ranges today normally don't take their herds above about 10,000 feet (though domestic sheep and goats, at least, can survive at 15,000 feet). We must also consider that the evidence of early occupation lies near the *east* end of the Tarim Basin, not at Kashgar, the westernmost point.

Skirting the mountains entails a much longer route, but one maintaining rather lower altitudes the whole way by staying down in the foothills. Starting from Tashkent, the traveler passes northward between the high peaks on the east and the Kyzyl Kum desert on the west. After a short climb over the Kara Tau ridge, the route swings east toward the Ili River along the cooler northern side of the thousand-mile-long Tien Shan range, a path that wandererring shepherds, much like those today in the Bosnian Alps, can follow one way or another to Ürümchi and beyond. Such a path would seem far easier for prehistoric herders following the pasturelands eastward, as it avoids the loftiest parts of both the Pamirs and the Tien Shan. (The highest peak, the 23,000-foot Khan Tängri, rises about at the corner where the east-west Tien Shan intersects the north-south Pamir range.)

At any of several places along this last stretch one can drift up the mountain valleys, with their lush summer grasses (plate 14b; map 8.1), over the top at not such killing altitudes, and down the streams on the other side to the Tarim River itself, flowing along the north side of the Taklamakan Desert. The roads today that cross the mountains southward to the oases of Kucha and Korla follow such routes. If you come down the tributary streams from the top, you need not cross days or weeks of desert to find the oasis at the bottom. You have water the whole distance for your family and flocks. This terrain, however, is too precipitous for those who want to farm along the way, being more suitable for plain herders.

Perhaps easier still, just beyond Ürümchi both the ancient and the modern traveler could wind through a gorge created by a small south-flowing stream, the White Poplar River, that cuts loose the Flaming Mountains—as bare and fiery red as Bryce or Zion—from the main range of the Tien Shan (fig. 8.3). This passage opens out into the Turfan and Tarim basins just west of Turfan (map 8.1), a natural gateway to exactly that area where prehistoric remains turn up. (The White Poplar River then joins the Alwighul River to flow east into the salty Ayding Lake, puddling in the very bottom of the Turfan Depression; see map 10.2). Loulan, with the earliest group of relics, lies two hundred miles due south of this gate, just beyond the hills of the Quruk-tagh on the path to Cherchen, while Hami and its site at Qizilchoqa lie three hundred miles to the east of it, a straight shot across the gravel desert.

The distribution of early sites with respect to this northern gateway thus makes the northerly route around the Tien Shan the most reasonable one, both for the Loulan immigrants of four thousand years ago (whose culture Stein, Hedin, Bergman, and Wang found widely scattered across the south slopes of the Quruk-tagh) and for the inhabitants we find at Cherchen and Hami a millennium later.

But if early oasis hoppers from Russian Turkestan could enter the Tarim Basin through this northern gate, so too could people from farther north— herders following their flocks across the grassy steppelands. That rather different ecological belt stretches east-west immediately north of the desert zone, running from the Carpathian Mountains (in modern-day Hungary and Romania) to the northwest corner of China, and it intercepts the route just traced from Russian Turkestan in the vicinity of the lakes Issyk and Balkash and the latter's tributary the Ili River (maps 2.9, 8.1). The steppe fostered its own pe-

FIGURE 8.3

Gorge of the White Poplar River through the barren red mountains separating Ürümchi from the Turfan Depression.

culiar forms of economy, and the form it took before 1000 B.C. suited the oases of the Tarim Basin far better than the later version, as we shall see.

Somewhere around 4000 B.C., when the revolutionary Neolithic idea of domesticating plants and animals reached the western Eurasian steppes from Syria and Mesopotamia, people living in those grassy zones enthusiastically took up raising cattle and sheep, but not tending crops. As anyone can imagine who has battled tenacious Bermuda grass in a flower bed, rooting out enough grass to clear entire fields for agriculture can be extremely tough. Now picture doing this without efficient shovels and hoes, using only, say, a digging stick. After all, this was still the Stone Age.

But ruminants can subsist on the grass itself, which has the very successful structure of growing from the bottom instead of at the top; it can thrive even while constantly nipped (or mowed) off. In fact the design and existence of grass in a sense made ruminants possible. So if humans protected the grass eaters from other predators, the people could then eat the ruminants.

Once they got the idea of domestication, some steppe dwellers thought to domesticate one of their own local grazing animals, the horse, a native of the Eurasian steppes. Our first evidence of horse taming comes from Ukraine around 4000 B.C. (map 2.9).

If you have sheep, cattle, and horses but aren't growing large crops of grain and hay, you'll have to keep moving around to find fodder for your herds. Sheep in particular force the issue; they bite off the grass right down to the roots, preventing cattle and horses from grazing in the same place. This is why sheep were so unwelcome among the cowboys of the Old West. But moving means taking everything with you.[2] The ingredient that made the nomadic lifestyle gel, therefore, was the wheeled cart, which appeared on the steppes north of the Black Sea and Caspian before 3000 B.C. David Anthony, an archaeologist who specializes in these early steppe cultures, summarizes the event as follows:

> The appearance of the Yamna horizon[3] at about 3500 BC was a cultural and economic watershed. The Yamna horizon (3500–2500 BC) represents the initial intensive occupation and exploitation of the Eurasian grassland environment, a breakthrough made possible by the combination of horseback riding, wheeled vehicles (almost certainly ox-drawn), grazing stock, and incidental cereal cultivation. . . . What set the Yamna horizon apart from its predecessors was its clear ability to exploit the deep steppe. . . .

What is usable in the "deep steppe"—the thousands of miles of grassland far from permanent settlements—is so widely scattered that you can't make a living in any one place, herds or no herds. Wheels, even on slow oxcarts, says Anthony, "provided the high-volume storage and transport abilities that were essential in order to exploit the dispersed resources of the deep steppe in a predictable and reliable manner." By carrying supplies of tools and food along, as well as shelter in the form of felt tents (plate 14b, fig. 2.10), the herders could manage on their own out in the wilderness for six, eight, even ten months at a time, returning once a year to the settled trade centers. There they could obtain materials from far away, such as obsidian or (later) metal for knives and other essential tools, as well as get grain and other cultivated foodstuffs to round out their diets. The earliest wheel yet found in the steppes—in Ukraine—dates to

---

[2] The alternative, abandoning raising sheep, is *not* a good option, however, because, although all three species provide meat, sheep are the only animals in this trio that produce fiber usable for cloth and clothing.

[3] *Horizon* is an archaeological term for a culture known from (horizontal) layers or levels in excavations. The Yamna or "pit grave" culture flourished on the Pontic-Caspian steppes during the transition from the Neolithic to the Bronze Age.

about 3200 B.C., according to Anthony. Soon after, with wheels under them, these people began to expand to the east, west, and south. (William of Rubruck, the Franciscan missionary who lived with the Mongols in the 1250s, says that "a wealthy Mongol or Tartar may well have a hundred or two hundred such carts with chests" of belongings, in addition to the carts carrying the "houses.")

So which of the two theories—herder-cultivators from the western oases or herders from the northern steppes—best fits our earliest immigrants into the Tarim Basin, our Loulan and Qäwrighul mummies? The argument still stands strong that these first immigrants needed to know not just how to tend sheep but also how to tame the bristling oases where the water was, if only to grow their crops of wheat. The clinching argument, however, may rest with some little twigs.

ALMOST EVERY known grave of the Loulan/Qäwrighul culture (see map 4.1) has proved to contain carefully bundled twiglets identified as ephedra. In Stein's graves on Mesa L.F. (fig. 5.2) and in Hedin's Grave 36 (fig. 5.8; also on a mesa), the "twigs," or stem sections, had been placed in little pouches neatly formed by tying up one edge of the mummy's shroud. Bergman found similar "twigs" with the bodies in Cemetery 5 on the Small River (figs. 5.5–5.6), as did Wang Binghua at Qäwrighul, where he unearthed the earliest mummies now in Ürümchi, radiocarbon-dated by the Chinese to 2000–1700 B.C.

Why ephedra? What was so precious about it, and why might the dead require it?

Ephedra (botanically *Ephedra spp*), a shrubby plant that lives primarily in desert regions, looks like the misfortunate union of a horsetail and a clump of Bermuda grass. Despite its often scrawny looks, it maintains a place in today's pharmacology since several species of the plant contain in their stem covering a water-soluble, adrenalinelike stimulant called ephedrine. The species *Ephedra sinica*, or Chinese ephedra (fig. 8.4), is one of these; the people of Xinjiang still gather and export huge truckloads of ephedra to China for medicinal purposes, where it is known as *má-huáng*, "yellow hemp." (Although dark green when growing, ephedra dries to a bright yellow color.) Another is the species that pioneers and native Americans spread across North America to make a beverage with the pleasant pick-me-up effect of coffee. In the West the plant still goes under the name of Mormon tea or desert tea. In stronger doses, ephedrine is especially effective in the treatment of asthma, giving part of its name to the common remedies Actifed and Sudafed. But it seems hardly likely that people living at barely subsistence level would pay such careful attention to promoting tea parties or preventing asthma attacks among the dead.

Worldwide, people generally surround their deceased with one or more of the

FIGURE 8.4

Ephedra, a shrubby horsetaillike conifer containing a stimulant drug in the stem covering. *Above:* Sprigs of *Ephedra sinica,* which grows in a bush shape. *Below:* Mediterranean variety of ephedra, which grows as ground cover. Packets of ephedra stems were buried with prehistoric mummies around Loulan. Ephedra still serves as a drug in both China and the West.

following: (1) favorite (or tainted) belongings of the departed; (2) things thought necessary for the spirit to reach and live comfortably in the next world; (3) things to keep the spirit from disturbing the living. The last two categories often merge: keeping the dead *there* keeps them away from *here*. For example, the Classical Greeks placed a coin in the dead person's mouth, ostensibly to pay the boatman Charon to ferry the soul across the river Styx to the land of the dead. Once there the spirit could not cross back to haunt the living. (The everyday Greek garb, a mere wraparound, had no pockets, so people habitually used their mouths for carrying coins. The comic playwright Aristophanes portrayed one of his stooges looking up in surprise and accidentally swallowing his small change.)

Ephedra doesn't fall into the first category, so it should find a place with the second and/or third.

A tremendous number of cultures, ancient and modern, New World and Old World, have believed that a second world exists beside our own, a world populated by willful but intangible beings known as spirits. In addition to their bodies, living creatures are thought to have impalpable "doubles" that animate those bodies and that leave for good as the creature dies. People without knowledge of modern physics and physiology typically believe that humans can catch glimpses of these spirits in reflective surfaces like lakes and mirrors (thus breaking a mirror brings bad luck), in shadows, and in dreams and hallucinations (where the spirits of dead people, as well as of the living, can come visit you or where you may even go and visit them).

To travel while still alive to the land of the spirits, you must induce hallucinations or other dreamlike states. The brain will produce hallucinations when fatigued by repetitive noises (such as the shaman's drum) or endlessly repeated motions (such as the shaman's dance). But psychoactive drugs, where available, will produce the effect much faster. Central Asia, like South America and the South Pacific, has a long history and large repertoire of mind-bending activities.

Upon finding a particular plant tied up so carefully in triple bundles in the Tarim mummies' shrouds, we should expect a hallucinogen, then, not a stimulant.[4] Why ephedra?

---

[4] Apparently ephedrine taken in sufficiently concentrated form can in fact cause a terrific high bordering on hallucination—and on cardiac arrest—as takers of an ephedrine-based street drug called Herbal Ecstasy have told me. Such high doses could probably not have been extracted from the amount of ephedra provided in a typical Loulan ephedra pouch, but one could experiment.

I have heard too that hallucination can occur when ephedrine is taken with alcohol—a substance intentionally produced in Egypt, Mesopotamia, and parts of Europe by this time, chiefly as wine, beer, and mead.

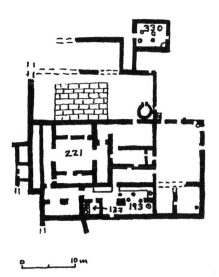
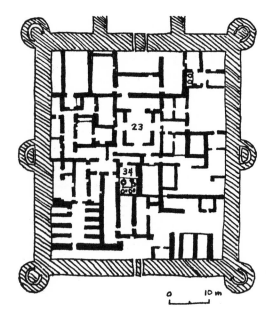

FIGURE 8.5

Typical religious complexes of ca. 2000 B.C. in Merv oasis (ancient Margiana), Turkmenistan. *Left:* Gonur Depe South: Room 137 was the White Room for fixing hallucinogenic drinks, with 3 storage vessels containing a residue of ephedra and hemp (marijuana); the adjoining Room 193 contained other utensils for beverage preparation; Room 221 was the central shrine, a courtyard encircled by corridors; Room 330 had a basin full of hemp. *Right:* Togolok 21: Room 34 was the White Room for fixing hallucinogens, with storage vessels containing a residue of ephedra and poppy; Room 23 was the central shrine, a courtyard encircled by corridors. (After Sarianidi.)

To understand this enigma, we must return to the early oasis settlements in Margiana and in particular to Sarianidi's excavations at Gonur Depe (map 8.1).

Gonur is the largest early Bronze Age settlement in the terminal delta of the Murgab River (ancient Margiana), which forms the first great oasis east of Anau and the other Late Neolithic towns of the Kopet Dagh. Strong fortification walls, originally twenty-five to thirty feet high with a circular tower at each corner, formed a slightly squashed square enclosing the domestic area. Right from the earliest level at Gonur, much of one quadrant of the fort held a large building full of ritual paraphernalia: some sort of temple (fig. 8.5 left).

This temple, like others built slightly later at nearby oasis forts, consists of a roofless courtyard (fig. 8.5: Room 221) surrounded on all four sides by long, skinny rooms. Close to this complex, the excavators always find a small room entirely plastered with white gypsum and fitted with three or more vessels set into a wall bench, also plastered white (Room 137). Inside the White Room vessels at early Gonur, Russian scientists found residues identifiable as ephedra and hemp, while at nearby Togolok 21 (map 8.1; fig. 8.5 right), the White Room residues deposited a few centuries later proved to contain ephedra and poppy. Both poppy and hemp (*Cannabis sativa*) still provide hallucinogenic alkaloids to people today, of course, as opium and marijuana (or hashish). So here we have a *connection*, at least, between ephedra and hallucination, just as we suspected. But still: why ephedra?

The ancient religious texts of Iran (the Avesta of Zoroastrianism) as well as those of India (the Vedas) refer to a sacred intoxicating beverage known as *haoma* in Iranian and *soma* in Indic.[5] (Both Indic and Iranian are branches of the Indo-European language family—the two that ended up farthest to the southeast of their siblings; see fig. 6.3.) By imbibing soma/haoma, we are told, one journeyed to the Other World to experience true reality as ordained by the deities, learning beyond all doubt that this world of *ours* is the illusory one. So important was this ritual drink—its name means simply "that which is pressed out, a pressed extract"—that the entire religion revolved around it, and consuming it constituted the central ritual. This relationship sounds remarkably like what we see in Sarianidi's temples in prehistoric Margiana, with their all-important White Rooms set up for extracting hallucinogens like opium and hashish.

Unfortunately, inherited knowledge of the ingredients of the soma/haoma beverage got lost centuries, even millennia, ago. In moving south into the Indian subcontinent, the Indic people moved out of the zone where the sacred plant grew and had to substitute "empty" plants for the religious ritual. The Iranians, for their part, eventually converted to Islam, a religion vehemently against intoxication of any kind. Haoma rituals (practiced up until then) died out except among a few unconverted Zoroastrians or "fire worshipers." Ever since Indo-Iranian studies became popular among Westerners a couple of centuries ago, scholars have argued over what the original soma/haoma was made from. The most famous theory was that the drug came from a psychedelic mushroom.

In 1989, however, two American scholars published a volume in which they exhaustively analyzed the evidence from every angle—botany, ethnography, folk medicine, and linguistics. Their evidence zeroes in on a plant called harmel (*Peganum harmala*) as the original Indo-Iranian hallucinogen. Harmel, a bushy plant much the shape of tumbleweed (itself a Eurasian steppe plant imported ac-

---

[5] Iranian *haoma* and Indic *soma* are linguistic cognates—that is, changed later forms of the same word.

cidentally into the New World), grows abundantly on the Iranian plateau and contains some very powerful psychoactive alkaloids, harmine and harmaline.

Prior to a performance of the Zoroastrian ritual of *Yasna,* it seems, a priest sat by himself in a specially equipped and consecrated space and pounded two types of twigs in a mortar partly filled with water. After squeezing the juice through a strainer into a sacred cup, the priest carried this drink through the temple to a second priest, who drank it while reciting certain liturgical texts. Evidence suggests that the drink always consisted of at least two different plants, but that the hallucinogen itself constituted one of them only if it was deemed necessary to visit the spirit world. Otherwise the preparer substituted an innocuous ingredient (see below). One can understand the reluctance to use the drug more than needed, after reading about the violent stomach cramps, vomiting, diarrhea, and such that harmine and harmaline cause.

Research also showed that the same mind-bending alkaloids occur in a New World plant, though not of the same family, in a vine called *Banisteriopsis caapi.* All around where it grows along the upper reaches of the Amazon, local tribes use it as transport to a magnificent Other World. Ethnographic descriptions, moreover, of how the South American drug takers act and of the world they visit sound eerily like the descriptions left by ancient Zoroastrians in their scanty surviving literature, including the strong insistence that the Other World, not this one, is the real world and that life as we know it is an illusion. (A South American anthropologist who went so far as to try the drugs himself found it hard for weeks afterward to shake off the conviction that the hallucinatory world was real and his daily life was not.) In fact the two religions are remarkably similar. But since they developed on opposite sides of the world, the close parallels must reflect simply the way that human brains react to this particular drug.

The Amazonian brew is also mixed from two plants, one of which modifies the effects of the hallucinogen. Indeed the psychoactive drug is so potent that the drug taker would not stay conscious long enough to perceive the psychic journey unless a stimulant were imbibed at the same time. The two American scholars concluded therefore that ephedra was added to harmel specifically to keep the person awake during the experience—and in fact that of all the pharmacologically active plants known from Iran, ephedra is by far the best suited to this purpose. Apparently the priests had learned to balance harmel and ephedra carefully as the ingredients of soma/haoma for trips to the spirit world. When "tripping out" wasn't necessary, something else—usually an extract of pomegranate wood—took the place of harmel in the sacred daily ritual, according to the evidence. Ephedra, however, a gentler drug than harmel, could always remain in the brew. When the Indic folk, who had already substituted something for harmel upon moving to northern India, moved yet farther south, out of the habitat even of ephedra, they substituted an inert "ephedra look-alike" for the second ingredient as well.

All this implies that the Loulan/Qäwrighul people tied ephedra into their burial shrouds as part of a ritual to help their dead reach the Other World, and that they must have come from an area where ephedra once tempered a hallucinogen. Furthermore, that area would have to be the oasis zone (or possibly Iran), where we see these rituals developing from 2000 B.C. onward—not the more northerly steppes. But in reaching the Tarim Basin, these folk moved away from the area where the hallucinogens known to them grew, and as in India ephedra must have remained as a now-empty but comforting ritual.[6]

Whether the ancestors of the Tarim people ever used harmel as the psychoactive coingredient is another matter; we know that early oasis hoppers were experimenting with hashish and opium and may not yet have discovered harmel, which (by all reports) grows principally to the south of the oasis zone on the Iranian plateau. (Ephedra, by contrast, grows widely in Russian Turkestan, Iran, and Chinese Turkestan, not to mention along the Mediterranean and in other areas.) New cross-cultural archaeological data show that the oasis settlers set up major ties to the south as they worked their way eastward. Thus the cult of the White Room had ready avenues for a rapid southward spread across the Iranian plateau.

Only two Indo-European branches, Indic and Iranian, show clear evidence of knowing about soma/haoma. Hence they must have picked up the use of these hallucinogens and the associated religious views after splitting off from the other Indo-European tribes. If the Loulan/Qäwrighul people, the earliest settlers into the Tarim Basin, spoke an Indo-European language, then, it would have to be Iranian or undifferentiated Indo-Iranian, not Tokharian. More specifically,

---

[6] Ironically, Flattery adds this footnote: "Alison Bailey Kennedy . . . reports that at Kew Gardens in 1984 she examined the plant specimens recovered by Sir Aurel Stein from graves near Turfan and described by him (1931) as *Ephedra* twigs, and discovered them to be in fact *Equisetum* . . ."—another genus of "horsetail" with no pharmacological content. (Equisetum, unlike ephedra, cannot grow in a desert but flourishes instead in a wet, marshy environment, available in the oases between the deserts. It superficially resembles ephedra in having short, tubular segments, but its surface is very raspy, rather than smooth like ephedra, the reason why it was most in demand for scrubbing pots.)

So, as with the Indic people, ephedra too may have suffered occasional replacement by a look-alike in the Tarim Basin. But the argument remains the same, perhaps becoming even stronger, since arguably only an important religious ritual would be likely to hang on so tenaciously in the face of such changes of available material. Symbols, and only symbols, need no direct tie to reality.

the packets of ephedra in the Loulan/Qāwrighul burials indicate that these ear-liest settlers immigrated from the desert-bound western oases, not from the northern grasslands.[7]

Such a conclusion actually makes more sense out of the apparent links be-tween the Hallstatt Celts and both the plaid twills of Hami and the later speak-ers of Tokharian. For it suggests that the Tokharians may have arrived not as the first wave of settlers around 2000 B.C. but as the bearers of the rather dif-ferent culture that turned up around 1200 B.C. near Hami.

Since Hami is in the northeastern corner of the region, once again the immi-grants must have slid in around the north side of the Tien Shan and through the gorge west of Turfan—roughly the path of China's later Road of the North and of the modern road running from Ürümchi through Turfan to Hami (maps 7.1, 8.1). But this time the wanderers with their sheep could well have approached via the grassy belt of steppe that connects the area north of the Caucasus zone (where archaeologists found the earliest plaids and twills we know of) with the northwest corner of the Tien Shan. Traces of twill technique have turned up in the Fergana Valley from about the same time (at the Chust-period site of Dal'verzin and at the slightly later site of Eilatan; see map 7.6).[8] Perhaps as they entered the Turfan Basin, the newcomers were deflected east by the Loulan people immediately to the south. Furthermore, the later centers of Tokharian culture, as known from inscriptions, are Turfan, Kucha, and Korla—precisely the oases that herders would find by following the grassy pasture along the streams as they came over the Tien Shan passes from the north.

This scenario makes some sense out of an interesting puzzle we have seen in the textiles—namely, that the technology of the cloth from the family tomb at Cherchen seems much more like a continuation and elaboration of the very sim-ple stuffs from Loulan than the plaid twills from Hami do. The plaid twills em-body a whole new batch of ideas presumably from the outside. If successive waves of people kept entering from the north, we can reasonably imagine that the later groups may only have tamped the earlier folk farther down (south-

[7] It is of course possible that groups from both the oasis zone and the steppe zone mingled along the way to the Tarim, bringing in and mixing two cultures so simple that little is left by which to distinguish their origins. The log circles around a few (but only a few) of the male burials find their closest parallels in the stone and wood grave circles of the Afanasievo and An-dronovo cultures to the north. The latter culture, which almost certainly represents (Indo-)Iranians, spread south into the oasis zone during the second millennium B.C., mingling there with the earlier oasis culture. The former seems, on many other grounds, to represent the best candidate for the ancestors of the Tokharians, having taken its soft-metal–using culture very far to the east late in the fourth millennium. The discovery of substantial textile remains at an Afanasievo site could prove very helpful in sorting out the picture.
[8] An impression of a zigzag twill turns up in the same area even later, in the late first millen-nium B.C., at Daraut Kurgan.

ward) into the basin, grabbing the more northern lands for themselves to settle on. There are any number of places on earth where we can see similar dynamics in the Neolithic or Bronze Age, where people got shoved over and scrunched up by newcomers, rather than overwhelmed and submerged—for example in the Caucasus, the Pyrenees, and pre-Columbian North America.

The herder-cultivators of Loulan and Cherchen, for their part, would then represent older "indigenes" with a simpler technology, the descendants of intrepid oasis hoppers from the west.

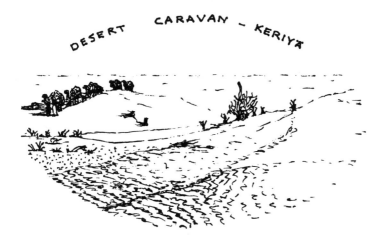

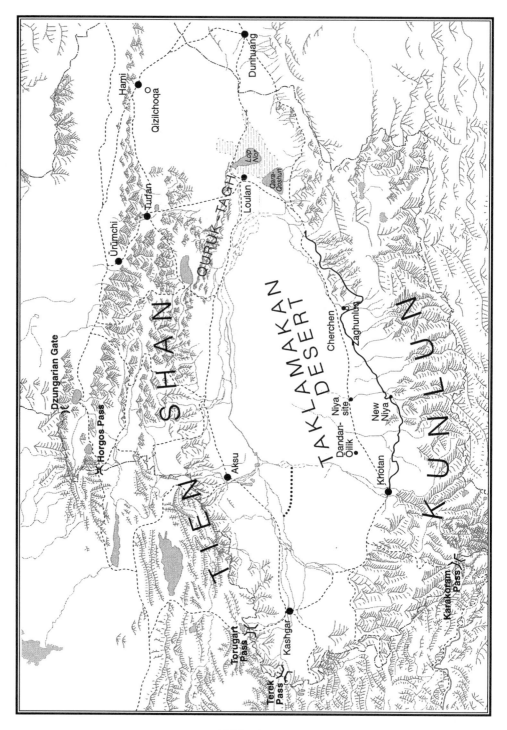

MAP 9.1

9

Pulses in the Heart
of a Continent

THE CENTER of a great continent is a mysterious place, especially to those who don't live there. We speak with awe of the Amazon Jungle, the Roof of the World, the Heart of Darkest Africa, the Australian Outback, and Innermost Asia. Until air travel triumphed, our most reliable roads were always the waterways, and what we couldn't reach by boat kept its aura of mystery, spawning tales of Gold-Guarding Griffins, Abominable Snowmen, and the like. An archaeologist tracking bygone civilizations finds that the cultures stop at mountain ranges but cross rivers freely. Even a "nearby" place like Bosnia has stayed mysterious because its limestone underpinning produced a land with no rivers running to the sea, or even to each other, only local sinkholes draining each disconnected and landlocked valley, where age-old traditions and hatreds could simmer oblivious of the world outside: the Heart of the Balkans.

Hard to reach and hard to traverse, the Tarim Basin, like Bosnia, has no rivers that reach the sea, but for quite different geological reasons. It does at least have rivers. Sitting smack in the middle of earth's largest landmass, the Tarim Basin receives meltwater from mountains on every side, in streams that

---

Opposite page: Physiographic map of major features of the Tarim Basin. In many cases the ancient sites are deep into what today is the central desert, the Taklamakan. The dashed line indicates the course of the Silk Road, while the solid line shows the modern paved road across the south. Note how far into the present desert both the ancient road and many of the southern sites are—an indication of increased dryness of the area.

flow together to become creeks and then rivers. The Tarim River system itself is 1,300 miles (2100 km) long in a wet year. But all that water either evaporates, or is used by living things, or sinks into the sandy floor of the basin, leaving the area unconnected with the rest of the world.

Such was not always the case. The geologic history of Innermost Asia is both complex and informative. From it we can piece together both why such splendidly preserved mummies should occur just here and why Stein, Hedin, and the other early explorers we have followed didn't find most of them.

It may be that they simply didn't look in the right place. But a careful glance at Stein's and Hedin's maps shows a powerful geological factor at work as well.

Sir Aurel Stein's chief interest lay in the spread of Buddhism from India into the Tarim Basin during the early centuries A.D.; to chase these relics was why he had come. In fact he viewed as a sort of "patron saint" the Chinese Buddhist pilgrim Xuanzang (older spelling: Hsüan-tsang, pronounced roughly *shwan tsahng*), who set out from China to travel the twenty-five hundred miles to India via the Tarim Basin in A.D. 628, at a time when the new Anglo-Saxon inhabitants of Britain were still writing runes and contemplating their first lessons in Christianity. He wanted to study Buddhism at its source and to bring back manuscripts that would instruct the Chinese in Buddhist thinking. Xuanzang actually succeeded in his mission—a feat we should remember the next time we complain about minor inconveniences like the airline's misrouting our luggage. The round trip took him seventeen years, and he wrote a record of it that Stein used (among other things) as a preliminary guide to what he should look for.

The Buddhist period sites that Stein found, like Niya and Dandan-Öilik (maps 9.1, 5.1), show on the maps as being typically thirty to fifty miles into the desert from the currently inhabited towns. *Sand-Buried Ruins of Khotan* he named his first major book.

What does that tell us? That the Taklamakan Desert is encroaching, that the rivers bringing the meltwater down from the mountains aren't getting so far as they used to before running out—that, in short, the Tarim Basin is considerably drier than it was fifteen hundred years ago.

Now double that. What about three thousand years ago, the date of the Cherchen finds?

We must remember that it takes only a little water to keep scrub and grasslands alive, and only a little bit less to kill them off. Differences that would be scarcely noticeable on the large scale of geologic time may make all the difference between life and death in areas poised on the border.

Dolkun Kamberi and his Ürümchi associates managed to find their mummies only six miles from a current town, Cherchen. But Dolkun remarks on the drying up of the bountiful southern "oasis corridor" into a series of small, disconnected areas that still have some water. "Today," he writes, "Chärchän county is like a lonely island in a sea of sand" thanks to the increasingly rapid encroachment of the desert. In the last forty years the road through the area has been moved out of the sand's way three times, displaced southward a full thirty kilometers (about nineteen miles). "But since 1971 [a mere twenty-five years]," Kamberi continues, "the natural environment has deteriorated more rapidly than ever before as a result of deforestation and the construction of dams up-river making reservoirs according to a government plan for new Chinese im-migrations into the region."

The Ürümchi archaeologists mention that they know of early sites so deep— a hundred miles or more—into the Taklamakan Desert that to dig them will re-quire the support not of modern four-wheel-drive Jeeps (which are hopeless in the deep, shifting sands) but of helicopters to bring supplies and personnel in and out, and global positioning systems to make sure the ground crew can al-ways be found in the shifting sea of sand. Only with such major technology, and for very short seasons each year, can human will and curiosity force the mighty desert to give up a few more of its secrets.

Over the last few thousand years, then, the Tarim Basin has grown drier, stranding deeper and deeper in the desert the places where people once lived. Some geological reports state that the area has *not* dried up appreciably in the last several millennia. But that depends on who is there to appreciate it. Sven Hedin had to crawl across a zone of dead, dry trees for the last two days of his seven-day search for water as he came out of the sand dunes.[1] Clearly water had fed those trees in the relatively recent past, yet by 1900 a wide swath contained none.

Another of the scientists on Hedin's Swedish team in 1928 was a geologist, Erik Norin, who labored to trace the geologic history of the region. He too no-ticed this "progressive advance of the desert especially in the southern part of the basin." He points out that "the sand [is] steadily encroaching upon the cul-tivable regions in the south and west, thus forcing cultivation towards the bor-der region of the Basin. As a result, the water used for irrigation of the new ground is absorbed to such an amount, that a considerable reduction of the vol-ume of the rivers follows and thus also a reduction in their extension. Yet, this does not account for all the facts." Extensive geological fieldwork also showed that the glaciers that feed the rivers along the south side of the Tarim Basin are retreating, sending less and less water down their courses as the centuries pass. Stein too proposed this as a cause of desiccation.

These rivers spring from the meltwater of glaciers south of the Tarim in the

---

[1] Recounted in Chapter 5.

Kunlun range (map 9.1), the northernmost of many east-west strings of mountains making up the huge mass we think of loosely as the Himalayas. (Technically the Himalayas form only the more southerly strings, closest to India, with the high plateau of Tibet, the Roof of the World, between them and the Kunlun; maps 9.1, 9.2). Even the Tarim River, which flows mostly along the north side of the Taklamakan Desert, receives much of its water from the southwest and in the past received great tributaries from the south. This broad configuration suggests that the basin's underpinnings are somehow tipped so that most of the water from the south ends up eventually on the north side, whether flowing on the surface or under the sand to get there. The Tarim River in turn finally ends at the northeast corner of the Tarim Basin; so the entire area is ultimately affected by the Kunlun meltwater.

Some of the Kunlun glaciers, according to Norin, survived from the last Ice Age, whereas others melted off completely after that time. (The last major phase of ice peaked about 18,000 years ago, when the famous cave paintings of the Upper Paleolithic were being produced, with reasonable warmth returning by about 8000 B.C., roughly when the Neolithic era began in the Near East with its new technology of domestication.) The radical reduction in glaciers produced a sizable period when the basin suffered even greater dryness than today. Later still the glaciers briefly re-formed. Says Norin: "Sub-recent terminal moraines [piles of ice-scoured rock debris deposited at the bottom end of a glacier] indicate an epoch in Post-glacial time when the amount of snow accumulating along the K'un-lun watershed was larger than now, causing an advance of the glaciers to this limit, from which the glaciers have since been receding."

Thirty years after Norin's report a California geologist named Joe Birman noticed in the California Sierra Nevada the leavings of a slight readvance of the ice that ended around 3000 or 2000 B.C. (Geological dating uses a much grander scale than archaeological, let alone historical, dating.) Curious as to whether this event was only local or—as he suspected—global, Birman traveled to a comparable latitude on the other side of the world, to eastern Turkey and the sources of the great Tigris and Euphrates rivers, which had watered the ancient civilizations of Mesopotamia (maps 4.4, 9.8). Despite political difficulties in eastern Turkey (the area was and still is a militarized zone), Birman discovered all sorts of evidence for a brief return of the ice there at about this same date, showing that this colder period had indeed occurred widely.

To the best of my knowledge, no other such global cold snap, causing a notable advance of glaciers at that latitude, has turned up in the geological record between the third millennium B.C. and fully historical times. So the last renewal of the Kunlun glaciers, and hence of the rivers along the south of the Tarim Basin, may date to around that time. They too fall at roughly the same latitude.

That suggests two things of great importance for the history of human habitation in the Tarim Basin. If indeed the Tarim Basin was even drier and less hospitable to life just before the brief and partial reglaciation than it is now, and if Norin's evidence for reglaciation truly dates to 3000 B.C. or slightly after, it seems unlikely that more than the tiniest handful of people could have lived there before then. But after that date, as the renewed supply of annual glacial meltwater pulsed seasonally down the rivers again, life in a wide oasis corridor around the Taklamakan would have become particularly lush and inviting, far more so than now. On these grounds the first attempt to radiocarbon date the Loulan/Qäwrighul culture, which gave 4500 B.C., seems highly unlikely, whereas the second attempt, which gave 2000 B.C., would be right in sync. Such relative wetness at that time would explain how these people came by forests of large trees to mark their burials as well as swamps thick with reeds for the matting that wrapped and cushioned their dead. Since then, as Stein's maps and Kamberi's observations attest, the basin has become ever drier.

ON THE huge scale of geologic time, however, this is only the tiniest tip of a much larger process of drying up in Central Asia. The sand-filled Tarim Basin once lay entirely under water. Hedin's summary of Norin's lengthy study begins as follows:

> In late glacial times, according to Norin, the whole Tarim basin was filled in by an enormous lake or inland sea, a Mediterranean Sea, of whose great volumes of water the historical lake of Lop-nor is the last disappearing survival. At the southern foot of the Kuruk-tag [just north and northwest of Loulan; maps 9.1, 4.1], Norin found the line of the northern shore of the Tarim lake, as he names the inland sea, extraordinarily sharply and clearly defined, and entered it on his map. The shore-line forms a terrace-shaped bank.

This may well be the ancient terrace on which Wang Binghua discovered the Qäwrighul cemetery with its cargo of mummies now in Ürümchi.

> Norin established that the north-eastern shore of the Tarim lake ha[d] in late glacial times been situated to the north and east of Lou-lan, and that the mighty lake, which together with its continuation towards the east ha[d] probably been as large as the Caspian Sea, ha[d] sent out long inlets towards the northeast. In this region the lake ha[d] been shallow and swampy. . . .

As Norin was able to determine by means of extremely accurate measure-
ments of altitudes, the crust of the earth has undergone age-long changes of
level since the Tarim lake disappeared; for the northern shore-line shows a
very pronounced fall from west to east. If Norin marks a point on the shore-
line to the north of Lou-lan with the value zero, then the same shore-line near
Aksu [850 km or 525 miles due west] has a relative height of 300 metres
[1,000 feet]. Further to the west the difference of altitude recedes again to 250
metres [800 feet].

That is, the Tarim Basin as we now know it has gradually bowed up in the middle, like a quilt over an awakening tabby cat, leaving the whole western half
much higher than the east end, where Loulan and Lop Nor are today, and the
center highest of all. Hedin continues:

> Through this movement of the earth's crust . . . the waters of the Tarim lake
> were thrown towards the east and formed in the eastern part of the basin a lake
> which Norin calls Great Lop-nor. . . . The almost complete absence of me-
> chanical deposits in the northern part of this new sea-bed indicates that the
> period of strongest melting of the ice-age had at that time already come to an
> end. . . .

This suggests why we find no Palaeolithic flint tools on the floor of the Tarim
Basin: it was underwater. The water, however, was fresh, and

> Norin supposes that men . . . dwelt on the shore of the Great Lop-nor; for on
> the north and west shores of the old lake he has found roughly-fashioned
> arrow-heads of jasper.

The next stage was gradual desiccation:

> Now the lake had entered a period in the history of its development when
> the peripheral inflow was not sufficient to replace the loss of water that it ex-
> perienced through the evaporation at the surface of the Great Lop-nor. Owing
> to this the lake shrank further and further back and was transformed into a
> constantly diminishing salt lake.

Eventually all that was left was the shallow salt-surrounded lake known to the
ancient Chinese annalists as the Lop Nor, filled with fresh water from the glacial
melt that funneled each year into the Tarim River.

By A.D. 330, however, the erratic seasonal swell of fresh meltwater had whipped the river away from its course past Loulan, the river swinging like a gigantic fire hose on the loose, overnight shifting its nozzle—the little Lop Nor—a good 200 kilometers (125 miles) to the south, forming the Qara-Qoshun (maps 9.1, 4.1), and then whipping it back again in the spring of 1921, after an interval of sixteen hundred years.[2] But such is geologic time, vast and completely insouciant of how many mere fish or humans it might inconvenience. The Tarim River is not alone in this whiplike behavior. The Danube now empties into the Black Sea through a channel seventy-five miles north of where it flowed in Roman times, and several times within historical record—most recently in the nineteenth century—the last stretch of China's Yellow River has flipped its mouth some two hundred miles during flood season, debouching either north or south of the Shantung peninsula (map 9.2). Each of these vast switches has caused enormous loss of life, giving the Yellow River the nickname China's Sorrow.

Virtually all the water in Central Asia comes from melting mountain snows. Rain itself never falls there—or so the guidebooks say, although our research team happened to drive into the town of Turfan just as it started to rain, one morning in June 1995. People stood around outside shaking their heads in amazement instead of seeking cover. The drizzle lasted an hour and then departed, perhaps not to return for decades.

Geology tells us why rain is so uncommon there and why precipitation of any kind is decreasing.

Eons ago—some twenty million years or so—when the continents as we know them still floated in separate pieces on earth's crust, the Indian subcontinent slammed slowly into the south side of Asia along a two-thousand-mile front, crinkling and squashing a huge mass of rock into what we know as the Himalaya Mountains (map 9.2). Tallest in the world, they are the deepest also, for like marshmallows floating in a punch bowl even more of their mass descends below the surface than rises above it. So thick is this rock mass—some 45 miles (72 km) thick—that it deflects a gravity pendulum away from true vertical. The gigantic barrier of the Himalayas helps keep the ocean out of Central Asia, for the whole Tarim area began sinking during the Upper Cretaceous Period, as the dinosaurs were dying out. It sank so far that the area just south of Turfan, the Turfan Depression, now rests more than five hundred feet below sea level (maps 9.2, 10.2). Recent research suggests, however, that the Tarim block itself is stronger than its surroundings, and, instead of crinkling up like the rest of the area, it has transferred pressure northward from the India-Asia collision,

---

[2] Hedin's expedition found evidence later that the river had probably whipped north and then south again once within this interval, somewhere between A.D. 1100 and 1600.

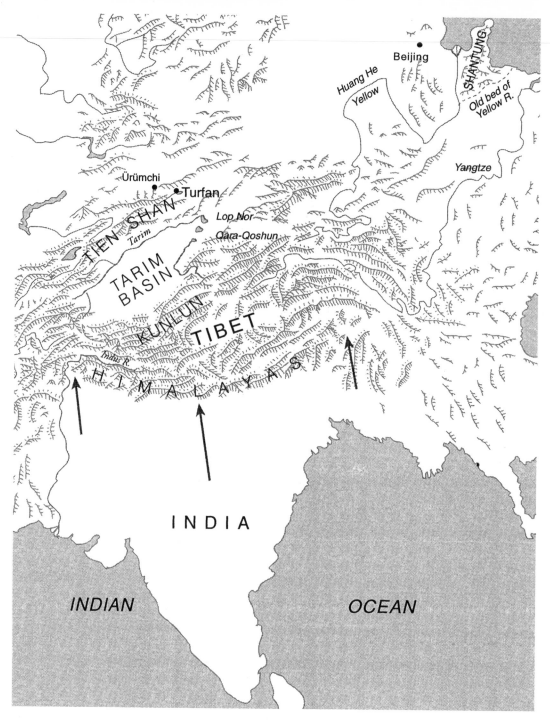

FIGURE 9.2

Twenty million years ago the Indian subcontinent, until then a northward-moving island, collided (arrows) with the Asian continent, shoving upward the Himalaya and Kunlun mountains plus the Tibetan plateau in between them. The hard block of the Tarim Basin didn't buckle but shoved north, pushing up the Tien Shan. The high mountains form a rain shadow, collecting all the moisture from the tropical air moving north from the Indian Ocean before it gets to the Tarim Basin. In recent times the mouths of both the Tarim River and the Yellow River (Huang He) have flopped back and forth over considerable distances.

causing the rise of the Tien Shan range that lines the Tarim along a thousand-mile-long front to the north. But all these mountains keep out rain as well as seawater.

When moisture-laden tropical air pushes northward over India each June from the Indian Ocean, it starts to dump its load. Air typically loses its burden of water whenever it gets either cooler or higher (thus thinner). The land, being higher than the sea, forces this warm, wet air upward, and down come the torrential monsoons. Then the traveling air hits the Himalayas, and up it goes some more. The farther north the mass of air journeys, the higher and colder it becomes, dropping more and more of its moisture as it moves. By the time it has passed over the Himalayas, Tibet, and the Kunlun, *they* are covered with snow and precious little water remains to fall on the other side. In short, the mountainous mass casts northward a rain shadow. Similar rain shadows exist elsewhere: much of the Pacific coast is wet, but great deserts lie just east of the Coast Range in California, the Olympic rain forest in Washington, and the Andes in parts of South America. Tiny rain shadows occur all over the Hawaiian Islands in the lee of the sharp volcanic ridges. Thus on Oahu, the rains that constantly pelt the upper Manoa Valley have spent themselves by the time the air, forced up and over the Pali from the Windward Side, reaches the university and downtown Honolulu. Three city blocks there can make a big difference in the year-round weather.

Inch by inch the Himalayas continue to push upward, slowly increasing the height of the barrier over a vast time. By the end of the Ice Ages, too little moisture reached Central Asia to offset evaporation—evaporation that rapidly increased as temperatures rose worldwide. And so, lacking new water, the huge freshwater lake that Norin named the Great Lop Nor began to shrink, like a puddle of water in a hot skillet.

If the water in the skillet were salty, it would leave a crust of hard, dry salt in the lowest dent in the pan as it boiled dry. So it was with the Lop Nor. After several millennia of evaporation, the small amounts of salt dissolved in typical runoff water had concentrated enough to make the lake brackish, then downright salty like the sea, and eventually much *more* salty than the world's oceans. The Dead Sea and the outlet lake of the Caspian, also landlocked, are like that.

At 20 to 25 percent salts the Dead Sea is so salty that essentially nothing can live in it, and if you should hazard swimming in it, as my grandfather once did, you will find it buoys you much higher than usual. Our family album shows Grandfather floating on his back with his Plimsoll line running midway between spine and bellybutton.

The Caspian Sea, having half the salinity of ocean water, supports copious life, but its "outlet" doesn't: that little knob midway down its eastern shore

FIGURE 9.3

Map of the Caspian Sea, its principal tributaries (the Volga and the Ural rivers), and its "outlet" (the Kara-Boghaz-Gol), a gigantic shallow lake where the water simply evaporates. The area due east of the Caspian is almost entirely a desert, the Kara Kum (Black Sand).

(map 9.3; the baby's rattle, if you imagine the shape of the Caspian as an upside-down swaddled baby facing east). At this spot a half-mile-wide cascade of Caspian water races down a rocky chute and leaps over a final waterfall into a

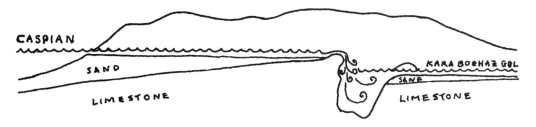

FIGURE 9.4

Cross-sectional structure of the straits and falls leading from the Caspian Sea down to the Kara-Boghaz-Gol. (Not to scale; after Garbell.)

ten-foot-deep, four-thousand-square-mile puddle called the Kara-Boghaz-Gol, Turkic for Black Gorge Lake (fig. 9.4). Blobs of the white chemical foam whipped up on the surface at the falls blow away for miles across the desert like tufts of cotton candy, while the water in the shallow lake cooks—titrates—in the desert sun. Here the dissolved chemicals soon reach saturation (about 30 percent of the brew; ocean water is less than 4 percent salts) and deposit themselves as beds of crystals on the surrounding rocks and flatlands. The Russians, to their surprise, found it more economical to set up a chemical collection plant for sodium sulfate (Glauber's salt) here on the isthmus between the Caspian and the Kara-Boghaz-Gol than to do so at the mouth of the Volga. That meant they had to ship the product four hundred miles up the Caspian before sending it on up the Volga to the paper factories that use it, but the preconcentrated nature of the water in the Kara-Boghaz-Gol made this much the cheaper method.

The fish coming down the chute get a surprise too. When they land in the water at the bottom of the falls, the concentrated salts kill them, and they are picked off as an easy meal by the eagles, pelicans, and gulls waiting on handy rocks and sandbars nearby. What the birds don't eat, the desert foxes and the nomads do, plucking the fish off the far shores of the Kara-Boghaz-Gol, where they wash up conveniently pickled by the brine. Wandering Turkmenian shepherds collect them by the bagful for future use, a rare bounty of nature in a harsh land.

The last step is for the pan to boil dry, leaving great shimmering flats of crystallized chemicals behind, such as can be seen today around Mono Lake and Great Salt Lake in the western United States. Beds of this sort made of sodium chloride (our table salt) occur in several parts of the world, mostly laid down in earlier ages and covered up by later deposits. The beds may run as much as 10,000 feet (3000 m) thick, as do, for example, the great Zechstein deposits under Germany. Other layers underlie parts of Austria and Central Europe and include the salt formations of Hallstatt that preserved the early Celtic plaid twills (see Chapter 7). The salt bed east of the Tarim's terminal lake stretches for some 150 miles, according to Stein's and Norin's early maps (see map 4.1). Nor is this salt flat alone out there. The Swede charted several smaller salt beds northwest of the Lop region, filling basins here and there in the Quruk-tagh (Dry Mountains); other beds occur near Cherchen, where the locals discovered the ancient cemetery full of mummies while digging salt for their own use (see Chapter 2). Indeed, maps of the Tarim Basin are peppered with names containing *tuz,* the Turkic word for "salt," and these salt flats formed some of the most punishing terrain that Stein and his pack animals had to traverse.

Stein left us a sharp picture of the largest of the salt beds, encountered as he traced the ancient route between Loulan and Dunhuang (map 4.1), "a vast salt-encrusted plain" which he deemed "the true bed of the ancient sea":

> Within half a mile from the "shore" the salt surface, so far tolerably uniform, turned into a seemingly endless expanse of crumpled puckered cakes of hard salt. The edges of the buckled-up slabs of salt, rising at an angle, protruded often a foot or more above others crushed in beneath them. . . . The ragged edges invariably showed the white of pure salt, while the upper surfaces of the cakes generally had a greyish hue, probably due to the admixture of fine dust.
>
> Progress over this hummocky *shōr* [a native name for the salt crust] was tryingly painful to the feet, even when protected by stout boots. . . . After we had covered two miles . . . , the surface became even more trying than before. It now looked exactly like a choppy sea overrun with "white horses", one to two feet high and suddenly turned to hard salt. . . . The camels, moreover, found a fresh source of trouble from here onwards in the shape of strange gaping cavities, usually from three to four feet in depth and somewhat less in width at their mouth, which studded the ground, often in close proximity to each other. Their sides were invariably encrusted with heaped-up floe-like blocks of rather darker salt . . . leaning at sharp angles. . . .

The salt crust everywhere was so hard that they could scarcely drive iron tent pegs into it, and it cut the camels' soles so badly that the drivers had to resort to an effective, if painful, local custom of sewing protective leather patches directly onto the camels' feet. The white-encrusted humps, in places up to fifteen feet high and eroded into strange, rounded shapes, gave Stein an idea that these were the "White Dragon Mounds" mentioned in first century B.C. Chinese accounts of the route from Dunhuang to Loulan. Those travelers had also labored across this difficult ground slowly on foot. At one point Stein even found a trail of perfectly preserved early Chinese copper coins that had dribbled one by one from the pack of some ancient wayfarer too tired to notice. No surprise that the old track cut across the salt-encrusted former lake bed at its narrowest point (map 4.1).

The modern terminal lake of Lop Nor still carries fresh water. (*Nor* or *nur* is, in fact, the Mongol word for "lake.") The Tarim River empties into it, bringing fresh meltwater, amplified by many tributaries, for some six hundred miles along the north side of the Tarim Basin; but the lake is much reduced in size. In 1941 Norin mapped the Lop lake as fifty miles long and twenty-five miles wide at its widest, near its southern end, while rumor has it that today almost no water remains.

AS WE come to see how this part of the world got so dry and so salty, we also learn why such wonderfully intact mummies lie precisely here. Dryness and salt: these are the factors that preserved them so splendidly. On a geologic scale the increasing dryness of the climate precipitated out the great salt beds of the Tarim Basin and helped desiccate the bodies when buried. But on the microscopic scale salt also *causes* dryness because it is a moisture hog; it absorbs water more easily than almost anything else around, so it tends to rob its surroundings of moisture. (That's why people used to put a few grains of rice in the salt shaker in damp climates: to absorb enough moisture back out of the salt that it would still shake.) Thus the presence and attributes of salt have aided greatly in the preservation of dead bodies as mummies, which occur precisely in the driest, saltiest part of Central Asia. The tomb diggers at Cherchen, in fact, had spaded through sandy topsoil into a layer of salt, so that the tomb walls consisted of pure salt.

The other geological trait that helped in mummification was the dry air of the desert. As Konrad Spindler, the archaeologist in charge of Ice Man, said, "the prerequisite of mummification by dehydration is a position in a dry but airy atmosphere." Ice Man died in a light snowstorm that covered his body with loose snow full of dry air. Thus desiccation could proceed quickly while the snow cover protected the corpse from predators. Loose sand can trap air too, and in the absence of rain, salty sand can rapidly absorb the body's moisture. This process must occur faster than microorganisms can eat the water-filled tissues. Spindler passes along an estimate that the entire process of mummification takes place in as little as a few weeks to a few months.

It is no accident, then, that the "coffins" containing well-preserved mummies near Loulan were shallow and had no bottoms—just wooden sides with hides over the top. The bodies lay on mats on the salty earth, which under the right conditions could suck them dry. In the much larger Cherchen tomb, the tomb builders had worked to provide real air space under the man's body by digging a foot-deep channel down the middle of the floor, across which they laid small branches to support the willow mats on which the man's body would lie (fig. 2.14). The two women who were placed directly on the earth near his feet did not survive so well, especially the one squashed into the corner where airflow would have been worst (fig. 3.1). The woman at his head, however, lay on the mats with her middle (The wettest part of a body) over the end of the channel, and she came through in excellent condition. One suspects that the protein pastes used both at Cherchen and in the Andes to promote mummification drew away moisture and that the ancient "undertakers" used them deliberately for this reason. Like the Egyptians and unlike those cultures that do their best to hasten separation of flesh from bones at death, some of the ancient settlers of the Tarim Basin clearly *wanted* their deceased to mummify.

The best conditions for mummification may be signaled in fact by the mummies' heavy clothing. The Tarim Basin is extremely hot in the summer—temperatures of 120–130° F are quite usual—and fiercely cold in winter, far below zero. The relatively heavy, dark clothes, unsuitable for summer, suggest that these particular persons died in the cold season and, like Ice Man, mummified so well because the bodies became very cold very quickly, then dried while in a frozen or near-frozen state. Not all Tarim burials produce mummies; many other corpses from these same sites were reduced to mere skeletons, including the unusually deep burials of men inside the log circles near Loulan (figs. 4.6, 5.3). The soil's temperature changes much more slowly down deep than it does at the surface, so that in a cool climate like that of Europe a body decomposes far more slowly in a deep grave than in a shallow one. (So the extra depth of the fanciest burials suggests that the Loulan folk may have moved recently from a much more temperate climate, where such extra work for the elite would be worth the trouble.) But in the Tarim Desert, apparently, deep sand was too warm in both summer and winter to keep the body from decomposing. Shallow sand, providing little insulation, wouldn't preserve a body from rot in summer, but in winter it could well act as the perfect refrigerator while the body dried to a mummified state. Once thoroughly dried, the mummy would not react to ensuing heat.

THE HEART of the Asian continent contains another pulse besides the grand geologic ebb and flow of ancient seas, salts, rivers, lakes, mountains, and temperatures. Within the limited time frame of human history, Eurasia has sent out wave after wave of emigrants—the Mongols, Huns, and Indo-Europeans, to name a few. Scientific study of ancient bones has shown that during the four million years since "ape-men" began walking on their hind legs, Africa functioned as the primary source of human dispersal, sending out one humanoid species after another until finally settling on *Homo sapiens sapiens* as its best model, maybe 250,000 years ago. But once our direct ancestors had wandered forth from Africa and across Eurasia to populate the world, new centers of expansion developed outside Africa, one of them in the heart of Eurasia. We can see this in the archaeological, the genetic, and most particularly the linguistic evidence. To understand this last type of evidence, we must briefly pick up another thread.

When did humans begin to speak? We now think we have trapped that elusive date. A rapid evolutionary push about 150,000 to 100,000 years ago radically changed the shape of our throats and mouths. The changes shortened the jaw, moved the tongue forward, and introduced a right-angle bend into the system where the now-horizontal mouth turns down into the throat (fig. 9.5). These alterations had several effects: they made it harder to breathe, easier to choke on food, and easier to die of infections from impacted teeth (caused by scrunching up the same number of teeth in a shortened jaw). They also made possible the production of rapid spoken speech, something we doubt the contemporary Neanderthal people could produce, although their brains may have hummed with the symbolic thinking prerequisite to language. In language evo-

FIGURE 9.5

Evolution of the vocal tract (passage from lips and nose to windpipe) from our nearest living relative, the chimpanzee (left), to humans (infant, center; adult, right). Compared with the gentle curve of the chimp's air passage, adult humans have a sharp, right-angle bend, making strong breathing (as when running) much less efficient, and the human jaw is much shorter (leaving less room for teeth). From age 3 months on, the human tongue (now differently shaped) fills much less of the mouth/throat cavity and is differently anchored, having both the space and musculature to articulate speech sounds. Note how the newborn baby's tract is intermediate between those of the chimp and of the adult human—another case of individual development recapitulating evolution. The small lens shape at the top of the windpipe represents the vocal cords (inside the larynx, protruding as the Adam's apple), which make the vibrations we call voice.

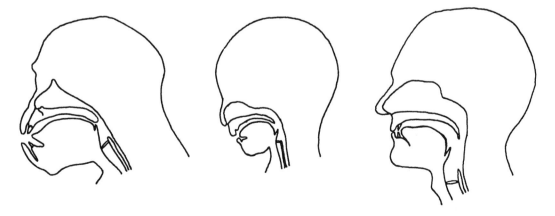

lution, as in the acquisition of language by children, the brain runs the mouth. That is, there's no need to learn the intricacies of language if you have nothing to say: cognition comes first and drives the effort to obtain means to express it. The humanoids with the new mouth type were much more liable to kick the bucket early than were their fellows; they survived as the "fittest" of the humanoid lot because the ability to speak far outweighed all the inadvertent physical disadvantages. After all, language is the most powerful tool we've got.

Eighty to forty thousand years ago modern human populations expanded across Europe and Asia, eventually reaching New Guinea and Australia before heading to the Western Hemisphere. By 40,000 B.C. people were also carrying far and wide such new language-mediated behaviors as religion and art (things that other animals don't have or do), the existence of which shows that language was fully evolved by that time.

That being so, the language families we know today should reflect something of how our modern human population moved out across the planet.

Dr. Johanna Nichols, a linguist at the University of California, Berkeley, became intrigued with how to extract such embedded information from language. She applied sophisticated statistical analyses to a large sample of human languages from all over the world, including a few of the earliest languages ever recorded in writing, five to four thousand years ago. Some areas of the world, she learned, tended to pile up remnants of languages—"residual zones" she called them: areas like the Caucasus Mountains, the Pamir-Himalaya ranges, New Guinea, and the Pacific coast of North America. Other areas, which she named "spread zones," became centers from which waves of people radiated, taking their languages with them. The great spread zones include, for example, Mesoamerica, the South Pacific islands, part of sub-Saharan Africa (accounting for the recent spread of Bantu languages there), and—the most famous, perhaps the most active spread zone of all—the central Eurasian steppes (maps 2.9, 9.6). From this last zone we can document a series of linguistic spreads periodically over the last five thousand years.

The first of these Eurasian expansions was proto-Indo-European (see Chapter 6). Since the daughter branches share words for soft metals, earlier linguists concluded that all the Indo-Europeans (in effect, the proto-Indo-Europeans) already knew in common how to use them—principally gold, silver, copper. Therefore they must already have entered the first age of metals, the Bronze Age, before splitting up, and that would put the Indo-European breakup somewhat after 3000 B.C., when the use of soft metals became widespread. Recent archaeological finds from Turkey, however, show that people back at 7000 B.C. were already picking up hunks of raw copper and investigating their properties, hammering and abrading them into hooks, pins, and other small items. (Copper sometimes occurs naturally in pure form, and Anatolia is one place where it does.) So a somewhat earlier date is not unthinkable.

Next came massive expansions, during the third and second millennia B.C., of the Indo-Iranian branch of Indo-European. During this time Indic speakers got all the way to India, while Iranian tribes flowed into an area running from southwestern Siberia, Russian Turkestan, and the Iranian plateau all the way to western Ukraine (map 9.6). Demonstrably Indo-Iranian and even specifically Indic names and vocabulary words turn up in written records of the Near East in the Bronze Age, starting soon after 2000 B.C., words like *ashva-*, the Indic word for "horse," and names of typical Indo-Iranian deities like Mitra and Varuna.

Seven or eight centuries later a new wave of people emanating from somewhere in Central Asia snuffed out the Bronze Age cultures of the Mediterranean. Big black destruction layers throughout Greece, Turkey, Syria, and on down to the gates of Egypt attest to the extent and seriousness of the devastation. Only the Egyptians managed to beat the invaders off, in a pair of great battles ending in 1190 B.C. The pharaoh Rameses III depicted these battles, one on land and the other in the Nile Delta, on the stone face of his huge mortuary temple at Medinet Habu, in Thebes in Upper Egypt (map 9.6).

Interestingly, the intruders the Egyptians fought don't appear to have been steppe folk themselves, but rather some peoples displaced southward, dominolike, by incursions from the northern steppes into lands bordering the Mediterranean Sea. Like the boll weevil, they were jus' lookin' for a home. Later, when the dust settles and the smoke blows away, we find the Hittites, for example, living in Syria, just south of their former home in Anatolia, while Anatolia is filled with new Indo-European groups like the peak-hatted Phrygians (see Chapter 2).

During the Late Bronze Age the Hittites had learned how to smelt iron (which requires a far higher temperature than copper) but had kept the process secret by means of a royal monopoly. Thus the Hittite king Hattusilis III, about 1275 B.C., composed a letter to an Assyrian king who had requested presents of this wondrous iron, answering that he was sending an iron dagger but that his royal friend would have to wait awhile for anything more since the smiths had not finished processing this year's batch of ore. Nearly a century earlier Tutankhamon had received such a kingly dagger. But the demise of Hittite hegemony in 1200 B.C. shattered the royal monopoly, releasing the secrets of smelting iron. So began the Iron Age.

Although Indo-European groups such as the Greeks, Romans, and Celts continued to expand and contract in the west, the next great pulses from Inner Asia

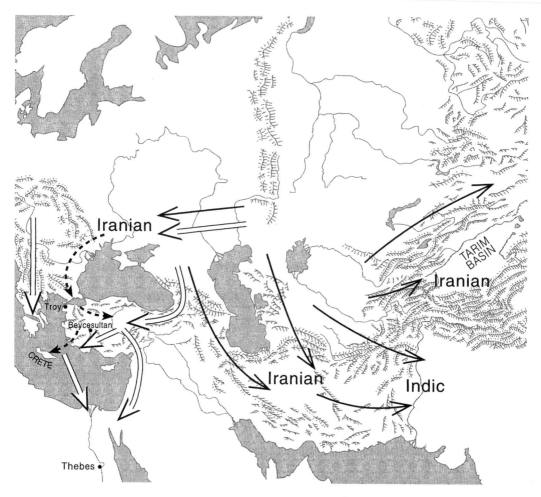

FIGURE 9.6

Mass migrations of the Bronze Age. Dashed arrows show a movement of peoples in southeastern Europe around 3000 B.C. Solid arrows show the deducible directions of spread of Indo-Iranians in the 2nd and 1st millennia B.C.; the eventual attested distribution of Indo-Iranian languages is labeled. Hollow arrows show the directions of movement of the Sea Peoples, who attacked and destroyed many civilized areas of southeastern Europe and the Near East around 1200 B.C. In this movement people pushing south into Greece and Turkey dislodged others, who in turn pushed south toward Egypt.

spread other language groups about. Beleaguered Europeans chronicled their arrival. The terrible Huns (a Turkic-speaking group led into Central Europe by Attila in the fifth century A.D.) came first, followed in rapid succession by the Avars (Turkic invaders of the sixth to eighth century, finally evicted from Hungary by Charlemagne), the Bulgars (Turkic speakers who invaded the Balkans in the seventh century and left their name to Bulgaria), the Magyar (Finno-Ugric ancestors of the modern Hungarians who swept into Hungary in the ninth century[3]), and the Seljuk Turks (who began invading Turkey in the eleventh century). These were chased in the thirteenth century by the most feared invaders of them all, the Mongol hordes,[4] who killed 90 percent of the population around Kiev and penetrated as far west as Budapest, burning that city on Christmas Eve of 1241. Then to the surprise of the terrified Europeans, the Mongol invaders abruptly wheeled and rode away, back to where they had come from. Why leave now, abandoning such rich booty? Far away in Mongolia their king had just died, and when the warriors received the news, they stampeded home to elect a new leader. They never again gathered enough momentum to invade so far west, although they continued to harry the Russians for centuries. No wonder the Russians are still jumpy about their borders.

All six of these groups spoke Uralo-Altaic languages (fig. 9.7). Magyar (Hungarian), still spoken in Hungary, belongs to the Uralic half, being a distant relative of Finnish, while the other five are Altaic. The Altaic superfamily includes Mongol, Tungusic, and the Turkic tongues. To Turkic belong not only the Huns, Avars, Bulgars, Seljuks, and the Ottoman or Osmanli Turks now in Turkey, but also the Uyghurs, who by the tenth century had moved from Siberia into the Tarim Basin, today the Uyghur Autonomous Region. As Johanna Nichols points out, each of these language spreads seems to have its center farther and farther east within Eurasia (map 9.9).

Europeans to the west and Tarim peoples to the south were not alone in suffering from a spreading plague of steppe horsemen. China too, at the east end of the steppes, records its share of distress from barbarian onslaughts. Repeatedly in the first millennium B.C., the Chinese wrote in despair of the fierce Xiongnu (see Chapter 6), probably ancestors of the Huns, who excelled in ra-

---

[3] Stamp collectors will know that Hungarian stamps say "Magyar" on them. English still uses a name obsolete fifteen hundred years ago.

Many examples of such misnomers exist. For example, the Chinese call themselves the Middle Kingdom, conceiving of themselves—as so many nations do—as being the center of the universe, whereas Western Europe still uses a name derived from the Qin (Ch'in) Dynasty, which flourished in the late third century B.C. The Russians, for their part, use a name for China *(Kitai)* belonging to the nearest Asian group with Chinese admixture that the Russians knew of in the tenth century A.D., the Khitans, people who lived somewhere in Mongolia and Manchuria. Similarly, the Greeks for twenty-five hundred years have called themselves *Héllēnes,* whereas the Romans (from whom we took our cue) called the Greeks by the name of the first Greeks they got to know, those who founded the first colony (Cyme) on Italian soil and who happened to be called *Graii* or *Graeci.*

[4] The English word *horde* is thought to come from the Mongol word for an encampment, *orda* or *ordu.* Because everyone had his (or her) own tent plus many carts full of baggage, the populous camps spread over enormous territory. The meaning eventually got transferred from the camp itself to the size of the group.

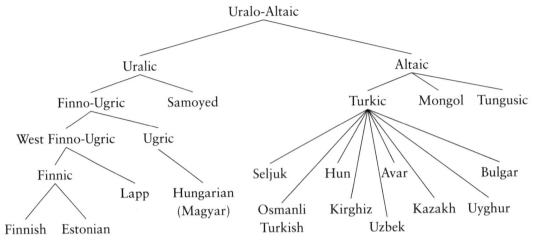

Tree chart showing the relationship among some of the languages in the Uralo-Altaic family, which extends across much of northern Eurasia. (Not all the modern descendants have been listed.)

pacity. Chinese defense troops even adopted nomad-style horse riding and trousers, around 400 B.C., to meet and fight the intruders on their own swift terms. Numerous Iranian words to do with wheeled transport, magic, medicine and the like (see Chapter 6), borrowed early into Chinese, tell us that Iranian expansion reached all the way to China at some point in the Bronze Age.[5]

Finally, A.D. 1260, after two thousand years of skirmishing, the Central Asian nomads won. Led by the great Kublai Khan, the Mongols overpowered the Chinese altogether and set up their own government on Chinese soil. For a short while this Mongol domain stretched from the Pacific Ocean to the Black Sea, the largest empire ever assembled before modern times.

What makes these pulses occur? What causes Central Eurasians suddenly to hop onto their horses and flatten everything to either side of them, like so many locusts? And why should the heart of the spread be shifting east?

Surely one important factor in their dominance is the periodic appearance of some politico-military genius like Attila or Genghis Khan, one able to organize and inspire a group of followers to overwhelm and incorporate neighbors into a bigger group that can in turn annex still more neighbors and so forth. The most effective leaders set up empires that reached all the way to Europe; the less

[5] In fact, three graves excavated just north of Beijing, at Baifu, belong to a "northern" culture contemporary with China's great Bronze Age culture, about 1000 B.C. But this culture and its graves possess quite different characteristics that link them with Western horses and Caucasoid peoples. See Chapter 10 and fig. 10.5.

effective ones, perhaps, merely started those dominolike shoving matches that we have noted here and there among the recorded disturbances. Brilliant leaders may explain pulses, but not why central Eurasia should be the heart of so many.

Perhaps we are back to geology and ecology. All these steppe people lived from their great herds of sheep, cattle, and horses. As we have noted, however, it takes only a little water to keep grasslands alive and only a little bit less to kill them off. Studies of climate suggest that in addition to long-term worldwide changes like the Ice Ages, each region has its own small cycles. For example, Southern California experiences a fairly rapid shift between serious drought and flooding rainstorms on a cycle of about eleven years. When the rains come and the dry washes (by now full of houses built by irresponsible developers) fill with water, the destruction makes national news. Although the Eurasian steppes may be subject to short pulses of this sort too, we suspect that a longer cycle of greening followed by drought operates over two to three centuries. When the grass dries up, herds and herders must move or die.

Hunters have always followed the food, but hunting doesn't support a large population. Herding does. So a new ecology began when people near the western end of the grass belt or steppes got the idea that one could domesticate animals and then herd them for a living. Archaeology tells us that domestication first began in the hilly zone running in an arc to the east, north, and west of Mesopotamia—the so-called Fertile Crescent (map 9.8). We have evidence for domestication in Syria before 8000 B.C., first for domestic dogs, then for domestic sheep and wheat. Goats, cattle, flax, barley, legumes, and other species soon followed. These cultigens made possible the change to a settled way of farm life nicknamed the Neolithic Revolution.

Two big breakthroughs of importance to the steppes occurred around 4000 B.C., however. One, first noticed and worked out in the 1980s by the English prehistorian Andrew Sherratt, has been dubbed the Secondary Products Revolution. Sherratt noticed evidence that prior to about 4000 B.C. people used their domestic animals only as a supply of meat and hides, killing all but a small breeding flock as yearlings. But then archaeological finds show a change: people get the idea of harvesting useful things from their living animals, so they start keeping them alive to a ripe old age. Vessels for milk and milk products appear (food), processing of wool begins (clothing), and use of draft animals to pull a more efficient plow commences (energy). Getting your food and clothing from a *live* animal means you can hoard wealth on the hoof.

The second change was the domestication of the horse, which we know first from a Ukrainian horse jawbone of about 4000 B.C. that shows special tooth wear from chewing on a man-made bit. As people grew more skilled in con-

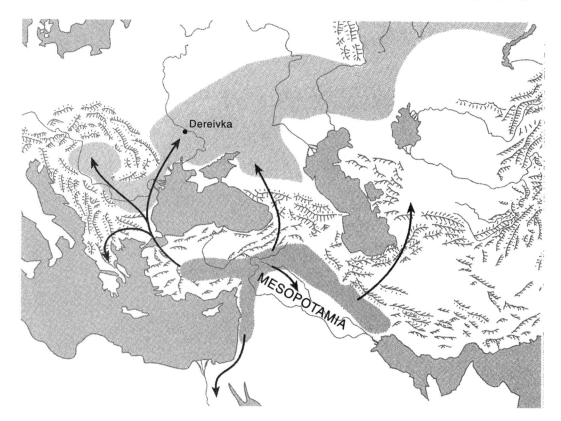

FIGURE 9.8

Map showing the so-called Fertile Crescent (darker shading, curled around Mesopotamia and into Anatolia), where the domestication of plants and animals began over 10,000 years ago. The arrows show roughly how it spread into other areas—e.g., across the Bosporus into southeastern Europe, across the Caucasus into the steppes (lighter shading), and across the Iranian plateau and the Kopet Dagh into the oasis zone.

trolling horses, they could use these splendid beasts to manage not just little flocks but vast herds of sheep and cattle. And so the stage was set for steppe no-madism, the first lifestyle that made living in the grasslands efficient.

Clearly we should not expect pulses of invading herdsmen to stream out of the Asian grasslands until after this new nomadic lifestyle had both begun and had time to take hold and develop. We could, however, expect that the first peo-ple who worked out the powerful economy of large-scale herding should be the first to mow down their neighbors.

Who might they have been? Let's look at the timetable. The newly woolly sheep seem to have spread into southeast Europe from the Near East by about 3500 B.C., and we can probably assume the same for spreading into the steppes.

Around 3000 B.C., we pick up a pulse of intruders out of the Ukrainian steppes into western Anatolia, with the founding of Troy and other important sites, and movement—dominolike?—into Crete from Anatolia (map 9.6). Our first surviving evidence for felt—another crucial ingredient in developing the life of the Eurasian nomad—occurs soon after, around 2600 B.C., at Beycesultan in central Turkey (map 9.6).

Were these first "pulsars" Indo-Europeans? Perhaps; or perhaps their close kin.[6] Being Indo-European is technically a linguistic attribute, requiring linguistic data to pin it down. But the timing of the first noticeable pulses matches nicely with the linguists' internal evidence for when the Indo-Europeans started splitting up.

The geography matches too. The proto-Indo-Europeans must have lived east of the Dniepr River (map 7.6, 9.9)—must, because they did not know of an important tool that developed in Central Europe from 5500 B.C. on: the warp-weighted loom. As one moves east, the Dniepr is where the archaeological evidence for that tool stops. Those Indo-Europeans who ended up farthest to the south and east used other looms, and those who ended up west of the Dniepr *borrowed* from other languages all their words to do with the warp-weighted loom. So they could hardly have spent the Neolithic living right there in Central Europe, where it was invented. This line of the Dniepr, east of which the proto-Indo-Europeans must have lived, lies not far from the textile zone that yields the earliest-known plaids and twills. In short, the evidence from that central industry, cloth, suggests that the proto-Indo-Europeans (by definition, this linguistic group before it spread out) lived on the Pontic and Caspian steppes, the area where the horse was domesticated and the nearest steppeland to the Near East and its crucial ideas of domestication.

We have another fix on where the proto-Indo-Europeans lived: Johanna Nichols's observation that the centers of linguistic spread shift farther and farther east (map 9.9). The Mongol invasions—the latest—stem from far, far to the east (map 9.9, area 4); the ancient Turkic center—providing the next earlier pulse—lay to the west of Mongolia along the upper Yenisei River (area 3). Be-

---

[6] I am thinking in particular of the Anatolian language family, which has yet to be proved on linguistic grounds to be a daughter of Indo-European rather than a cousin. (My archaeological hunch is that they are cousins.) I have long suspected these early intruders into western Anatolia, via Troy, to be the Luwian branch of the Anatolian family, while their strange, hollow spindle whorls (see Chapter 8) suggest they came ultimately from far to the east, rounding the north side of the Black Sea on their way west. Some of the yet earlier inhabitants of Eurasia, whether a large group or small, must also have belonged to still older trunks and branches attached to this linguistic line of descent, for the stock that gave *rise* to the Anatolian and Indo-European languages (as recorded and reconstructed) had to have lived somewhere.

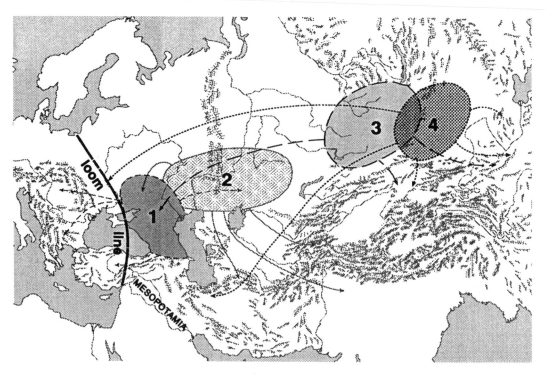

FIGURE 9.9

Map of postulated successive spread zones of language groups in Eurasia. Circles indicate postulated starting zones and arrows approximate directions of spread. (1) Indo-European (whose starting zone cannot lie west of the line marking the east edge of the warp-weighted loom, a basic tool unknown to the proto–Indo-Europeans), before 3000 B.C.; (2) Indo-Iranian, before 2000 B.C.; (3) Turkic, before A.D. 400; (4) Mongol, before A.D. 1000. Note that the centers of the movements keep shifting east, along the steppe belt and away from Mesopotamia and the Fertile Crescent (where animal domestication began).

fore them, the Indo-Iranians started from still farther west (area 2; although scholars argue whether that point was just east or just west of the southern Ural Mountains). At any rate they spread south into today's Iran (ancient Persia) and India and west into Ukraine. The earliest of the lot was the spread of the proto-Indo-Europeans. If we place their old center west of the Indo-Iranian starting area but east of the warp-weighted loom, there they are again on the steppes north of the Caspian and the Black Sea or Pontus (area 1).

The first people to work out nomadism would have had such an edge over everyone else that they must have been the first to overrun their neighbors' pasturage. It looks more and more likely that the Indo-Europeans got their original edge this way, just happening to be the people sitting in the right place, the

East European steppes, at the right time, the fourth millennium. They have been spreading ever since.[7]

One more tool is now being developed to help solve these puzzles of how groups of people spread: the analysis of human DNA. Studies already show something of how human populations spread. In Europe alone five ancient expansions can be detected by DNA analysis, three of which can be traced in Central Asia, in particular among the Uyghurs. As we learn more about which genes control what, we may eventually be able to follow unusual traits like blue eyes or very tall stature, which we can trace now in the archaeological record only through random findings of ancient paintings and of skeletons.[8] Adequate DNA samples from a variety of mummies like those in Ürümchi, compared with modern and ancient populations, will help enormously in sorting out the picture.

The samples, however, must come from bodies fresh out of the ground, properly taken to avoid contamination. Genetic material that old is badly degraded, and the polymerase chain reaction that makes multiple copies of DNA fragments is much more inclined to work on DNA that's in good condition than on the scrappy stuff. So even a couple of flakes of skin from the excavator's hand or scalp can contaminate the sample and skew results. The Italian geneticist Paolo Francalacci recently succeeded in taking adequate samples from a newly excavated mummy of about 1200–1000 B.C. at Qizilchoqa, as well as samples from several other mummies. To provide cross-checks against contamination of one or another sample, he tried to select tissue from several protected places on each body. Of the specimens taken, he reports that he was allowed to analyze five samples from two individuals.

Results suggest connections with Central Europe—just as the linguistic and

---

[7] Nichols would place the Indo-European center far to the east of the Urals, yet that not only clashes with her own observation of the centers' moving east, but more seriously, it ignores the fact that these rapid spreads clearly result from the new lifestyle of nomadic herding. Vast expanses of steppe separate the Urals from the ancient centers of the Near East; that region is too far east to fill the bill. The cradle of the lifestyle and thus the first center of spread had to be far enough west to receive the key ideas of domestication from the Near East—and to receive them first.

[8] The occupants of the Shaft Graves at Mycenae, who depicted horse chariots on their gravestones and were almost certainly early Greeks (ca. 1600 B.C.), were over six feet tall. (Since later Philistine sites are full of pottery derived from Mycenaean models, it has been suggested that Goliath was an over-six-footer of Mycenaean descent—a veritable giant when pitted against the local five-foot Mediterranean stock.) Mallory also cites evidence of a tall, robust Cro-Magnon type (associated in the late Palaeolithic with the northern forest steppe) turning up in Ukraine already in the fifth millennium. These tall skeletons occur in the Dniepr-Donets culture, thought by many to be one of the key ingredients of early Indo-European culture. But all we have at the moment are a few tantalizing signposts in the dark; we badly need the light DNA can shed.

textile analyses do. But far more needs to be done to clarify the picture, both by analyzing more samples from new excavations and by continuing to analyze the genetic components of the modern population of Xinjiang (as is being done currently by the Chinese Academy of Sciences). Such studies await us in the twenty-first century.

DANDAN-ÖILIQ PAINTED PANEL
1st mil. AD

SILK COCOONS

LOOM, COMB

REEL?

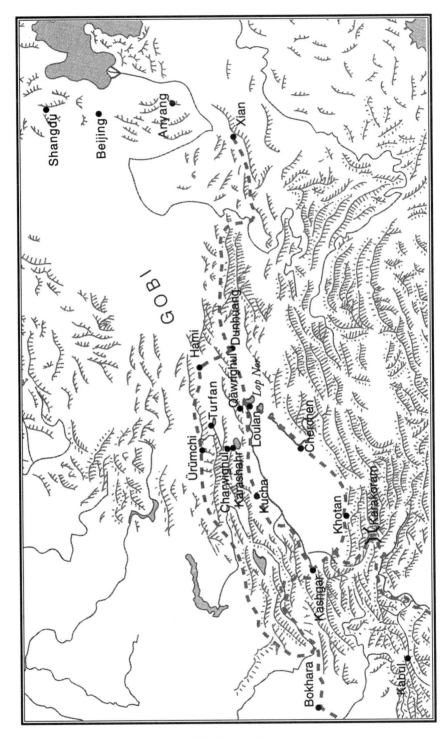

MAP 10.1

10

Sands of the Silk Road,
Sands of Time

MANY CULTURES have come and gone in Central Asia in the last four thousand years, and not all the Ürümchi mummies come from the early sites around Loulan, Hami, and Cherchen. The sands enveloping later burials were just as thirsty, just as ready to preserve bodies and their clothing (map 10.1).

For example, deep in the Flaming Mountains above Turfan, amid the barren red hills of a Mars-like landscape, lie several ancient sites near the village of Subeshi (map 10.2, fig. 3.15) that date "merely" to 700 B.C. and later. (Thirty-five hundred miles away the Greeks were just emerging from their long Dark Age and starting to develop the ideas of art and politics that would so influence Western civilization.) One of these sites is a tiny village atop a steep, dusty-beige hillock. It overlooks the Toyuq River tumbling in the gorge at its foot, carrying ice-blue meltwater from the snowy peaks above to the gray-brown gravel flats, or *sai,* below. Stone grain grinders and fire-darkened hearths lie scattered about among small sections of house walls, and one can still make out and marvel at the long, steep path the inhabitants descended to fetch water every day. A small tributary stream bed cuts off the back side of the hillock; thick, hexagonal slabs of dried white mud pave its floor, like the tiled lavatory of a giant, evidence of

Opposite page: Locations of various ancient sites mentioned in Chapter 10, including Shangdu, the summer capital of the Mongol emperors of China, where Marco Polo claimed to have served Kublai Khan.

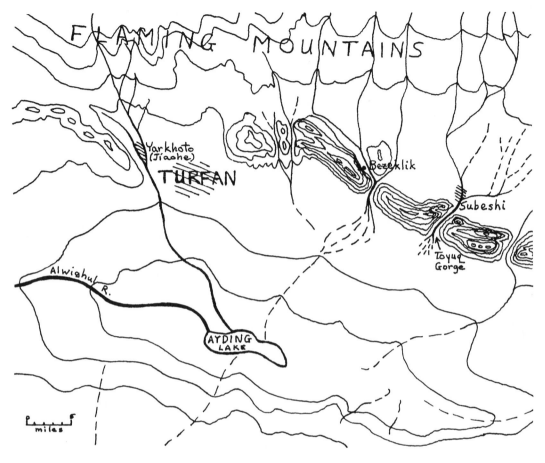

FIGURE 10.2

Map of the Turfan Basin, more than 500 feet below sea level at its lowest spot (the salt-water Ayding Lake). The mid-1st millennium B.C. sites near the village of Subeshi lie on the west side of the Toyuq Gorge. The Buddhist monastery of Bezeklik is cut into the west side of the next gorge to the northwest; the paintings in its caves date to the late 1st millennium A.D.

a flash flood from whenever the last hard rain fell—a decade or a century ago.

A short way upriver, on a flat terrace of barren, sandy gravel, lies a cemetery of the mid- to late first millennium B.C. (fig. 3.15). From its graves the Ürümchi archaeologists pulled several colorfully arrayed bodies. One woman (fig. 10.3) wore a copious woolen skirt striped horizontally in shades of red, yellow, and brown, with a dark felt hat rising high above her to two conical peaks like a twin-steepled church. The pelt used to make her long coat had the fur turned inside for warmth, and neat leather slippers protected her feet. A gigantic leather mitten encased her left hand, the sort of protection a falcon owner might wear,

FIGURE 10.3

Woman from cemetery at Subeshi, near Turfan, mid-1st millennium B.C. Note the twin-peaked hat (the left point is partly lost), the leather mitten and slippers, and 2 small pouches (below the hand without a mitten), one shaped like a chili pepper and the other with a comb peeking from the top. (After Newbury.)

and she possessed two little pouches, one the shape of a long, narrow chili pepper and the other containing a round-topped comb.

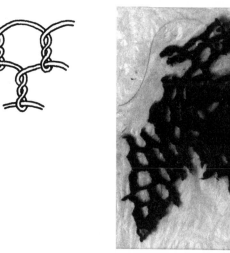

FIGURE 10.4

One of the types of woolen hairnets found at Subeshi, 1st millennium B.C.

Elsewhere a felt-hatted man lay dressed for the millennia in sheepskin boots and coat, while a second man displayed the most interesting sewing job yet dug up in the Tarim Basin. He had undergone chest surgery, and the two incisions were sewn up with horsehair.

Two other women had bound their long tresses into black hairnets made in either needle techniques or *sprang* (fig. 10.4).[1] Yet another female—her skeleton found beside the remains of a man—still wore a terrifically tall, conical hat just like those we depict on witches riding broomsticks at Halloween or on medieval wizards intent at their magical spells.

And that resemblance, strange to say, may be no accident. Our witches and wizards got their tall, pointy hats from just where we also got the words *magician* and *magic,* namely, Persia. The Persian or Iranian word *maguš (cognate with English *might, mighty)* denoted a priest or sage, of the Zoroastrian religion in particular. The three Magi, or Wise Men, said by the New Testament to have followed an unusual star to Bethlehem at the time of Jesus' birth, received their name from this group. Magi distinguished themselves with high hats; they also

[1] Sprang is rather like playing cat's cradle with dozens of threads at once. You simply twist the tightly strung parallel threads around each other one after another, pushing the twists to both sides—as in cat's cradle—until there isn't room to do any more. Then you darn one thread in crosswise to hold the twists from unwinding, and there you have a nice stretchy net. The ancient Egyptians knew such techniques, as did Neolithic farmers in northern Europe. Elderly peasants in parts of Greece, Scandinavia, and Central Europe still ply these crafts.

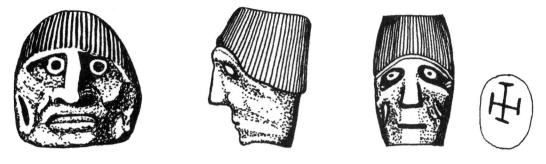

FIGURE 10.5

Early Chinese sculptures of "Caucasoid" facial types, with big noses, deep-set round eyes, and wide, thin mouths. *Left:* Bone carving from Anyang, capital of the Shang Dynasty (1500–1100 B.C.). *Center:* Two small carvings of mollusk shell used as tips of hairpins, ca. 780 B.C., from a palace 60 miles west of Xian. *Right:* Ancient Chinese character for **mʸag* ("magician") incised on top of rightmost figure's hat, identical in form to the "Cross Potent" sign used by Western magicians in the Middle Ages. (After Mair.)

professed knowledge of astronomy, astrology, and medicine, of how to control the winds and weather by potent magic, and of how to contact the spirit world. We have already explored (in Chapter 8) the relation between the Indo-Iranians' knowledge of herbs—specifically harmel and ephedra—and their experiences of visiting the spirits. In the conical hats of Subeshi we have yet more evidence suggesting Iranians in the area. But at this date, late in the first millennium B.C., their presence is not surprising, since soon afterward we begin to get inscriptions along the south side of the Tarim Basin, some written in a provably Iranian dialect.

In addition to first drawing international attention to the unexpectedly western mummies in Ürümchi, Victor Mair also surprised Orientalist circles by demonstrating that the Old Chinese word **mʸag²* must come from the same source as *magic*: Persian *maguš*. Ancient Chinese **mʸag* denoted powerful individuals at the Chinese courts who, according to Mair's researches, "were primarily responsible for divination, astrology, prayer, and healing with medicines"—pretty much the same list of specialties that the magi had. Furthermore, the Chinese references to and representations of such round-eyed Western "magicians" (fig. 10.5) considerably antedate the Subeshi conical hats

---

² The asterisk in front of the word indicates that its ancient pronunciation has been reconstructed by linguists from their understanding of the regular sound changes that have occurred over the centuries. A Chinese "character" denotes first and foremost the meaning of a word, and some characters consist solely of a meaning radical. Any further information about its pronunciation, included in some of the characters, was ambiguous even when originally encoded (chiefly of the sort used in charades: "Sounds like X") and has also undergone subsequent sound changes. So what we know about the sounds of an ancient Chinese word comes at least as much from other considerations as from its written form.

of the first millennium B.C. Some go back even to the Shang Dynasty (1500–1100 B.C.). If this were the only evidence of early contact between Iranians and Chinese, one might dismiss it, but Mair has also accumulated a long list of early linguistic borrowings from the West. Most interesting to archaeologists is the word for a chariot *(chē,* from something like **klʸag),* a prestigious device that also came into China during the Shang Dynasty. That word is Iranian too, and it gives some idea of how these Westerners managed to travel so far.[3]

The linguistic street may even have been two-way. Mair also suggests that the typical European words for silk (such as English *silk,* borrowed ultimately from Greek *sērikós* "silken; Chinese") are related to the oldest reconstructable Chinese word for silk, **sʸə(g)-.*[4] That word too may have spread from the mouths of Iranians headed back west.

In fact, the ubiquity of Iranians across Eurasia becomes more and more striking as material accrues. When written records began in the Tarim Basin in the early centuries A.D., the whole southern chain of oases—the southern half of the basin—was occupied by speakers of Iranian, the most prominent being the Sakas of Khotan, who had climbed over the Pamirs from the west to get there. The northern string of oases (Aksu, Kucha, Turfan, etc.) teemed at that time with Tokharians, who, however, may have arrived only with the plaid twills late in the second millennium B.C. Well before that, to go by the loanwords and depictions of Big-Noses in China, Iranian magi had already ingratiated themselves into the courts of the Shang Dynasty in northern China, where the emperor and his nobles would hardly move without consulting diviners first. (William of Rubruck, A.D. 1250s, described this trait among the Mongol rulers also.) Even the name of Dunhuang, that ever-strategic site where the Gansu Corridor opens westward into the Central Asian desert basins (map 10.1), appears to be Iranian in origin. According to Mair's linguistic research, the name is related to a group of Iranian words for watchtowers, fortified posts, and means of holding a borderland. Moreover, the characters selected by the ancient Chinese scribes to denote *Dunhuang* include the radical for "fire." (The Iranians,

---

[3]With Old Sinitic **klʸag* compare Greek *kyklo-* ("wheel"), from which English has borrowed *(bi)cycle.*

Three graves excavated just north of Beijing, at Baifu, belong to a "northern" culture contemporary with the great Bronze Age cultures of China, about 1000 B.C. But this culture and its graves possess rather different characteristics from the Shang tombs, traits that link them with western horses and Caucasoid peoples.

[4]The presumed presence of a final velar stop (*k* or *g*) suggests that the Greek noun *Sēr* for "an Oriental" is a back formation from *sērikós* "silken; from the Orient" on the common model of Greek adjectives ending in *-ikos,* rather than the adjective coming from the noun as is usually supposed.

Greeks, Chinese, and others used fire signals to send long-distance messages from one watch post to the next.) The mesa sites on which Stein found so many remains of the Loulan/Qäwrighul culture—see Chapter 5—suggest in fact that an extensive watchtower system already existed in the eastern Tarim Basin long before the Chinese arrived. And the presence of ephedra, as we have seen, suggests the possible arrival of Iranians in the Loulan area as far back as 2000 B.C.

Yet other East-West connections turn up in the first millennium B.C. Excavations during the 1980s, carried out by Lü Enguo and others of the Xinjiang Institute of Archaeology at the Bronze and Iron Age site of Charwighul (just north of Karashahr: map 10.1; not to be confused with Qäwrighul, a millennium earlier and 180 miles southeast), revealed a series of large cemeteries containing some two thousand tombs, six hundred of which have been opened so far. They cluster near a circular altar of gravel placed at the highest spot in the area. Each stone-lined gravepit is enclosed by gravel: the earliest flatiron-shaped, younger ones stirrup-shaped, and the most recent circular. Near the tip of the flatiron-shaped enclosures, excavators usually found a sacrificial hole containing the skull and legs of a horse, a constellation reminiscent of the similar deposit above Cherchen Man's tomb (fig. 3.1). The Charwighul cemetery has been dated to 1200–400 B.C., so the early tombs, the flatiron-shaped ones, are contemporary with the great burial excavated at Cherchen.

Such sacrifices of horse skull and legs have come to light rather earlier and farther west. Earliest are those from the Srednij Stog culture (central Ukraine), 4500–3500 B.C., and its successor the Yamna culture (extending from western Ukraine to the southern Urals), 3600–2200 B.C. Both cultures are strong candidates for gestating the proto-Indo-Europeans. At 2600 B.C. we find the skulls and forelegs of cattle positioned around the gold-filled "royal" tombs of Alaca Höyük in central Anatolia, among people argued to have arrived recently from the Pontic steppes. Then, around 2000 B.C., head and foreleg sacrifices of horses turn up at Krivoe Ozero and other sites of the Sintashta-Petrovka culture on the border between eastern Russia and Kazakhstan (map 10.6). Exactly at these sites too the earliest evidence for the development of spoke-wheeled chariots occurs. Solid-wheeled carts are too heavy for horses to pull, especially with inefficient harnessing. Until people learned to hold the harness low on the horse's chest, the breastband that takes the weight would slide up and squeeze the horse's windpipe and neck veins when the animal pulled hard—counterproductive, to say the least. Greek paintings from 500 B.C. show uncomfortable ways of holding the breastband low, but the efficient "modern" traction harness took over in Europe only in the twelfth century A.D.

So the Eurasian invention of lightweight spoked wheels—an outgrowth, it seems, of experimenting with bending wood for making a more efficient bow—

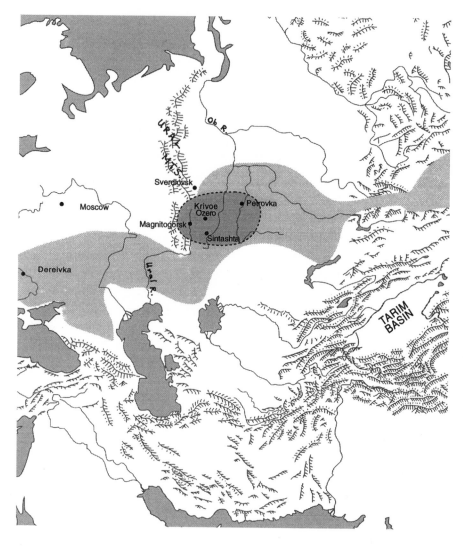

FIGURE 10.6:

The earliest evidence for spoked wheels, about 2000 B.C., has turned up at sites like Sintashta, Petrovka, and Krivoe Ozero, in the steppe area just east of the southern Ural Mountains.

revolutionized transportation and warfare all over the ancient world during the second millennium B.C. Numerous features directly paralleling peculiarities of the early Indo-Iranian culture suggest that these northeasterly people, the inventors of the spoke-supported rim, were Indo-Iranians too.

The various mummies and their belongings thus show us that people in general and Iranians in particular had long been moving through Central Asia by several paths, living along the trackways, and leaving their dead to mummify in the sands beside them.

The first history books indicate much the same. The Greek writer Herodotus led the way, coining the very term *history* in the fifth century B.C. while researching the course of the wars between the Greeks and the Persians.[5] He mentions the vast eastward extent of the Persian Empire, which King Darius himself boasted as extending to Gandhara, the modern plain of Peshawar in northwestern Pakistan. Although hostilities kept Herodotus from going to Persia—he did visit as many places important to the war as he could—he reported all he could hear tell of it. Unfortunately for our purposes, that was far more about customs than about the geography. But Herodotus was an excellent observer. At one point he remarks in disgust at the glee the Persian magi seemed to take in killing victims for their famous divinations, but then he concludes philosophically, "But as for this custom, let it be as it was established long ago; I will return to my narrative."

Alexander the Great, who lived a century later, did not let others stand in his way. He went to Persia himself. In 334 B.C., having subdued his enemies in Macedonia, Greece, and the Balkans (receiving, among others, a warily friendly embassy of Celts), he set out to conquer Asia and "the barbarians" who had attacked Greece 150 years before. Landing first at Troy, on the northwest tip of Anatolia, he sacrificed to the gods who had helped the Greeks conquer that corner of Asia 900 years earlier. He had studied Hellenic history well—his tutor none other than Aristotle. By 331 B.C. Alexander had fought his way across Anatolia, Syria, and Babylonia to the Tigris River and beyond (map 10.7). Upon entering one conquered city, he found a famous Greek statue of two tyrant slayers, an artwork carried off by the Persian king who sacked Athens in 480 B.C. Delightedly he sent the piece back home to Greece—both because he admired Greek art and as a political statement. The next year, moving into what is now Iran, he captured the royal city and palace at Pasargadae, called Persepolis ("Persian City") by the Greeks, and put such a hoard of gold from its royal treasury back into circulation that the "world" gold market got its first Black Monday. Then, after some moving about to secure his flanks, he marched east again.

First Alexander swung northeast into the area of Bactria, on the Oxus River, which he conquered with little fighting but much hardship in the cold mountains. The Greek colonies he set up in this province were they that two centuries later recorded the arrival and eventual departure of the Tókharoi (i.e., the Greater Yuezhi chased out of the Tarim Basin by the Xiongnu; see Chapter 6).

---

[5] The Greek word Herodotus used is *historia,* meaning "research, a seeking out." The Persians of course are Iranian, and what today is called Iran was still called Persia when I was a child.

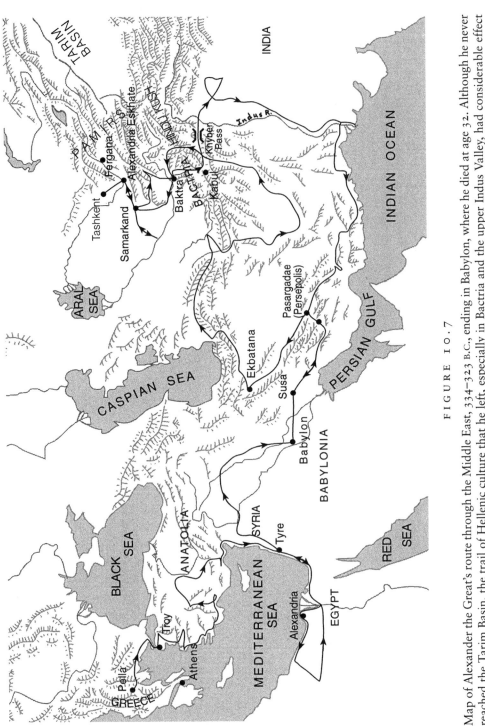

FIGURE 10.7

Map of Alexander the Great's route through the Middle East, 334–323 B.C., ending in Babylon, where he died at age 32. Although he never reached the Tarim Basin, the trail of Hellenic culture that he left, especially in Bactria and the upper Indus Valley, had considerable effect on the Tarim cultures of the next millennium.

Alexander himself got as far northeast as the point where the Syr-därya flows out of the Fergana Valley into the desert plains. There in 328 B.C. he founded one of many towns he built along the way and named after himself, this one Alexandria Eskhate—Alexandria the Farthest.

After many adventures in Bactria, including his marriage to a beautiful captive named Roxane, Alexander turned south in 327 B.C. to conquer the Indus River valley, today's Pakistan, entering via its northwestern tributary, the Kabul River, and the Khyber Pass. In Gandhara (Peshawar), as elsewhere, he built cities on the Greek model and moved on. By 325 he and his army had reached the mouth of the Indus, and, after a brief sail in the Indian Ocean, he began to work his way overland back toward home, some three thousand miles away to the northwest. He got as far as Babylon before falling sick of a fatal fever, and in June of 323 B.C. Alexander the Great died at the age of thirty-two. According to one tradition, his body was encased in honey to preserve it for the long journey back to his beloved city of Alexandria in Egypt, where he wished to be buried.[6]

Alexander was dead, but Greek influence in Central Asia was not. In Bactria in particular, Greek rulers and colonists remained and spread their canons of art among the other inhabitants. Thus when the Greater Yuezhi, or *Tókharoi*, originally from the Tarim Basin, eventually left Bactria for northern India, they took Greek ideals with them to their new kingdom of Gandhara, where the Kabul and Swat rivers flow together into the upper Indus (maps 10.1, 6.1). Converted to Buddhism, the Yuezhi/Tókharoi merged the Greek and Indian traditions into the delicate style known today as Gandharan or Greco-Buddhist art, which came to flower early in the first millennium A.D. Then they carried it north with their Buddhist teachings over the Karakoram Pass to Khotan and the other oases of the southern Tarim Basin, where Stein was so startled to find it when he arrived and began excavating in 1900.

Back and forth, to and fro. The passing of ideas between East and West clearly has a long history, and dry, sandy Central Asia served as the main corridor until quite recently. Some have tried to wish away the evidence for such transcontinental contacts, believing that independent invention confers the greatest glory. But global research shows that isolation, not contact, is enemy to a progressive and vibrant civilization. The Tasmanians, for instance, cut off for several thousand years from the rest of humanity, not only made no progress but actually backslid, losing one important skill after another, such as how to make bone tools (including needles for sewing clothes—an inconvenient loss) and how to haft handles to stone blades (to make tools capable of felling trees

---

[6] Honey contains so little water that it dehydrates to death any bacteria that try to live on it. Like dry sugar, it can be used as an emergency antiseptic and/or preservative.

and hollowing out boats—a fatal loss). New contacts among diverse peoples, on the contrary, spark creative new ways of looking at things. For example, every major improvement in writing systems came when new arrivals said, in effect, "This is wonderful—but there must be an even better way. . . ."

There was, in fact, an amazing amount of traffic all over Central Asia long before the Silk Road came into being. That great east-west passage became established as a trade route only during Roman times, concurrent with China's Han dynasties (202 B.C. to A.D. 220). And trade flourished. Chinese silk became the envy of upper-class ladies of the Roman Empire while Central Asian costumes and dances became the rage among ladies of the Han court, along with Roman glass.

The Mesopotamians had first managed to produce glass back around 3000 B.C. The making of glass from scratch requires melting silica, traditionally in the form of quartz sand, at a temperature of around 3000° F and then cooling it slowly to form a noncrystalline solid. The temperature can be dropped a full thousand degrees by adding an alkaline flux (such as soda, lime, or potash) to the quartz and going through a two-stage firing process, although the second firing must be held at 2000° F (1100° C) for many days. Such a feat was so difficult with the primitive furnaces of ancient times that it almost certainly happened only once to begin with, presumably by accident. Once the first glass had been produced, however, more glass could be made by using old pieces of glass as a catalyst for speedy fusion, so the furnace stokers didn't have to maintain the high temperature for very long. (Collecting broken glass, or *cullet*, for this purpose became a regular occupation in the ancient Near East. Recycling is an old idea.) The Mesopotamians kept the secret of glass close for many centuries, making and exporting finished objects and also glass ingots for remelting and shaping elsewhere. In fact glass ingots molded into round buns and colored cobalt blue to imitate the sacred lapis lazuli were found recently in a shipwreck of about 1300 B.C. off the south coast of Turkey. By that time the Egyptians too had become skilled glassmakers. With the invention of glassblowing in the first century B.C., the Romans and others in the West came to excel in creating dainty vessels of multicolored glass, giving full value for the delicately colored silks of China.

The term *Silk Road* is actually quite modern, originally coined in German *(Seidenstrasse)* in the late nineteenth century by Ferdinand, baron von Richthofen, a German scholar, explorer, and geographer (and a relative of the "Red Baron," Manfred, baron von Richthofen, famous flying ace of World War I). This handy label for the important arteries bringing silk westward soon settled specifically onto the braided cable of roads that passed through today's

FIGURE 10.8

View from the ancient ruined city of Yarkhoto across one of the 2 deep gorges that nearly surround it and make it a natural fort. The ruins date largely from the early 1st millennium A.D., but the highly defensible mesa had been occupied well before that. The cliffs, which cut down through the barren terrain a full 100 feet (30 m) to the greener riverbeds, give a good idea of the terrific erosion typical of the area.

Xinjiang. There, in the first millennium A.D., the Chinese already occupied key fortified towns like Yarkhoto (also called Yarghul or Jiaohe: fig. 10.8, map 10.2) to protect the merchants who connected China with Bactria, Syria, and the Mediterranean as well as with the Indus Valley. Richthofen preceded Hedin and Stein into Central Asia, and the later explorers often relied on Richthofen's maps.[7]

In Western lore the most famous of all travelers along the Silk Road was Marco Polo, the Venetian trader who composed a book about going to China and back in the thirteenth century A.D. In fact, his father Nicolo and his uncle

[7] The Qilian Mountains south of the Gansu Corridor are also known as the Richthofen range, in his honor.

Maffeo had made the trip earlier, in the company of emissaries returning from Bokhara to the court of Kublai Khan, the brilliant Mongol ruler who had finally conquered China for the Mongols in 1260. The elder Polos visited Kublai during that same decade, impressing him with their culture, it is said. Kublai even gave them letters for delivery to the pope, requesting a delegation of learned men from the West to instruct him in Christianity and Western knowledge.

In 1271 the elder Polos set out for China again, this time with young Marco and two Dominicans. The Dominicans soon turned back, daunted by the hardships, but the Polos, according to Marco's later account, continued eastward, crossing the Pamir range to Kashgar and the Tarim Basin. From there they followed the Road of the South through Khotan to Cherchen, then toiled northeast across the deserts surrounding the Lop Nor and Turfan, and finally across the forbidding Gobi Desert to the corner of northern China where the khan held court—in the summer at Shangdu and in the winter a little farther south at what is now Beijing (map 10.1). (Shangdu is immortalized in poetry by Samuel Taylor Coleridge as Xanadu: "In Xanadu did Kubla Khan / A stately pleasure dome decree. . . .") There Marco says he entered the service of the khan, diligently studying the principal languages of the khan's domain and acting as his envoy all over eastern Asia for seventeen years. The khan, he explained, was an anthropologist at heart and particularly enjoyed hearing about the customs of his far-flung subjects. So Marco enterprisingly took notes wherever he went, to edify his royal patron with a full report upon returning from a mission.

In 1295, after two dozen years away, the Polos finally returned much travel-worn to Venice, where, as with Odysseus long before them, their own household did not recognize them. During a year of enforced leisure, the result of capture by the Genoese in a Venetian-Genoese battle in 1298, Marco Polo finally dictated a "Description of the World" to a fellow captive, one Rusticiano of Pisa, who apparently took down the original manuscript in a dialect of French. Translated then into Italian and finally into other languages, this book became the first description of the Far East widely read in the West, and Marco Polo became known as Marco Milioni—Marco of a zillion tales.

Recent scholarship questions whether Marco Polo ever reached China at all. His account contains errors, certainly; but more to the point are major omissions that ring false, such as his mentioning Chinese block-printed money while giving no description of printing. In Marco's day, 150 years before Gutenberg and several centuries before paper money in the West, such technology was revolutionary. Nor does he mention Chinese calligraphy, the Great Wall of China, tea drinking, bound feet, or a host of other things that virtually every other Western traveler has rated high among the noteworthy sights and customs. Surely someone who spent seventeen years living there and running errands for the king could hardly have missed them. His text in fact reads more like an account pasted together from others who had been there, while he himself sat somewhere in the Middle East.[8] (Most of his terms for things Chinese are actually Persian words or words filtered through Persian. What happened to all those principal languages of the khan's domain that he said he studied?) The book is certainly not organized as a viable itinerary, rather—as its title says—as a "description." Moreover, if you were the khan, with half the world groveling at your feet, would you have instantly picked some young whippersnapper—and a foreign devil at that, just arrived from parts unknown—as your most trusted envoy?

But Marco wasn't the only source of questionable tales. Later writers have credited him with introducing many important Chinese inventions into the West, such as gunpowder, magnetic compasses, noodles, ice cream, and ravioli (Chinese *jiaozi*), even though we have no evidence whatever that he brought them. In ancient Greece every story of an event requiring prodigious strength gravitated to Herakles (Hercules), and so it was in early Renaissance Europe, where Marco Polo's name attracted everything thought to have come from China.

Whoever did introduce them to Europe, these and other Oriental inventions and commodities had tremendous impact on Western culture, and they came largely by way of the Silk Road. In the early period that we've explored in this book, most of the movement was west to east, but later the flow largely reversed, and China's influence on Europe became enormous. Chinese gunpowder alone forever changed the Western way of life and death. The reverse flow shows clearly among the Tarim mummies too. Between 2000 and 1000 B.C. they are entirely Caucasian in their features, whereas by 300 B.C. bodies with Mongoloid features mingle with the Westerners—e.g., at Charwighul. The Tokharian paintings of A.D. 600 to 1000 show Buddhist devotees of many races—Chinese, Indian, Mongol, and Turkic types, as well as fair-haired, blue-

---

[8] Some of his sources were excellent; the book is not totally fabricated. Various archaeological findings corroborate one passage and another. But other sections throw doubt either on whether he visited these places himself or on his truthfulness. For example, he claims that the Polos were the first "Latins" the khan had seen (although William of Rubruck, two decades earlier, had found the khan's court fairly crawling with Westerners, including several native speakers of Latin-derived languages) and that the Polos designed catapults to help Kublai Khan win a siege that took place well before they could have got there. (Mongol historical sources say the khan brought in two famous Persian engineers specifically to make such machines.) But intellectual imperialism was a common enough custom in Europe at that time.

eyed, white-cheeked Caucasians. The mummies tell the same tale, with ever-increasing percentages of Turkic, Mongol, and finally Chinese types. In fact the last mummy in the Ürümchi Museum gallery is that of a Chinese general. He is far smaller than Cherchen Man, with a very different facial structure.

If you walk the streets of Ürümchi today, you will see mostly Chinese faces—except in the bazaars. There amid the babble of spice sellers, noodle vendors, and cloth merchants you will still hear many varieties of Turkic languages, Uyghur and Kazakh being the most prominent (fig. 9.7), and see many non-Chinese faces and modes of dress. And here and there you will spot someone with honey blond hair, perhaps even blue eyes. Dolkun Kamberi himself is such a one, a full-blooded Uyghur with light brown hair and a European-looking face (fig. 10.9). One day, when Victor Mair had stuffed me and Irene and Dolkun into a cab to go to the museum, we heard Dolkun chortling in the front seat

FIGURE 10.9

Dolkun Kamberi and Irene Good in the desert hills near Subeshi. Kamberi, like many other Uyghurs, still shows Caucasoid genetic traits (round eyes, high-bridged nose, light brown hair) like those of the early mummies in Ürümchi.

after giving directions to the driver. When we asked what was so funny, Dolkun replied that the driver had just asked him how he came to speak perfect Chinese since he was obviously a foreigner. "I grew up in Ürümchi!" he exclaimed. But he looked like us, not like the driver.

From 1924 to 1928 the Russian-American painter and philosopher Nicholas Roerich traveled from India through the Tarim Basin and Mongolia. His log of that difficult journey, published in 1929 as *Altai-Himalaya,* afforded me my first glimpse of Chinese Turkestan when I encountered it, with its yellowed paper and intriguing end map, in my father's library when I was a child of fourteen. I still find Roerich's description of the Tarim Basin impossible to put down: how he struggled over the eighteen-thousand-foot passes northward from "India" (now Pakistan) into the Tarim Basin—from blizzardy passes as high as the highest mountain in Europe down to the edge of the worst desert in the world—and finally dragged gratefully into the market city of Khotan, only to be put under house arrest by its preemptory and suspicious ruler. Escaping eventually from the dark and airless little hovel where he was detained, he made his way along the caravan road north to Kashgar, with its colorful bazaar filled with merchants, camels, horses, and textiles.

Road? Calling the Silk Road a road is like calling a strand of spider silk a rope. The fabled Silk Road, one learns, consisted of no more than a dusty and evanescent track skirting the oval of the terrible Taklamakan Desert, where mere humans and animals have no chance against the searing heat and landmarkless wastes of traveling dunes that make up its interior. Instead of cutting across that impassable center, the track skittered by two-, five-, and fifteen-day marches from one water source to the next, whether brackish wells or bright streams of meltwater tumbling down from the surrounding ring of mountains. In either case, at these life-giving spots one could refill the precious canteens of water for both people and pack animals before toiling onward. The dusty traveler could often see the oases miles ahead, splashes of emerald green against the monotonous gray-brown wasteland (plate 15b). Khotan to Kashgar constituted the north-south leg of the journey skirting the west end of the basin. From Kashgar the track turned east across the north side of the basin, heading toward Kucha, Karashahr, and Turfan, centers of the ancient Tokharian kingdoms.

Hidden from the rest of the world for a thousand years, the Tokharians had come to light a scant two decades before Roerich's journey. Most spectacular of the remains he saw were the magnificent frescoes in the Buddhist monastery of Bezeklik near Turfan (plate 15b), found by the German explorer Albert von LeCoq. As he visited these painted cells, perched in the ocher-red rocks above an emerald gorge, the artist Roerich looked with wonder on ancient portraits of these forgotten people (plate 16), with their often light brown beards and elegant mustaches, their blue eyes and white skin, proudly donating bags of money to the Buddhist monasteries for good works. Musing on their fortune, Roerich wrote into his diaries: "So, before the eyes of history has come a nation, from whence is unknown; nor is it known how it scattered and disappeared without a trace."

The mummies lying in state in Ürümchi are making that story known again. And Dolkun, pointing to his own Caucasian face and pale brown hair, answers when his audience asks why all those early Caucasians disappeared: "We are not gone—we are still here. . . . *I* am still here!"

LOULAN

Notes on Sources

FIVE OF the color photographs—plates 1, 5a, 9, 10b, 11a—were taken by Jeffery Newbury/©1994 and reprinted with permission of *Discover Magazine*.

For complete bibliographical information, see the Bibliography. What follows is a list of specific page references to the sources of quotations, drawings, and other information, together with some brief explanatory descriptions of sources that may be helpful to the curious reader.

CHAPTER 1

Evan Hadingham's April 1994 *Discover* article "The Mummies of Xinjiang" includes full-color photographs by Jeffery Newbury. Victor Mair's article in *Archaeology* "Mummies of the Tarim Basin" (1995) also contains some of Newbury's photos (printed backwards) as well as some of Mair's. In 1996 *National Geographic* published Thomas Allen's article "Xinjiang," including in its last section, "The Silk Road's Lost World" (pp. 44–51), Reza's photos of some of the mummies, sites, and artifacts.

Konrad Spindler tells the story of the prehistoric Ice Man, found mummified in an Alpine glacier in 1991, in his book *The Man in the Ice* (1994).

For the origin and development of textiles as a key industry in early times, see my two earlier books: *Women's Work—The First 20,000 Years* (1994) and *Prehistoric Textiles* (1991). The latter also gives a full account, with photographs, of the ancient European plaid twills (pp. 166–69, 186–95).

CHAPTER 2

The slashed cloak from Gerumsberg, Sweden, is further described in my book *Prehistoric Textiles*, pp. 192–94, with references to the original Swedish publications.

Dolkun Kamberi describes the excavation of the Cherchen site in English in a short, illustrated paper, "The Three Thousand Year Old Chärchän Man Preserved at Zaghunluq" (1994). The man's tomb, Tomb 2, is described in detail on pp. 5–7, and diagrammed on pp. 9–12. The quotation about the spoons with ocher comes from p. 6. Zaghunluq and its setting are described on pp. 2–4.

I describe the economic place of textile crafts in the prehistoric and Classical world in *Women's Work—The First 20,000 Years.*

Further discussion of both knitting and *nalbinding* can be found in Richard Rutt's *A History of Hand Knitting* (1987).

Drawings of some of the hats (figs. 2.6, 2.7 right; 2.8 left) are based in part on photographs in *The Ancient Art in Xinjiang, China* (1994), no. 253–54. (A photo of Cherchen Man's white overcoat occurs there as no. 255.) The Phrygian hats in the center of fig. 2.8 come from scenes of the Judgment of Paris, in which Paris is typically tagged as coming from Anatolia, not Greece, by having Phrygian headgear. The upper head is found on an engraved Etruscan mirror in the Louvre, Paris (Br 1734); the lower head is on a painted Roman relief in the Tomb of the Pancratii, Rome.

For early domestic horses and tooth wear at Dereivka, see David Anthony and Dorcas Brown, "Looking a Gift Horse in the Mouth" (1989). A recent overview of the whole question, with a photo of the Dereivka skull, appeared in the *Los Angeles Times* (1995) in "Scientist Trots Out New Equine Theory," by M. Mycio. Henri Moser, a Swiss adventurer of a century ago, recounts many interesting firsthand observations of the dynamics between impoverished herders and farmers of Russian Turkestan in his fast-reading book *À travers l'Asie centrale* (1885).

For theories of perturbations on the steppes, see the introduction by Christopher Dawson to his edition of descriptions of *The Mongol Mission* (1955), p. ix.

An early Egyptian shirt purportedly of the First Dynasty was published by Sheila Landi and Rosalind Hall in "The Discovery and Conservation of an Ancient Egyptian Linen Tunic" (1979); other early sleeved shirts appear in Hall's article "Garments in the Petrie Museum of Egyptian Archaeology" (1982). See also my books *Prehistoric Textiles,* pp. 146–48, for the Egyptian shirt, and *Women's Work,* pp. 134–37, for discussion of the history of sleeves in early times.

My thanks to Joe Rhode of Disney Studios for letting me examine his Tibetan wool coat.

Fig. 2.14 is based on Dolkun Kamberi's descriptions and diagrams in "The Three Thousand Year Old Chärchän Man Preserved at Zaghunluq."

CHAPTER 3

Dolkun Kamberi describes the burials of both the women and the baby in his excavation summary, "The Three Thousand Year Old Chärchän Man Preserved at Zaghunluq," pp. 4 and 6. Figure 3.1 is based on his diagrams on pp. 9–12.

William of Rubruck's wonderfully observant memoir of his Asian travels, written for Louis IX of France (St. Louis), has been translated by Christopher Dawson as part of his book *The Mongol Mission.* The quotations on felt come from pp. 101 and 94. I also present a discussion of the history of felt, with further references, as Chapter 9 of *Prehistoric Textiles.*

The felt, textiles, and other finds at Pazyryk, now housed in the Hermitage Museum in St. Petersburg, are fully described and well illustrated by Sergei I. Rudenko in his tome *The Frozen Tombs of Siberia* (1970). Fig. 3.3 is based on fig. 59 of the original Russian edition of 1953, which is clearer than its nearest equivalent, fig. 31, of the English version. A photograph of the carved Cherchen spindle, serving as a principal source for fig. 3.4, appears as fig. 218 of the catalog *Rūran ōkoku to yūkyū no bijo* (1992).

The films of Bosnian folklife were made as part of a documentary series by Ankica and Vlatko Petrović for Sarajevo television. Dr. Ankica Petrović is a noted ethnomusicologist; her husband directed Sarajevo TV for many years. Since the films were made, most of the age-old lifestyles that they tried to record have been destroyed by the latest Balkan wars. Only a few of the films themselves survived, brought to the United States by the Petrovićes as cultural treasures.

My thanks to Elizabeth Ettinghausen for letting me reproduce a portion of the Persian wedding painting, fig. 3.9, in her collection.

For plaiting techniques: Noémi Speiser has collected a wide variety into her book *The Manual of Braiding* (1991), including the balanced ribbing technique (which is what many of the ornate flat bands appear to be) and *kumihimo*. Several books on making *kumihimo* exist—for example, *Creative Kumihimo* by Jacqui Carey (1994). Fuller details of the Aegean weights suitable to making *kumihimo* cords and other evidence of cloth made up from narrow bands in that area are set out in my article "Minoan Women and the Challenges of Weaving for Home, Trade, and Shrine" (1997). My thanks to Paul Barber for crafting the *kumihimo* stand seen in fig. 3.11 and to the Art Department at Occidental College for providing me with the clay and work space to make the weights.

Discussion of what we know about embroidery before 500 B.C. can be found in *Prehistoric Textiles*, pp. 159–62, 198–200, 203, etc. The earliest-known brocades, from the Swiss pile dwellings, are discussed on pp. 134–40.

Irene Good presents her analysis of the cashmere fibers, with a photomicrograph (fig. 1), in "Bronze Age Cloth and Clothing of the Tarim Basin: The Chärchän Evidence" (1998).

I published a color photograph of the scrolled tapestry from Pazyryk in *Prehistoric Textiles* (plate 4, right), and a drawing and discussion of its design appear in Rudenko's *The Frozen Tombs of Siberia*, plate 157A–B and pp. 204–05. *Scientific American* also published a short article on this key site in 1965: "Frozen Tombs of the Scythians," by M. I. Artamonov.

CHAPTER 4

Map 4.1 is based on maps 25–26, 29–30, and 32–33 found in Sir Aurel Stein's *Innermost Asia* (1928, vol. 4), and on fig. 36 (p. 163) of Folke Bergman's *Archaeological Researches in Sinkiang* (1939). Stein's excellent, detailed maps are the best maps of the Tarim Basin readily available in the West still today.

The reconstructed portrait of the Loulan "Beauty" is reproduced on p. 51 of Thomas Allen's article "Xinjiang."

Tamar Schick, an Israeli archaeologist interested in prehistoric weaving, published a comb with such wear marks in the article "A 10,000 Year Old Comb from Wadi Murabba'at in the Judean Desert" (1995).

The domestication of einkorn in the Early Neolithic has just been pinpointed through DNA to where the Fertile Crescent crosses the Euphrates; see Manfred Heun et al., "Site of Einkorn Wheat Domestication Identified" (1997). For a fuller account of the development of woolly sheep, see *Prehistoric Textiles,* pp. 20–30, and for the development of looms, see pp. 79–125.

The Qäwrighul cemetery was excavated by Wang Binghua of the Xinjiang Institute of Archaeology in 1979. A brief English summary of his findings, "The Content of Qäwrighul Historical Culture," appeared on pp. 20–22 of the abstracts submitted to the "mummy conference" held in Philadelphia in April 1996. More accessibly, but with fewer details, Kwang-tzuu Chen and Fredrik Hiebert summarize the graves of this culture in their paper "The Late Prehistory of Xinjiang in Relation to Its Neighbors" (1995), especially pp. 251–57 (with full references to the Chinese-language literature on the subject).

Norman de Garis Davies spent much of his life carefully copying Egyptian tomb paintings when they were fast deteriorating, to preserve them as a precious record of human history. The ground loom in fig. 4.5 (top) is drawn from his copy of the Middle Kingdom tomb of Khnumhotep, as published by H. Ling Roth in *Ancient Greek and Egyptian Looms* (1913), fig. 6. The two vertical looms (fig. 4.5 bottom) are drawn from his copy of the murals in the New Kingdom tomb of Neferronpet, found in Davies's book, *Seven Private Tombs at Kurnah* (1948), plate 35. A history of the development of these looms is given in *Prehistoric Textiles,* pp. 79–91, 113–16.

Fig. 4.6 is based on a postcard (purchased from a street vendor in Ürümchi)—similar to excavations photographs seen at the museum. One gets one's data where one can.

Sven Hedin describes the vagaries of the Kum-darya (alias Qum-därya, Kuruk-darya, Quruk-därya) and the Lop Nor in his book *Across the Gobi Desert* (1932), especially pp. 361–78. The quotation about Marco Polo occurs on p. 361; those about finding Loulan and surveying the old lake basin (starting "On the 28th") come from pp. 362–63, and those about his laborious marches in the dry riverbed (starting "How well I") on p. 367.

CHAPTER 5

Jeannette Mirsky has compiled a well-researched biography of Stein, from his birth in Budapest in 1863 to his death in Kabul in 1943, in her book *Sir Aurel Stein, Archaeological Explorer* (1977).

Marc Aurel Stein's first journey of 1900–01 was published in three forms: *Preliminary Report on a Journey of Archaeological and Topographical Explorations in Chinese Turkestan* (1901), *Sand-Buried Ruins of Khotan* (1904), and *Ancient Khotan* (1907). He relates the story of Islam Akhun briefly in *Preliminary Report,* pp. 64–68, and more fully in *Sand-Buried Ruins,* pp. 449–59. His second journey Stein described in the two-volume work *Ruins of Desert Cathay* (1912). The quotation beginning "Ever since my plans" comes from vol. 1, p. 337.

Sven Hedin tells the gripping story of his "Death March" in Chapters 19–22 (pp. 146–79) of *My Life as an Explorer* (1925). The quotations come from pp. 169–70.

Finding Kharoṣṭhī tablets at Loulan is described by Stein in chapter 8, p. 141, of his book *On Ancient Central Asian Tracks* (1933). This very interesting overview of his travels, which he wrote some years later with the knowledge of hindsight, has been reprinted in paperback by University of Chicago Press (1974; different pagination, fewer illustrations).

The history of the Chinese name form *Loulan* was reconstructed by the great Sinologist Bernhard Karlgren and quoted by Folké Bergman in his tome *Archaeological Researches in Sinkiang* (1939), p. 44. The material on substrate loans in the local Prakrit was worked out by T. Burrow, "Tokharian Elements in the Kharoṣṭhī Documents from Chinese Turkestan" (1935).

The quotations concerning Stein's second trek to Loulan come from Chapter 9 of *On Ancient Central Asian Tracks*: the three short ones beginning "rows of fallen" on pp. 148–49 and the long one beginning "a small ruined fort" on pp. 154–55 (original edition). The quotations beginning "head and face" and "a fence" come from Stein's *Innermost Asia*, p. 264, and he mentions ephedra on p. 265. Fig. 5.2 is drawn from Stein's photo 173 in *Innermost Asia*; the same photo was reproduced as fig. 67 in the original edition (only) of *On Ancient Central Asian Tracks*.

Wang Binghua mentions finding *Ephedra sinica* in his report "The Content of Qäwrighul Historical Culture," pp. 21–22.

The quotation sequence beginning "revealed a method" comes from p. 735 of Stein's *Innermost Asia*; the sequence beginning "The graves were marked" is from p. 734; fig. 5.3 is drawn from photo 336.

Hedin's summary of Bergman's Lop Nor findings, from which the brief quotations are taken, appears in *Riddles of the Gobi Desert* (1933), pp. 292–93.

The reader interested in learning more about radiocarbon dating can consult a book like R. E. Taylor, *Radiocarbon Dating: An Archaeological Perspective* (1987), which gives both historical and technical overviews of the subject, together with an explanation of the problems of calibration.

P. V. Glob discusses the Egtved burial and many other interesting Bronze Age finds in Denmark in his highly readable book, *The Mound People* (1970). Fig. 5.4 was drawn from his photos 18, 20, and 21. My thanks to Andrew Sherratt for communicating to me the tree ring date of the Egtved coffin.

I first drew attention to the long history of the string skirt in *Prehistoric Textiles*, pp. 255–58, elaborated it in *Women's Work*, pp. 54–69, and attempted a definitive history of it up to modern times in the article "On the Antiquity of East European Bridal Clothing" (1995). The first two have photos of the Egtved skirt, which is in the National Museum, Copenhagen.

The quotations about Cemetery 5 on the Small River come from pp. 9–10 of Bergman's introduction to Vivi Sylwan's book *Woollen Textiles of the Lou-lan People* (1941); the quotation beginning "the loin-cloths" is on p. 10. Sylwan herself discusses the construction of the loincloths on pp. 56–67 (plates IX–XI). Fig. 5.5 and 5.6, showing Cemetery 5, were drawn from Bergman's photographs plates IIIb and IXb in his book, *Archaeological Researches in Sinkiang*. Fig. 5.7 was drawn from his photos of loincloths in plates 26 (woman's, above), 12 (woman's, below) and 11 (man's). Fig. 5.8, the mummy from Grave 36, was done from a drawing published as fig. 1 (p. 11) in Bergman's preface to Sylwan's book, itself done from a photo by Parker C. Chen; the quoted description ("This single grave") comes from pp. 11–12.

Bergman refers to the Chinese opinion of the Loulan people "resembling birds and wild beasts" on p. 12 of his preface to Sylwan's book, without citing his sources.

CHAPTER 6

The Tokharian inscription in fig. 6.2 was copied from E. Sieg and W. Siegling, *Tocharische Sprachreste* (1921), no. 252, which they discuss on p. 127. The Kharoṣṭhī inscription was copied from a photograph of document 310 that Stein found in house XV at Niya, printed in Stein's *Preliminary Report,* plate XI.

Sir William Jones made his statement in a speech entitled "Third Anniversary Discourse" delivered to the Asiatic Society of Calcutta in 1786.

For the essential facts about chasing the name of the Tokharians, see the introduction to Douglas Q. Adams's volume, *Tocharian Historical Phonology and Morphology* (1988), pp. 1–6. Another highly useful source for the history of studying all the Central Asian languages and scripts is Holger Pedersen's book *The Discovery of Language* (also published as *Linguistic Science in the 19th Century;* 1962). T. Burrow analyzes the early substrate loans in his article "Tokharian Elements in the Kharoṣṭhī Documents from Chinese Turkestan."

The Chinese scholar quoted on the subject of *Hú* is Chen Chien-wen of the Taiwan Normal University, who presented a paper entitled "Further Studies of the Racial, Cultural, and Ethnic Affinities of the Yuezhi" at the "mummy conference" (Chen, 1998). The quotation starting "deep eye sockets" is on p. 777; early descriptions of skin color occur on pp. 773–74.

The story of early Chinese relations with the Xiongnu (or Hsiung-nu) and other western barbarians was compiled around 100 B.C. by the "Grand Historian" of the Han court, Sima Qian (old spelling: Ssuma Ch'ien), using many ancient sources that have since perished. His very interesting volume, the *Shiji* (or *Shih-chi*), was translated by Burton Watson as *Records of the Grand Historian of China* (1961; revised using the newest orthography, 1993). The history of the Xiongnu occupies Chapter 110 and the story of Zhang Qian, Chapter 123 of this great work. The quotation starting "Formerly they" and the sequence beginning "the Yuezhi originally" come from vol. 2, p. 234; "rich and fertile" from p. 232; and the passages beginning "the Loulan and Gushi" and "west of the Yutian" from p. 233.

Statistics about the Great Wall of China come from William Watson's easy-reading and well-illustrated introduction to the archaeology of China, *Early Civilization in China* (1972), p. 69.

Chang Tsung-tung lists dozens of possible and probable Indo-European loans into early Chinese, backed up by proposed patterns of sound correspondence, in his treatise "Indo-European Vocabulary in Old Chinese" (1988). Material on early loans, especially wheels and chariots, occurs also in various papers given at the "mummy conference"—e.g., Alexander Lubotsky, "Tocharian Loan Words in Old Chinese" (1998), especially pp. 382–85. See also Robert Bauer, "Sino-Tibetan *kolo* 'Wheel' " (1994) and much of Victor Mair's work in the Bibliography.

The etymologies of the mountain names are discussed by Lin Meicun, "Qilian and Kunlun—The Earliest Tokharian Loan-words in Ancient Chinese" (1998). Chen Chien-wen tells of the manuscript mentioning the late kingdom of Yuezhi in his paper "Further Studies of the Racial Affinities of the Yuezhi," p. 777.

The archaeology of names in Greece was worked out in a seminal article by J. B. Haley and Carl Blegen, "The Coming of the Greeks" (1928). A brief discussion of the distribution of Baltic, Slavic, Iranian, and Finno-Ugric water names in East Europe, with a map, occurs in Zdeněk Váňa, *The World of the Ancient Slavs* (1983), pp. 13–17.

Etymologies of many of the English words for textiles and clothing (including *felt* and *mantle*) appear in *Prehistoric Textiles,* along with a pilot study (Chapter 12) of how to use linguistic analysis of word strata in the service of archaeology, while clothing as an ancient system of showing status and identity forms a main theme of *Women's Work.*

Any scholar of Turkic linguistics wishing to analyze the origins of Turkic textile vocabulary might begin with Gunnar Jarring's work *Garments from Top to Toe: Eastern Turki Texts Relating to Articles of Clothing* (1991), and contact me for my file of material.

Vivi Sylwan comments on the quality of felt at Loulan on p. 96 of her book *Woollen Textiles of the Lou-lan People.*

The Tokharian words for a weaver can be found on p. 11 of Douglas Adams's *Tocharian Historical Phonology and Morphology.*

CHAPTER 7

The drawing of the mummy from Qizilchoqa, fig. 7.2, was done from Victor Mair's 1993 field photograph on p. 32 of his *Archaeology* article "Mummies of the Tarim Basin."

The quotation from Hadingham about the Qizilchoqa mummies comes from p. 76 of his "The Mummies of Xinjiang." Unfortunately the excavator Wang Binghua has published little about this important site as yet.

Passages translated into English from the old records of clothes and bodies found in the salt mines are quoted by K. Spindler in *The Man in the Ice,* pp. 63–64. The main publication of the Hallstatt/Hallein cloth remains, however, is Hans-Jürgen Hundt's detailed analysis in German, in the journal of the Roman-Germanic Museum in Mainz, appearing serially from 1959 to 1962 and 1967 to 1969. See the bibliography under Hundt in my book *Prehistoric Textiles* for complete citations, and pp. 186–94 for a descriptive summary in English of his findings. Hundt discusses the "heathen rock" and the early records on pp. 66–67 of *"Vorgeschichtliche Gewebe aus dem Hallstaetter Salzberg"* (1959); he describes the garment with nits on p. 141 of an article of the same name from 1960; and the white-ground cloths from Hallein on pp. 14–16 of *"Neunzehn Textilreste aus dem Duerrnberg in Hallein"* (1961).

Albert von LeCoq gives his cure for lice in *Auf Hellas Spuren in Ostturkistan* (1926), p. 37.

Irene Good's original analysis of the plaid twill given to Mair was published by Mair in "Mummies of the Tarim Basin" (1995)

Wang Luli published a photograph (no. 3) and sketchy description (pp. 1–2) of a Qizilchoqa plaid in *The Great Treasury of Chinese Fine Arts* (ed. Huang; 1990). Using my thread count from the top half of this photo, Rebecca Ashenden of Shelburne Falls, Massachusetts, wove the exact replica shown in plate 13b.

The evidence for the start of twill-woven textiles is assembled, with full bibliography, in *Prehistoric Textiles,* pp. 167–68, 186–96, 211–12; the first evidence for plaids (including Tsarskaja) is on pp. 168–69. Evidence for the development of woolly sheep occurs on pp. 20–30 and the data for the origin of looms on pp. 79–125, 213, 249–55.

In fig. 7.7 the horizontal ground loom was sketched from a wooden model of an Egyptian weaving shop found in the Eleventh Dynasty tomb of Meketre, ca. 2000 B.C. The warp-weighted loom comes from a tiny Greek jar from Corinth, ca. 600 B.C. The vertical two-beam loom was composed from several such painted on the tomb wall of Neferronpet, at Thebes, Egypt, ca. 1250 B.C. More complete photos and drawings of these monuments appear in *Prehistoric Textiles,* on pp. 85 (fig. 3.6), 106 (3.24), and 114 (3.30) respectively, with further bibliographical references.

The current evidence for the origin and spread of the proto–Indo-Europeans, a much-labored subject, is set out most neutrally, thoroughly, and readably by James Mallory in his book *In Search of the Indo-Europeans* (1989). See also David Anthony, "The Archaeology of Indo-European Origins" (1991).

The two loom depictions on Hallstatt urns are reproduced and discussed in *Prehistoric Textiles*, pp. 56 fig. 2.15, 106, 213 fig. 8.1, and 295 fig. 13.3. Central Asian nomads weaving on narrow ground looms are pictured in Albert von LeCoq's *Land und Leuten in Ostturkistan* (1916), plate 24.2, and in George Cressey's *Asia's Lands and Peoples* (1963), p. 167.

I have reconstructed much proto–Indo-European textile vocabulary, with its notable lack of words for large looms, in *Prehistoric Textiles*, pp. 260–82.

CHAPTER 8

The most readily available book on recent archaeological work in Russian Turkestan, and on the spread of the Kopet Dagh cultures into and across the oases, is Fredrik T. Hiebert's *Origins of the Bronze Age in Central Asia* (1994). Most of my discussion comes from Hiebert. The preface of his book, written by C. C. Lamberg-Karlovsky of Harvard's Peabody Museum, discusses some of the problems scientists had in working around the Iron Curtain. Another useful resource is a special section of the 1994 (vol. 68) issue of *Antiquity* devoted to "The Oxus Civilization: The Bronze Age of Central Asia" (p. 353ff.), with articles by scholars from both Russia (L. P'yankova, V. Sarianidi) and the West (Lambert-Karlovsky, Hiebert, Francfort, Moore, Miller, Meadow).

Raphael Pumpelly published the Anau finds in *Excavations in Turkestan; Expedition of 1904* (1908). I discuss the strange whorls at Anau and their implications, with illustrations and a map, in an essay "The Weight Chase" in *Prehistoric Textiles*, pp. 303–10.

The quotation about reorganizing the water supply comes from George Cressey, *Asia's Lands and Peoples*, p. 166.

The two quotations about life in the deep steppe come from pp. 204–06 of David Anthony's "The Archaeology of Indo-European Origins" (1991). The quotation from William of Rubruck comes from p. 95 of Dawson's edition of *The Mongol Mission*.

Ephedra in the Loulan area graves is mentioned by Stein in *Innermost Asia* on p. 265; by Bergman in *Archaeological Researches in Sinkiang* on p. 136 and in his introduction to Sylwan's *Woollen Textiles of the Lou-lan People*, pp. 9–10; and by Wang Binghua on pp. 21–22 of "The Content of Qäwrighul Historical Culture."

Aristophanes mentions people carrying coins in the mouth (and accidentally swallowing them) in *The Birds*, ll. 502–3.

The photographed samples of ephedra were found at the Huntington Gardens, Pasadena.

The range of beliefs and practices to do with body disposal and fear of revenants forms the core of Paul Barber's book *Vampires, Burial, and Death*. He discusses the notion of the double on pp. 167 and 179–88.

Viktor Sarianidi, of the Russian Academy of Sciences, lays out his findings of hallucinogens in the ancient temples of the Merv oasis on pp. 388–97 of "Temples of Bronze Age Margiana (1994). Fig. 8.5 is adapted from his fig. 2, p. 390, and fig. 4, p. 393. The psychedelic mushroom theory was presented by R. Gordon Wasson, *Soma: Divine Mushroom of Immortality* (1968).

The two American scholars mentioned are David Stophlet Flattery and Martin Schwartz, who wrote *Haoma and Harmaline: The Botanical Identity of the Indo-Iranian*

Sacred Hallucinogen . . . (1989). Flattery describes the Yasna ritual on p. 67 and discusses ephedra on pp. 72–76 and pomegranate on 76–80. The quotation about false identification comes from note 6, p. 73. The substitution of something inert for the hallucinogen is discussed on pp. 98–99 and the South American use of similar drugs on pp. 24–29 and 76.

Fredrik Hiebert published a map summarizing the known southward contacts of the oasis hoppers of Russian Turkestan as fig. 10.8 (p. 177) in *Origins of the Bronze Age Oasis Civilization in Central Asia*. Mallory discusses the archaeology of the Afanasievo and Andronovo cultures in his volume, *In Search of the Indo-Europeans*, especially pp. 223–29 and 263, with maps and drawings.

The Fergana Valley pot impressions of twills were published by Ju. A. Zadneprovskij in *Drevnezemledel'cheskaja Kul'tura Fergany* (1962), plates LXXIV–VI.

CHAPTER 9

Aurel Stein published *Sand-Buried Ruins of Khotan* (1904) as a description of his first trip.

The quotations from Kamberi about the current rapid desiccation come from his report "The Three Thousand Year Old Chärchän Man Preserved at Zaghunluq," pp. 2–4.

Erik Norin presents the results of his geological research in his book *Geologic Reconnaissances in the Chinese Tien-Shan* (1941). The quotations beginning "progressive advance" and "the sand" come from p. 30; that beginning "Sub-recent terminal moraines" from p. 31.

Stein mentions deglaciation as a principal cause of dryness in *On Ancient Central Asian Tracks* (1933), pp. 28–30.

The report of Joseph Birman's findings in Turkey appear in his article "Glacial Reconnaissance in Turkey" (1968).

Sven Hedin's summary of Norin's reports (from "In late glacial times" to "diminishing salt lake") is quoted piecemeal from pp. 376–77 of Hedin's *Across the Gobi Desert.* For a fascinating account of the dynamics of huge, silt-laden rivers that radically shift their beds, see John McPhee's *The Control of Nature* (1989), which uses the Mississippi as a primary example.

Statistics on the formation of the Himalayas came from *The Historical Atlas of the Earth* (1996), pp. 130–31. Additional information about the Tarim block and the formation of the Tien Shan comes from E. A. Neil and G. A. Houseman, "Geodynamic Models of Central Asia" (1996).

The geology and ecology of the Kara-Boghaz-Gol as the outlet of the Caspian form the core of a well-illustrated article by Maurice A. Garbell for *Scientific American* (1963): "The Sea That Spills into a Desert." Fig. 9.4 is based on his figure on p. 98. My thanks to Beatrice Hopkinson for supplying me with statistics on salt beds.

The entire fourth volume of Stein's *Innermost Asia* consists of maps, and Erik Norin reproduces a number of his own maps in his *Geologic Reconnaissances in the Chinese Tien-Shan*. These two sets of maps are still the best available in the West—done with such accuracy that I could locate on them the topographic features of the newly discovered sites described by current Chinese archaeologists. Additional topographic information should soon be available from LANDSAT images.

Stein's fullest descriptions of traversing the salt beds can be found in *Innermost Asia,* vol. 1, pp. 283–301. The first little quotations come from p. 299, and the long passage from p. 300. He discusses the "White Dragon Mounds" on p. 283 and the trail of coins on p. 290.

The quotation from Spindler about mummification can be found in *The Man in the Ice*, p. 154; the other information about the desiccation of Ice Man comes from pp. 154–55.

Deductions about the evolution of the vocal tract and its drawbacks are laid out by Philip Lieberman in *On the Origins of Language* (1975), especially p. 177. Fig. 9.5 is based largely on his diagrams on pp. 106–09. What data sources we have about the early developmental stages of human language and what we can infer from them are presented by E. J. W. Barber and A. M. W. Peters in the essay "Ontogeny and Phylogeny: What Child Language and Archaeology Have to Say to Each Other" (1992).

Johanna Nichols presents the bulk of her evidence in her book *Linguistic Diversity in Space and Time* (1992). A brief summary of her arguments within a wider context (including a confused map) is presented in Bruce Bower's article in *Science News* "Indo-European Pursuits" (1995).

Early copper tools from the Turkish site of Çayönü Tepesi are illustrated by Halet Çambel and Robert J. Braidwood in "An Early Farming Village in Turkey" (1970).

For a treatment of the Indic names, see, for example, Paul Thieme, "The Aryan Gods of the Mitanni Treaties" (1960).

An up-to-date discussion of the waves of people who ended the Near Eastern Bronze Age, including many of the battle depictions left by Ramesses III, can be found in Trude and Moshe Dothan's book *People of the Sea* (1992).

The Hittite letter about sending gifts of iron is discussed, for instance, by O. R. Gurney: *The Hittites* (1961), p. 83.

One very readable source for what linguists have deduced about the Uralo-Altaic family (and Indo-European too) is Holger Pedersen's fascinating book *The Discovery of Language*. See p. 109 for the linguistic pedigrees of the early Eurasian invaders.

The graves at Baifu, mentioned in note 5, are discussed by Mrea Csorba in "The Chinese Northern Frontier: Reassessment of the Bronze Age Burials from Baifu" (1996).

Andrew Sherratt's work on the Secondary Products Revolution appears in his article "Plough and Pastoralism: Aspects of the Secondary Products Revolution" (1981). Domestication of horses is discussed by Anthony and Brown in "Looking a Gift Horse in the Mouth," while the development of woolly sheep and the origins of felt (including the Beycesultan material) can be found in *Prehistoric Textiles*, pp. 20–30 and 215–22, respectively.

After my manuscript was written, Margalit Finkelberg published a paper, "Anatolian Languages and Indo-European Migrations to Greece" (1997), in which she marshaled a number of strong arguments in favor of the Anatolian language family being a cousin of Indo-European (not a daughter) and some interesting observations suggesting that the first wave of farmers coming into Europe at the start of the Neolithic might have spoken yet older branches from the tree that ultimately produced proto–Indo-European and proto-Anatolian.

Quantities of data concerning the extent of the warp-weighted loom, the etymological and semantic analysis of ancient Greek textile vocabulary, and the geographical conclusions that can be drawn from them are collected in *Prehistoric Textiles*, pp. 91–113 and 260–282. Mallory provides a whole book full of nontextile evidence for the geographic and temporal source of the proto–Indo-Europeans in *In Search of the Indo-Europeans,* also finally settling on the Pontic-Caspian steppes shortly before 3000 B.C.

DNA analyses of Eurasian populations and of some of the Xinjiang mummies were reported at the "mummy conference" by Luigi-Luca Cavalli-Sforza, "Genetic Geography and Ancient Migrations in Eurasia" (1996) and in greater detail by Paolo Francalacci, "DNA Analysis on Ancient Desiccated Ancient Corpses from Xinjiang (China): Further Results" (1998). Mallory's evidence for particularly tall people is cited on pp. 188 and 190 of *In Search of the Indo-Europeans.*

CHAPTER 10

Map 10.2 is based on a portion of map 28 in Sir Aurel Stein's *Innermost Asia,* vol. 4.

Further information about the Subeshi cemetery, with color photos of some of the finds (including the peak-hatted women), can be found in Hadingham's "The Mummies of Xinjiang," especially pp. 72, 76–77. For Jeffery Newbury's color photo of the woman from Subeshi (Subashi), from which fig. 10.3 was drawn, see also Mair's "Mummies of the Tarim Basin," p. 29.

Victor Mair lays out his theory of Iranian magi reaching ancient China in the article "Old Sinitic **mʸag*, Old Persian *maguš*, and English '*Magician*' " (1990). The quotation comes from p. 35; the discussion of the "chariot" word is on p. 45 and that of the "silk" word on p. 44. Fig. 10.5 is drawn from his collection of early Chinese images of Caucasoids, specifically from his figures 3 (Anyang: from Carl Hentze, *Funde in Alt-China*; 1967; plate XV), 1 and 2 (Chou-yüan palace, T45:2 and T45:6: from Yin Sheng-p'ing, "Hsi-Chou pang-tiao jen-t'ou hsiang chung-tsu t'an-so" [1986], pp. 46–49, figures on pp. 46–47).

The peculiar graves at Baifu, mentioned in note 2, are discussed by Mrea Csorba in "The Chinese Northern Frontier." She reproduces photos and drawings of the two shell figures of Caucasians (my fig. 10.5) as well as of another mustachioed, round-eyed face from a Baifu dagger hilt.

The origin of Dunhuang's name is tackled by Victor Mair in "Reflections on the Origins of the Modern Standard Mandarin Place-Name 'Dunhuang' . . ." (1991).

Lü Enguo describes his Charwighul cemetery site briefly in English in "The Discovery of and Research upon Charwighul Culture" (1996).

A short, well-illustrated account of the Sintashta-Petrovka culture and its evidence for early wheels and horse sacrifices was published by David Anthony and Nikolai Vinogradov in the same issue of *Archaeology* as the mummies: "Birth of the Chariot" (1995). Map 10.6 was extrapolated from information there. A highly accessible description of the royal tombs of Alaca Höyük can be found in Seton Lloyd's *Early Highland Peoples of Anatolia* (1967), pp. 20–29 and fig. 5–18 (head and hooves visible in fig. 11). The other evidence for the "head and hooves cult" is listed by Mallory in *In Search of the Indo-Europeans,* pp. 198, 206, 214.

The history of the traction harness is laid out by E. M. Jope in the chapter "Vehicles and Harness" in *A History of Technology,* edited by Charles Singer et al. (1956), vol. 2, especially pp. 552–53.

The passage quoted from Herodotus closes section 140 of Book 1 of his *Histories.* Alexander the Great's eastern campaigns are most conveniently summarized by J. B. Bury, *A History of Greece* (1913), pp. 728 and 734–808, and map 10.7 is based heavily on Bury's map opposite p. 770. An important—and very readable—ancient source is Plutarch's *Life of Alexander.*

For details about Tasmania and the pitfalls of isolation, see Jared Diamond, "Ten Thousand Years of Solitude" (1993). For the history of writing systems, see in particular I. J. Gelb, *A Study of Writing* (1963).

Samuel Kurinsky's very readable history of glassmaking, *The Glassmakers* (1991), was the source of many of the details on early glass. The glass ingots (pictured by Kurinsky on pp. 82, 89) were first found in 1986. The excavator, George Bass, reports on the diving of the Ulu Burun wreck in *National Geographic,* in "Oldest Known Shipwreck Reveals Splendors of the Bronze Age" (1987), with glass ingots pictured on p. 716.

A concise account of Marco Polo, the few things known independently about his life, and the circumstances of his composing the book can be found in the *Encyclopaedia Britannica* under "Polo." The interesting array of arguments against and questions about Marco Polo's journey are marshaled by Frances Wood in *Did Marco Polo Go to China?* (1995), from which this discussion is culled. Sir Henry Yule, Paul Pelliot, and other famous translators-annotators of Marco Polo had raised many of these doubts earlier without pursuing them systematically.

The Russian émigré painter and philosopher Nicholas Roerich (Nikolaj Rerikh; 1874–1947) traveled from India to the Tarim Basin and Mongolia from 1924 to 1928. The English version of his adventures appeared as *Altai-Himalaya* (1929); the quotation comes from p. 241. Museums of his colorful paintings exist in New York, England, and Russia.

Chap. 5, 2 petroglyph faces: from Bronze Age rock carvings at Kangjiashimenzi in the Tien Shan.

Chap. 6, ruined dwelling XV at Niya: from Stein's photo on p. 368 of *Sand-Buried Ruins of Khotan.* This house contained an ancient rubbish heap in which the Kharosthi inscription of fig. 6.2 was found.

Chap. 7, Turkic weaver, Kara-Khodsha: from Albert von LeCoq's photo 2, in *Land und Leuten in Ostturkistan.*

Chap. 8, desert caravan: from Stein's photo 282 of the dried-up Keriyä delta, p. 393 of *Ruins of Desert Cathay.*

Chap 9, painted wooden panel from Dandan-Öiliq: based on Stein, *Ancient Khotan,* pl. LXIII (and see discussion pp. 259–60). This mid-first millennium A.D. painting is the only early representation of weaving I know of from Central Asia. The woman seems to hold a weaving comb; the bowl holds silk cocoons.

Chap. 10, 2 wooden statues: from plate V of Bergman's *Archaeological Researches in Sinkiang.* Found in Cemetery 5 near Loulan, they are of uncertain date.

Bibliography

Adams, Douglas Q. *Tocharian Historical Phonology and Morphology.* New Haven: American Oriental Society, 1988.

Allen, Thomas B. "Xinjiang." *National Geographic,* vol. 189, no. 3 (March 1996), pp. 2–51.

Anthony, David. "The Archaeology of Indo-European Origins." *Journal of Indo-European Studies,* vol. 19 (1991), pp. 193–222.

Anthony, David, and Dorcas Brown. "Looking a Gift Horse in the Mouth: Identification of the Earliest Bitted Equids and the Microscopic Analysis of Bit Wear." In *Early Animal Domestication and Its Cultural Context,* ed. P. Crabtree, D. Campana, and K. Ryan, MASCA Research Papers in Science and Archaeology, vol. 6 suppl. (1989), pp. 98–116.

Anthony, David, and Nikolai Vinogradov. "Birth of the Chariot." *Archaeology,* vol. 48, no. 2 (March–April 1995), pp. 36–41.

Artamonov, M. I. "Frozen Tombs of the Scythians." *Scientific American,* vol. 212, no. 5 (May 1965), pp. 100–109.

Barber, Elizabeth J. Wayland. *Prehistoric Textiles: The Development of Cloth in the Neolithic and Bronze Ages, with Special Reference to the Aegean.* Princeton: Princeton University Press, 1991.

———. *Women's Work—The First 20,000 Years.* New York: W. W. Norton & Co., 1994.

———. "On the Antiquity of East European Bridal Clothing." *Dress,* vol. 21 (1995), pp. 17–29.

———. "Minoan Women and the Challenges of Weaving for Home, Trade, and Shrine." In *TEXNH: Craftsmen, Craftswomen and Craftsmanship in the Aegean Bronze Age* (= *Aegaeum* 16), ed. R. Laffineur and P. Betancourt. Liège: Université de Liège, 1997. Pp. 515–19.

Barber, E. J. W., and A. M. W. Peters. "Ontogeny and Phylogeny: What Child Language and Archaeology Have to Say to Each Other." In *The Evolution of Human Languages,* ed. John Hawkins and Murray Gell-Mann. Redwood City: Addison-Wesley, 1992. Pp. 305–52.

Barber, Paul T. *Vampires, Burial, and Death.* New Haven: Yale University Press, 1988.

Bass, George. "Oldest Known Shipwreck Reveals Splendors of the Bronze Age." *National Geographic,* vol. 172, no. 6 (December 1987), pp. 692–733.

Bauer, Robert. "Sino-Tibetan **kolo* 'Wheel.' " *Sino-Platonic Papers,* no. 47 (August 1994).

Bergman, Folke. *Archaeological Researches in Sinkiang.* Stockholm: Sino-Swedish Expedition no. 7, 1939.

Birman, Joseph. "Glacial Reconnaissance in Turkey." *Geological Society of America Bulletin,* vol. 79 (1968), pp. 1009–26.

Bower, Bruce. "Indo-European Pursuits." *Science News,* vol. 147 (February 25, 1995), pp. 120–21, 125.

Burrow, T. "Tokharian Elements in the Kharoṣṭhī Documents from Chinese Turkestan." *Journal of the Royal Asiatic Society of Great Britain and Ireland* (1935), pp. 667–75.

Bury, J. B. *A History of Greece.* New York: Modern Library, 1913.

Çambel, Halet, and Robert J. Braidwood. "An Early Farming Village in Turkey." *Scientific American,* vol. 222 (March 1970), pp. 50–56.

Carey, Jacqui. *Creative Kumihimo.* Somerset: Acanthus Press, 1994.

Cavalli-Sforza, Luigi-Luca. "Genetic Geography and Ancient Migrations in Eurasia." Abstract in Mair, 1996, p. 4.

Chang Tsung-tung. "Indo-European Vocabulary in Old Chinese." *Sino-Platonic Papers,* no. 7 (1988).

Chen Chien-wen. "Further Discussion of the Racial, Cultural, and Ethnic Affinities of the Yuezhi." In Mair, 1998, pp. 767–84.

Chen, Kwang-tzuu, and Fredrik Hiebert. "The Late Prehistory of Xinjiang in Relation to Its Neighbors." *Journal of World Prehistory,* vol. 9, no. 2 (1995), pp. 243–300.

Cressey, George B. *Asia's Lands and Peoples.* New York: McGraw-Hill, 1963.

Csorba, Mrea. "The Chinese Northern Frontier: Reassessment of the Bronze Age Burials from Baifu." *Antiquity,* vol. 70 (1996), pp. 564–87.

Davies, Norman de Garis. *Seven Private Tombs at Kurnah.* London: Egypt Exploration Society, 1948.

Dawson, Christopher. *The Mongol Mission: Narratives and Letters of the Franciscan Missionaries in Mongolia and China in the Thirteenth and Fourteenth Centuries.* New York: Sheed and Ward, 1955.

Diamond, Jared. "Ten Thousand Years of Solitude." *Discover,* vol. 14, no. 3 (March 1993), pp. 48–57.

Dothan, Trude, and Moshe Dothan. *People of the Sea: The Search for the Philistines.* New York: Macmillan, 1992.

Finkelberg, Margalit. "Anatolian Languages and Indo-European Migrations to Greece," *Classical World* vol. 91 (1997), pp. 3–20.

Flattery, David Stophlet, and Martin Schwartz. *Haoma and Harmaline: The Botanical Identity of the Indo-Iranian Sacred Hallucinogen "Soma" and Its Legacy in Religion, Language, and Middle Eastern Folklore.* Berkeley: University of California, 1989.

Francalacci, Paolo. "DNA Analysis on Ancient Desiccated Corpses from Xinjiang (China): Further Results." In Mair, 1998, pp. 537–47.

Garbell, Maurice A. "The Sea That Spills into a Desert." *Scientific American*, vol. 209 (August 1963), pp. 94–100.

Gelb, I. J. *A Study of Writing*. Chicago: University of Chicago Press, 1963.

Glob, P. V. *The Mound People*. Ithaca: Cornell University Press, 1970.

Good, Irene. "Bronze Age Cloth and Clothing of the Tarim Basin: The Chärchän Evidence." In Mair, 1998, pp. 656–68.

Gurney, O. R. *The Hittites*, 2d ed. Baltimore: Penguin, 1961.

Hadingham, Evan. "The Mummies of Xinjiang." *Discover*, vol. 15, no. 4 (April 1994), pp. 68–77.

Haley, J. B., and Carl Blegen. "The Coming of the Greeks." *American Journal of Archaeology*, vol. 32 (1928), pp. 141–54.

Hall, Rosalind M. "Garments in the Petrie Museum of Egyptian Archaeology." *Textile History*, vol. 13 (1982), pp. 27–45.

Hedin, Sven. *My Life as an Explorer*, trans. A. Huebsch. New York: Boni & Liveright, 1925.

———. *Across the Gobi Desert*, trans. H. J. Cant. New York: Dutton, 1932.

———. *Riddles of the Gobi Desert*. London: Routledge, 1933.

Hentze, Carl. *Funde in Alt-China: Das Welterleben in ältesten China*. Göttingen: Musterschmidt, 1967.

Heun, Manfred; R. Schäfer-Pregl; D. Klawan; R. Castagna; M. Accerbi; B. Borghi; and F. Salamini. "Site of Einkorn Wheat Domestication Identified by DNA Fingerprinting." *Science*, vol. 278 (November 14, 1997), pp. 1312–14.

Hiebert, Fredrik T. *Origins of the Bronze Age Civilization in Central Asia*. Cambridge, Mass.: American Schools of Prehistoric Research Bulletin 42, 1994.

Huang Nengfu, ed. *The Great Treasury of Chinese Fine Arts: Arts and Crafts*, vol. 6, *Printing, Dyeing, Weaving and Embroidery (I)*. Beijing: 1990.

Hundt, Hans-Jürgen. "Vorgeschichtliche Gewebe aus dem Hallstätter Salzberg." *Jahrbuch des römisch-germanischen Zentralmuseums Mainz (JRGZM)*, vol. 6 (1959), pp. 66–100.

———. "Vorgeschichtliche Gewebe aus dem Hallstätter Salzberg." *JRGZM*, vol. 7 (1960), pp. 126–50.

———. "Neunzehn Textilreste aus dem Dürrnberg in Hallein." *JRGZM*, vol. 8 (1961), pp. 7–25.

Jarring, Gunnar. *Garments from Top to Toe: Eastern Turki Texts Relating to Articles of Clothing*. Stockholm: Almqvist and Wiksell International, 1991.

Jope, E. M. "Vehicles and Harness." In *A History of Technology*, ed. Charles Singer, E. J. Holmyard, A. R. Hall, and Trevor I. Williams. New York and London: Oxford University Press, 1956. Vol. 2, 535–62.

Kamberi, Dolkun. "The Three Thousand Year Old Chärchän Man Preserved at Zaghunluq." *Sino-Platonic Papers*, no. 44 (January 1994).

Kurinsky, Samuel. *The Glassmakers*. New York: Hippocrene Books, 1991.

Landi, Sheila, and Rosalind M. Hall. "The Discovery and Conservation of an Ancient Egyptian Linen Tunic." *Studies in Conservation*, vol. 24 (1979), pp. 141–51.

LeCoq, Albert von. *Land und Leuten in Ostturkistan*. Berlin: Dietrich Reimer, 1916.

———. *Auf Hellas Spuren in Ostturkistan*. Leipzig: J. C. Hinrichs, 1926.

Lieberman, Philip. *On the Origins of Language*. New York: Macmillan, 1975.

Lin Meicun. "Qilian and Kunlun—The Earliest Tokharian Loan–words in Ancient Chinese." In Mair, 1998, pp. 476–82.

Lloyd, Seton. *Early Highland Peoples of Anatolia.* London: Thames and Hudson, 1967.

Lü Enguo. "The Discovery of and Research upon Charwighul Culture." Abstract in Mair, 1996, pp. 13–15.

Lubotsky, Alexander. "Tocharian Loan Words in Old Chinese: Chariots, Chariot Gear, and Town Building." In Mair, 1998, pp. 379–90.

Mair, Victor H. "Old Sinitic *mʸag, Old Persian *maguš*, and English 'Magician.' " *Early China*, vol. 15 (1990), pp. 27–47.

————. "Reflections on the Origins of the Modern Standard Mandarin Place-Name 'Dunhuang' with an Added Note on the Identity of the Modern Uighur Place-Name 'Turpan.' " In *Papers in Honour of Prof. Dr. Ji Xianlin on the Occasion of His 80th Birthday*, ed. Li Zheng et al. Nanchang: Xiangxi People's Press, 1991. Pp. 901–54.

————. "Mummies of the Tarim Basin." *Archaeology*, vol. 48, no. 2 (March–April 1995) 28–35.

Mair, V. H., ed. *Abstracts Submitted to the Conference on the Bronze Age and Iron Age Peoples of Eastern Central Asia.* Philadelphia, April 1996.

————. *The Bronze Age and Early Iron Age Peoples of Eastern Central Asia.* University of Pennsylvania Museum of Archaeology and Anthropology, and *Journal of Indo-European Studies* monograph series, 1998.

Mallory, J. P. *In Search of the Indo-Europeans.* London: Thames and Hudson, 1989.

McPhee, John. *The Control of Nature.* New York: Farrar Straus Giroux, 1989.

Mirsky, Jeannette. *Sir Aurel Stein, Archaeological Explorer.* Chicago: University of Chicago, 1977.

Moser, Henri. *À travers l'Asie centrale.* Paris: Librairie Plon, 1885.

Mycio, M. "Scientist Trots Out New Equine Theory." *Los Angeles Times*, March 14, 1995, H2.

Neil, E. A., and G. A. Houseman. "Geodynamic Models of Central Asia: Strong Tarim Basin or Weak Tien Shan?" *Geologic Society of Australia Abstracts*, vol. 40 (1996), p. 115.

Nichols, Johanna. *Linguistic Diversity in Space and Time.* Chicago: University of Chicago Press, 1992.

Norin, Erik. *Geologic Reconnaissances in the Chinese Tien-Shan.* Stockholm: Sino-Swedish Expedition No. 16, 1941.

Osbourne, R., and D. Tarling, eds. *The Historical Atlas of the Earth.* New York: Henry Holt, 1996.

Pedersen, Holger. *The Discovery of Language* (= *Linguistic Science in the 19th Century*), trans. J. W. Spargo. Bloomington: Indiana University Press, 1962.

Pumpelly, Raphael. *Excavations in Turkestan; Expedition of 1904.* Washington, D.C.: Carnegie Institute of Washington, 1908.

Roerich, Nicholas. *Altai-Himalaya.* New York: Dutton, 1929.

Roth, H. Ling. *Ancient Greek and Egyptian Looms.* Halifax: Bankfield Museum, 1913.

Rudenkno, S. I. *Frozen Tombs of Siberia*, trans. M. W. Thompson. Berkeley: University of California Press, 1970. Original Russian edition: *Kul'tura naselenija gornogo Altaja v Skifskoe vremja.* Moscow: Akademija Nauk SSSR, 1953.

Rutt, Richard. *A History of Hand Knitting.* Loveland, Colo.: Interweave Press, 1987.

Sarianidi, Viktor. "Temples of Bronze Age Margiana: Traditions of Ritual Architecture." *Antiquity*, vol. 68 (1994), pp. 388–418.

Schick, Tamar. "A 10,000 Year Old Comb from Wadi Murabba'at in the Judean Desert." *'Atiqot*, vol. 27 (1995), pp. 199–206.

Sherratt, Andrew. "Plough and Pastoralism: Aspects of the Secondary Products Revolution." In *Pattern of the Past: Studies in Honour of David Clarke,* ed. Ian Hodder, G. Isaac, and N. Hammond. Cambridge: Cambridge University Press, 1981. Pp. 261–305.

Sieg, E., and W. Siegling. *Tocharische Sprachreste.* Berlin: Walter de Gruyter, 1921.

Sima Qian: *See* Watson, Burton.

Speiser, Noémi. *The Manual of Braiding.* Basel: private publ., 1991.

Spindler, Konrad. *The Man in the Ice,* trans. E. Osers. New York: Harmony Books, 1994.

Ssuma Ch'ien: *See* Watson, Burton.

Stein, Sir Marc Aurel. *Preliminary Report on a Journey of Archaeological and Topographical Explorations in Chinese Turkestan.* London: Eyre & Spottiswoode, 1901.

———. *Sand-Buried Ruins of Khotan.* London: Hurst & Blackett, 1904.

———. *Ancient Khotan.* Oxford: Oxford University Press, 1907.

———. *Ruins of Desert Cathay.* London: Macmillan & Co., 1912.

———. *Innermost Asia.* Oxford: Clarendon Press, 1928.

———. *On Ancient Central Asian Tracks.* London: Macmillan, 1933. Abridged reprint: Chicago: University of Chicago Press, 1974.

Sylwan, Vivi. *Woollen Textiles of the Lou-lan People.* Stockholm: Sino-Swedish Expedition No. 15, 1941.

Taylor, R. E. *Radiocarbon Dating: An Archaeological Perspective.* New York: Academic Press, 1987.

Thieme, Paul. "The Aryan Gods of the Mitanni Treaties." *Journal of the American Oriental Society,* vol. 80 (1960), pp. 301–17.

Váňa, Zdeněk. *The World of the Ancient Slavs.* Detroit: Wayne State University Press, 1983.

Wang Binghua. "The Content of Qäwrighul Historical Culture." Abstract in Mair, 1996, pp. 20–22.

Wang Luli: *See* Huang Nengfu.

Wasson, R. Gordon. *Soma: Divine Mushroom of Immortality.* New York: Harcourt, Brace, and World, 1968.

Watson, Burton. *Records of the Grand Historian of China.* New York, 1961; revised, using the newer orthography: New York: Columbia University Press, 1993.

Watson, William. *Early Civilization in China.* New York: McGraw-Hill, 1972; London: Thames and Hudson, 1966.

William of Rubruck: *See* Dawson, Christopher.

Wood, Frances. *Did Marco Polo Go to China?* Boulder, Colo.: Westview Press, 1995.

Yin Sheng-p'ing. "Hsi-Chou pang-tiao jen-t'ou hsiang chung-tsu t'an-so." *Wen-wu,* vol. 1 (1986), pp. 46–49.

Zadneprovskij, Ju. A. *Drevnezemledel'cheskaja Kul'tura Fergany* ["Ancient Farming Culture of Fergana"]. (*Materialy i Issledovanija po Arkheologii SSSR* 118). Moscow: Akademija Nauk, 1962.

The Ancient Art in Xinjiang, China. Ürümchi: Xinjiang Art and Photography Press, 1994.

Rūran ōkoku to yūkyū no bijo ["The Kingdom of Loulan and the Eternal Beauty"]. Tokyo: Osahi Shinbunsha, 1992.

Index

This index is alphabetized without regard to word breaks, because people don't agree where word breaks go in the foreign place names. Abbreviations are: d = definition, m = map, p = picture.